T0330189

Work and Labour Relations in Global Platform Capitalism

International Labour
and Employment
Relations Association

ILERA PUBLICATION SERIES

The ILERA publication series covers the general theme of comparative labour and employment relations. Books in the series focus on comparative analysis of labour and employment relations, broadly interpreted to comprise all aspects of work including labour policy, labour market analysis, labour relations and collective bargaining, human resource management, and work- and workplace-related topics.

Trade Unions and Migrant Workers
New Contexts and Challenges in Europe
Edited by Stefania Marino, Judith Roosblad and Rinus Penninx

Organizing Matters
Two Logics of Trade Union Representation
Guy Mundlak

Work and Labour Relations in Global Platform Capitalism
Edited by Julieta Haidar and Maarten Keune

Work and Labour Relations in Global Platform Capitalism

Edited by

Julieta Haidar

Associate Professor, Workers' Innovation Centre (UMET-CONICET), Buenos Aires, Argentina

Maarten Keune

Professor of Social Security and Labour Relations, AIAS-HSI, University of Amsterdam, the Netherlands

ILERA PUBLICATION SERIES

Edward Elgar
PUBLISHING

Cheltenham, UK • Northampton, MA, USA

International Association of Labour and Employment Relations
Geneva, Switzerland

Published by
Edward Elgar Publishing Limited
The Lypiatts
15 Lansdown Road
Cheltenham
Glos GL50 2JA
UK

Edward Elgar Publishing, Inc.
William Pratt House
9 Dewey Court
Northampton
Massachusetts 01060
USA

In association with
International Association of Labour and Employment Relations
4 route des Morillons
CH-1211 Geneva 22
Switzerland
ISBN 978-92-2-034984-7

A catalogue record for this book
is available from the British Library

Library of Congress Control Number: 2021947653

This book is available electronically in the **Elgar**online
Political Science and Public Policy subject collection
http://dx.doi.org/10.4337/9781802205138

ISBN 978 1 80220 512 1 (cased)
ISBN 978 1 80220 513 8 (eBook)

Printed and bound by TJ Books, Padstow, Cornwall

Contents

Figures

Tables

Contributors

Cora Arias, Workers' Innovation Centre (CONICET-UMET)

Helena Barnard, Gordon Institute of Business Science, University of Pretoria

Graciela Bensusán, Universidad Autónoma Metropolitana-Unidad Xochimilco

Janine Berg, International Labour Organization

Premilla D'Cruz, Indian Institute of Management Ahmedabad

Mark Graham, Oxford Internet Institute, University of Oxford

Julieta Haidar, Workers' Innovation Centre (CONICET-UMET)

Isis Hjorth, Oxford Internet Institute, University of Oxford

Simon Joyce, University of Leeds

Maarten Keune, AIAS-HSI, University of Amsterdam

Vili Lehdonvirta, Oxford Internet Institute, University of Oxford

Wing-Fai Leung, King's College London

Petar Marčeta, AIAS-HSI, University of Amsterdam

Nicolás Diana Menéndez, Workers' Innovation Centre (CONICET-UMET)

Ernesto Noronha, Indian Institute of Management Ahmedabad

Uma Rani, International Labour Organization

Héctor Santos, Instituto de Investigaciones Dr. José María Luis Mora

Nick Srnicek, King's College London

Mark Stuart, University of Leeds

Kurt Vandaele, European Trade Union Institute

Mariano Zukerfeld, Centro de Ciencia, Tecnología y Sociedad, Universidad Maimónides (CONICET)

Introduction: *Work and Labour Relations in Global Platform Capitalism*

Julieta Haidar and Maarten Keune

INTRODUCTION

Since the 1990s, and in particular since the 2008 crisis, digital platforms have progressively ascended to the centre of contemporary capitalism, giving rise to so-called platform capitalism (Srnicek 2016). Platform capitalism is an authentically global phenomenon as around the world platforms have come to play a major role in social networking, retail, business services, delivery of food and other products, domestic and care work, streaming, the development of artificial intelligence, transport, etc. Global platform capitalism is epitomised by a group of very large transnational companies like Alibaba, Facebook, Alphabet, Amazon, Tencent or Uber. And then there is a large, and ever-growing group of other, smaller platforms, some also with a global reach and others focusing on specific groups of countries. Through their rapid growth, digital platforms are increasingly shaping social relations, consumption, work and labour relations around the globe.

In this volume, we present an analysis of work and labour relations in global platform capitalism. We focus our analysis on labour platforms – digital platforms that organise labour processes by matching labour providers (mainly self-employed workers) with clients and consumers. Labour platforms charge rents over the fees paid through the platform and use algorithmic management methods to exercise disciplinary control, to a varying degree, over task allocation and performance (Gandini 2019).

Labour platforms can be divided into online and offline platforms (De Stefano 2015). Online platforms connect a multiplicity of clients and individual workers through the internet, with work being done remotely. The scope of online platforms is global, transcending geographic boundaries and creating atomised global labour markets. Some of these platforms require complex services or 'macrotasks' with higher skill levels, such as translation or design (e.g. Upwork, Workana). Others cover a multiplicity of simple 'microtasks' or 'click work' (e.g. Clickworker, Amazon Mechanical Turk) such as the categorisation of pictures, transcription of speech, participation in surveys, etc., that require lower skill levels.

Offline platforms connect clients and customers with workers who perform their tasks physically in a given geographic space. Some services are developed in public spaces, such as passenger transport (e.g. Uber, Cabify) and delivery (e.g. Deliveroo, Glovo) and others in private spaces, such as home repair (e.g. IguanaFix, Jobin) or domestic and care work (e.g. Helpling, Aliada). Offline platform work generally involves physical tasks like driving or cleaning; however, the workers are also continuously interacting through apps with the platform to receive orders or instructions, accept or decline tasks and receive evaluations.

Labour platforms have become significant sources of controversies, tensions and ambiguities. On the one hand, they have become important sources of work and income. This tendency seems only to be strengthened by the COVID-19 pandemic as many have retreated into their private homes and predominantly have digital social interaction, increasing demand for the services of labour platforms. Also, the economic crisis and job losses resulting from the pandemic make labour platforms a possible shelter for unemployed workers. In addition, the platforms claim that they provide high levels of autonomy and flexibility to workers regarding when and how much they work. On the other hand, it is often argued that the work that labour platforms create is precarious and exploitative, that they raise the control of capital over workers to new heights, and that platform workers lack legal protection and collective representation.

In this volume, we discuss these controversies, tensions and ambiguities surrounding labour platforms theoretically and empirically, and situate them within the broader development of global capitalism. The volume brings together authors from different parts of the world, takes a global perspective and studies a selection of continents, countries and types of online and offline platforms. It is divided into three main parts. The first is a largely theoretical part that situates platform work in the wider context of contemporary capitalism and includes chapters by Nick Srnicek, Mariano Zukerfeld and Petar Marčeta. The second part discusses labour platforms from the perspective of the international division of labour as well as their embedding in local labour markets and contains chapters by Janine Berg and Uma Rani, Vili Lehdonvirta, Isis Hjorth, Helena Barnard and Mark Graham, and Wing-Fai Leung, Premilla D'Cruz and Ernesto Noronha. The third part focuses on the labour process and labour relations and incorporates chapters by Simon Joyce and Mark Stuart, Cora Arias, Nicolás Diana Menéndez and Julieta Haidar, Kurt Vandaele, and Graciela Bensusán and Héctor Santos.

In this introduction we present in five sections our main propositions, which can be summarised as follows: (1) labour platforms are at the frontier of capitalist development, comprising both important continuities and meaningful novelties; (2) labour platforms generate new dependencies and a new international division of labour between the global North and South; (3) labour platforms are capital's latest attempt to increase control over the labour process; (4) labour platforms are built on and foster the ideal of the entrepreneurial self; and (5) labour platforms are riddled with tensions between dependency and autonomy, the shape of which influences the extent and ways in which workers organise. In discussing these five propositions we make ample use of the subsequent chapters of this volume that analyse various aspects of them in detail.

1   LABOUR PLATFORMS AND THE DEVELOPMENT OF CAPITALISM

The emergence and growth of labour platforms cannot be understood as driven by the availability of digital technologies but are an expression of longer-term tendencies we can observe in the global political economy. Labour platforms represent profound innovation that embodies the frontiers of capitalist change, but they are also products of earlier developments and demonstrate continuities with the past. In this section we provide a discussion of several major and closely interrelated aspects of capitalist development of the last few decades that are relevant in this respect. We present the main arguments in a concise way here, while in the subsequent sections their most salient features are discussed in detail.

To begin with, the rise of labour platforms is part and parcel of the development of capitalism as a mode of production that continuously seeks to optimise the labour process. Where in the first post-WWII decades Fordism was the dominant mode of organising the labour process, since the 1970s, in the post-Fordist era, a series of new types of management and work organisation have been devised (Boyer & Durand 1997; Lepadatu & Janoski 2020). These range from lean production, Toyotism and flexible specialisation, to McDonaldization, project-based organisations and agile management. They all in their own way attempt to optimise the labour process, some emphasising standardisation, external labour flexibility, low wages and tight control and others focusing on increasing autonomy, internal flexibility, skills development and career planning.

Labour platforms can be considered one of the frontiers in this process of optimisation and the latest manifestation of the capitalist labour process. As will be discussed in more detail below, they combine the latest digital technologies with their own specific organisational, managerial and discursive strategies to optimise the use of labour. This includes unilateral and untransparent algorithmic management methods to strengthen efficiency, flexibility and control and the circumvention of the wage relationship to reduce costs and risks and again to increase flexibility. They also involve the construction of workers as entrepreneurs, emphasising their autonomy and responsibility for their own success and fostering intense competition between them.

Labour platforms also constitute the next level in the ongoing process of global fragmentation of economic activity, aiming to exploit differences in labour and other costs between countries and continents, and to optimise value chains. Since the 1970s we can observe the decline of the large integrated firm in the global North, which progressively started to subcontract and outsource production to optimise cost efficiency and profits and reduce risks. Over the years, this process of fragmentation acquired a decisively global character as capital started to massively offshore activities to geographical locations more advantageous in particular in terms of labour costs (Gereffi 2011, 2014). Massive offshoring took place first in manufacturing but gradually also in a wide range of services, resulting in complex and fragmented global value chains in which predominantly Northern capital orchestrates the global distribution of profits and risks (Gereffi 2014).

Labour platforms take this fragmentation a step further. This is especially true for online labour platforms which facilitate the outsourcing and offshoring of a growing range of service activities not to companies but to an infinite pool of freelancing and competing individuals across the globe. They allow firms and individual clients to access individual workers on all continents in an instant and to seek out the most favourable price-quality combinations. As will be discussed in the next section, this results in a new international division of labour which includes elements of the pre-industrial putting-out system.

In their own way offline platforms also contribute to a new international division of labour, not because work crosses borders but because many of the workers on offline platforms are migrants, coming from other countries. Although they are often overqualified for the work they do, for migrants that have a hard time finding jobs, platform work has the advantage of low entry barriers and the promise (although not necessarily the reality) of earnings that compare favourably to other job opportunities they have access to in the host country. In this way, labour platforms offer migrant workers much-needed opportunities to improve their livelihoods while simultaneously reproducing discrimination and degrading working conditions (van Doorn et al. 2020; van Doorn 2017).

Apart from the optimising and fragmenting of existing activities, labour platforms also play a role in capitalism's drive to bring more and more areas and activities under capitalist relations (Silver 2003), or, as Streeck (2017) phrases it, to 'ultimately commodify everything'. Labour platforms have a threefold importance in this striving for commodification. One is that platform work, generally not subject to employment and social protection regulations, often replaces or crowds out work that previously did enjoy such protection, thus recommodifying labour (Marčeta in this volume; Aloisi 2015). As will be discussed in the next section, this applies in particular to the global North where it contributes to the growth of precarious work. Another is that labour platforms commodify labour previously not subsumed by the capitalist mode of production (Marčeta in this volume). This can concern previously non-commodified activities as well as the incorporation of geographical areas or groups of persons that were previously largely outside the reach of the capitalist mode of production. Finally, labour platforms, like all other platforms, engage in the continuous accumulation of data about all aspects of their activities. There is a lively debate concerning the extent to which this data is commodified and whether it is part of a process of value creation or rather value appropriation (Fuchs 2014; van Doorn & Badger 2020). Two chapters in this volume contribute to this debate and do so from different perspectives: Srnicek argues that platforms mainly engage in value appropriation through rents instead of value creation, whereas Zukerfeld does argue that platforms produce value but claims that there are different types of exploitation through which capital obtains a surplus value at the expense of exploited actors, which do not necessarily occur in the context of labour relations.

The accumulation of data is also closely related to a further aspect that has been vital for the development of labour platforms, that is the financialisation that gradually got its grip on global capitalism from the 1970s (Deutschmann 2011; van der Zwan 2014). In the previous decades, growth rates in the global North had started to decline, resulting in less profitable investment opportunities for investment capital. At the same time, high savings rates, an increased money supply, low interest rates and public policy liberalising the financial sector fostered a swift increase in available equity and venture capital and investors desperately started to look for new and highly profitable investment opportunities, a tendency which sharpened after the financial crisis of 2008.

Labour platforms promise to provide such opportunities, in two different ways. On the one hand, because of their capacity to capture value by charging rents for each transaction that the platform facilitates (e.g. each delivery, Uber ride, executed click task or completed translation). Here the interest of investors is in the novel and lean business model of labour platforms which makes them potentially very profitable ventures. On the other hand, as mentioned above, labour platforms continuously accumulate data about their own processes, markets, customers, etc. This data is first of all used to improve their own operations but, more importantly, they potentially represent value in a broader but yet indeterminate sense as well:

> [...] whereas the value of this monetary rent can be dynamically determined by the platform, the value of data rent is fundamentally indeterminate insofar as it derives from speculative and performative practices. Platforms engage in constant

data accumulation because of the potential value this data, once processed by their analytics software, might embody or give rise to [...] Yet captured data also attract venture capital and grow financial valuations, to the extent that investors expect data-rich platform companies to achieve competitive advantages by creating data-driven cost efficiencies, cross-industry synergies, and new markets. (van Doorn & Badger 2020: 3)

As a result, venture capital and other investors have shown great interest in the platform economy and massive amounts of capital have been invested in labour platforms and in platform companies in general, in particular after the financial crisis (Langley & Leyshon 2017; Kenney and Zysman 2016). It is important to underline that these are essentially rentier-type investments that do not engage in value creation but in rent and value appropriation. In this sense, platforms are exemplary for financialised capitalism in which rentiers, i.e. finance owners and financial institutions, have become core actors in the economy, not contributing to productive investments but strongly increasing their income, at the expense of stagnating real wages and increased house-hold debt (Streeck 2017; van der Zwan 2014; Standing 2016). The fact that these massive investments in platforms have a non-productive character also explains why the enormous growth of many platform companies has not been accompanied by accelerating economic growth in the global North; indeed, they may rather undermine growth by extracting value from the productive economy (Srnicek in this volume).

Finally, the rise of labour platforms was facilitated by the fact that over the previous decades neoliberalism had established itself firmly as the quasi-hegemonic governmentality of capitalism in most parts of the world, even though in a geographically variegated way (Harvey 2005; Brenner et al. 2010; Peck 2013). Two dimensions of neoliberalism are particularly important for the understanding of the emergence and growth of labour platforms. One, which will be discussed in more detail below, is the rise of the ideal of the entrepreneurial self (Bröckling 2013) fostering the continuous construction of workers as entrepreneurs, autonomous subjects who are responsible for their own destiny.

The other is that the neoliberal era is increasingly becoming a state of post-democracy, in which both economic and political power is '[...] increasingly being exercised by international business interests ranging at will over transnational territories beyond the reach of nation-states – the level at which democracy remained largely trapped' (Crouch 2016: 71). Large corporations are less and less subject to the rules of the market, and rather strive for monopolistic or oligopolistic status; they are also less and less subject to the rules of democracy, freely moving their financial assets across borders, escaping regulations of some countries and imposing their own rules in others (Crouch

2004, 2016). This is particularly true for platform companies, today the largest, most globalised and most powerful companies (Drahokoupil and Piasna 2017; Degryse 2019).[1] They have become the main example of capitalism unbound. Existing regulations and regulators often do not have the capacity to deal with the digital nature of in particular online platforms, which means they easily transcend the nation-state and seem to escape geography. Similarly, the novelty of their activities and business models often means that there are no clear standards to govern them, allowing for unchallenged self-regulation by the platforms. And where regulators try to enforce compliance from platforms, the latter invest heavily in lobbying and court battles to protect their interests.

This also applies in terms of labour and social security regulations (ibid.). Online platforms in particular easily avoid (national) regulations since these do not foresee digital employment relations in which client and worker may be located on different continents and digital platforms are the entity closest to the figure of the employer. Deciding which regulations apply where and how to enforce them presents an array of serious problems, as does the question of how to organise online platform workers through trade unions or other organisations. Consequently they often only have access to the protective standards and arbitration or mediation procedures which the platforms themselves establish (if any). This leaves the workers without real protection against precarious employment conditions and abusive practices.

Offline labour platforms, operating in defined geographical spaces where it is clear which labour and social security regulations should apply, engage in extensive political lobbying and fierce court battles in order to evade such regulations. Their main strategy is to deny that they are employers of the workers working for their platform, and in this way refusing workers employee status and the protective labour regulations and social security rights this status brings (Bensusán and Santos in this volume; Marčeta in this volume; De Stefano, 2015). Platforms like Uber or Foodora constantly lobby politicians and are involved in court cases around the world to try and safeguard their non-employer status. On top of this, the strategies of trade unions to organise and protect offline platform workers are still in their infancy (Arias et al. in this volume; Vandaele in this volume).

In this way, the neoliberal hegemony has created an ideological and regulatory environment in which labour platforms can lower costs and increase flexibility and control by placing themselves outside the reach of labour and social security regulations. This connects neoliberalism to the starting point of this section, i.e., capitalism as a mode of production that continuously seeks to optimise the labour process, and exemplifies the interconnections between the various aspects of capitalist development and the ways in which they have favoured the rise of labour platforms.

2 LABOUR PLATFORMS IN THE GLOBAL NORTH AND SOUTH

With the expansion of platform capitalism, labour platforms have become global phenomena. However, as demonstrated in several chapters in this volume (Vandaele; Bensusán and Santos; Berg and Rani; Lehdonvirta et al.; Lueng et al.), their local manifestations and impacts vary due to the uneven global distribution of capital, the structural and institutional features of local labour markets and the international division of labour. To capture this tension, in this section we examine two main issues. One is how labour platforms shape the relationships between the global North and the global South, in particular through online labour platforms. The other is the specific impact of labour platforms on local labour markets.

Concerning the relationships between the global North and South, we identify two quite distinct but not mutually exclusive perspectives. The first focuses on exploitation and underlines how Northern capital utilises labour platforms as a new way to get access to ever-cheaper labour and to exploit workers in the global South. The second centres on opportunities and emphasises that labour platforms offer countries and workers in the South valuable prospects for development.

The exploitation perspective starts from the observation that most of the online labour platforms are financed by capital from the global North, most of the demand for labour on these platforms also originates in the North, while most of the work is done by workers from the global South (Lehdonvirta et al. in this volume; Graham et al. 2017). In this way, online labour platforms increase the dependency of the South on Northern capital and make it vulnerable to its whims. They also orchestrate a new international division of labour in which workers in the South are digitally subordinated to capital and clients in the North.

Lueng et al. (in this volume) argue that the global character of these platforms results in a new international putting-out system of labour (NIPL). Whereas historically the putting-out system of home-based artisanal workshops preceded the movement of work to the factories of the industrial era, labour platforms are reversing this development and are moving work back to the homes of individuals (Kenney & Zysman 2016), principally in the global South. The NIPL allows the clients from the North to reduce the costs of labour, management, supervision, equipment and real estate and to transfer many of the risks traditionally borne by employers and investors onto the shoulders of Southern workers.

Additionally, nominal hourly rates in the South are often substantially lower than in the North (Lueng et al. in this volume; also Berg and Rani in this volume). Workers from the South suffer from 'liabilities of origin', as clients act according to country stereotypes, facilitated by the respective information platforms present on the workers (Lehdonvirta et al. in this volume). For example, clients from the North expect workers from the South to accept lower rates than their Northern counterparts, even when they have the same skills and experience. This discriminatory behaviour goes against the supposedly meritocratic nature of platform work, where earnings should above all depend on one's own capacities and commitment. Indeed, equal human capital does not mean equal earnings in the global platform labour market (ibid.).

Moreover, workers in the South often accept lower rates because of the lack of better opportunities in their local labour market. This is further strengthened by the fact that labour demand on online platforms far outstrips labour supply (ibid.), fomenting competition between workers and causing downward pressure on pay rates. Indeed, many platform workers (from South *and* North) would like to work more hours but are confronted with the limited availability of work. However, this affects workers from the South more as platform work is often their only or main source of income, while in the North it is generally an additional source of income to complement insufficient wages in the main job (Berg & Rani in this volume). As a result, workers from the South have fewer alternative opportunities and less bargaining power. Furthermore, in many cases they have to adapt their working hours to the requirements of their clients in the North, leading to extensive night work. And on top of these disadvantages workers from the South are also confronted with racist language and remarks in their interactions with Northern clients as well as competing workers from the North (Lueng et al. in this volume).

The opportunities perspective instead argues that online labour platforms offer workers and countries in the global South important opportunities to make good use of capital from the North. A number of governments in the global South view such platforms as a way to strengthen their economy and labour market and therefore as an important element of their development strategies (Berg & Rani in this volume; Soriano & Cabañes 2020). They argue that labour platforms offer an important new source of income and a way to mitigate the brain-drain caused by the outward migration of well-educated workers. In this view, labour platforms can substantially reduce the need to attract productive capital from abroad and all the concessions this may require.

Also, platform workers in the South see several positive sides to online platforms. To restate a point made above in a more optimistic way, for the more highly skilled workers in particular hourly pay is often substantially better than the earning opportunities on their local labour markets, even if it might be below that of workers from the North. Moreover, when pay rates are converted to purchasing power parity, online platform workers in the South may actually earn more than their Northern counterparts (Berg & Rani in this volume).

Apart from pay, other positive aspects underlined by platform workers are the (real or fictious) flexibility and autonomy concerning when, where and how much they work, opportunities to build networks with new contacts all over the world, and opportunities to learn new skills (Lueng et al. in this volume).

In our view, these two perspectives both offer useful interpretations and are not mutually exclusive. They show that the North-South relations created by online labour platforms are full of contradictions and tensions. Online platforms are largely populated by workers from the global South but orchestrated by capital from the North, leading to exploitation, dependency, inequalities and discrimination. At the same time, they offer workers from the South earning, learning and autonomy opportunities that they lack in their local labour markets. These opportunities are the reason that workers often express their satisfaction with platform work, despite its exploitative character.

The other issue that we want to discuss here is the differential effect labour platforms, both on- and offline, have on local labour markets. As mentioned above, a key characteristic of labour platforms is that they (attempt to) circumvent local labour market and social protection institutions. They create informal employment which, according to the ILO (2018) is employment that is not, in law or in practice, subject to national labour legislation, income taxation, social protection or entitlement to employment benefits. It is important however to underscore that the level of informality differs dramatically between the global North and South. Whereas in 2016, 61.2 per cent of global employment was informal employment, in Western Europe, USA, Canada and Australia informality was below 20 per cent, which contrasts with 53.1 per cent in Latin America, 68.2 per cent in Asia and the Pacific and 85.8 per cent in Africa (ibid.).

The differences in levels of informality stem from the (partial) decommodification of labour in the North labour during Les Trente Glorieuses of the post-WWII era. In this period, labour market-related risks were to an important extent collectivised through protective employment and social regulations and strong trade unions (Esping-Andersen 1990). However, in recent decades the trend has been one of recommodification, as employers seek to evade or weaken protective institutions, and trade unions have been losing strength in most countries and sectors (Streeck 2017; Keune & Pedaci 2020; Doellgast et al. 2018). This is manifested by the growing use of, among others, temporary contracts, zero-hour contracts, on-call contracts, bogus self-employment, and outsourcing. Labour platforms can be considered the latest manifestation of this process of recommodification, contributing to the further weakening of labour protection (Marčeta in this volume). At the same time, the recommodifying effect of platform work in the North is limited since it is more often a complement to a formal job and a way to earn additional income in the context of stagnation of wage growth and increasing labour market insecurity.

In most of the global South, decommodification did not take place to the same extent and was often limited to parts of the public sector and large enterprises. Precarious work lacking protection is a structural feature of the labour markets in the South. Labour platforms consequently do not necessarily contribute to the weakening of protection but largely reproduce the low level of protection of the historically large informal sector (Bensusán et al. 2017). Or as Lueng et al. (p. 146, in this volume), discussing online platform work in India and China, phrase it: 'Unfortunately, workers' rights and collective bargaining are not well developed in either country, and therefore, with online employment, Upworkers are as vulnerable as their offline counterparts'. Platform work in the South can therefore more easily be interpreted as simply another source of (informal) work and income, without the connotation of recommodification. Consequently, the novelty of platform work in the South resides not so much in its precarious nature but, as mentioned before, in the alternative employment opportunities it provides as well as the possibilities for better earnings than those available on the local labour market.

Labour platforms create a new international division of labour and affect local labour markets in a variegated way along the North-South divide. However, it is noteworthy that they do not seem to challenge the traditional gender division of labour. In this respect, Berg and Rani (in this volume) show that inequalities between men and women, to the detriment of the latter, transcend geography. Women in both global regions emphasise their need or preference to work from home, indicating a persistence of the traditional gender division of labour in which domestic work and care responsibilities predominantly fall on women's shoulders. On top of this, women earn less than men from platform work in both global regions, suggesting that, instead of transforming such fundamental cultural traits, labour platforms tend to reproduce them.

Thus, labour platforms are global phenomena but geography continues to matter, both in the relationships these platforms create between the global North and South and in the way they affect local labour markets. In the following sections we will discuss in more detail the commonalities and geographical specificities around three core dimensions of labour platforms: the labour processes and algorithmic management methods workers are subject to, the process of constructing the subjectivity of the workers according to the ideal of the entrepreneurial self, and the challenges they pose in terms of collective workers' organisation.

3   PLATFORMS AS MODES OF ORGANISING AND
        CONTROLLING THE LABOUR PROCESS

The definition of platforms as companies that organise labour processes enables us to recognise the existence of processes of valorisation of capital and of asymmetrical social relations between capital and labour (Joyce & Stuart in this volume). On the basis of these premises we discuss how labour platforms organise and control the labour process underlining three characteristics. The first is that platforms constitute a hybridisation of different historical attempts by capital to close the existing gap between the productive capacity of labour power and its effective application in the service of capital. The second is that these efforts, in platform capitalism, are permeated by a new form of management, so-called 'algorithmic management' (Rosenblat & Stark 2016; Möhlmann & Zalmanson 2017). The third is that the control exercised by the platforms leads to the obliteration of the distinction between work and life, or between working time and free time, intensifying the tendency towards the real subsumption of society under capital.

With regards to the first characteristic, over the course of capitalist history, capital has developed different attempts to capture the productive capacity of labour power. We can distinguish at least three attempts which have been com-bined at different points in history (Vercellone 2020). The first is the technical division of labour (principally through Taylorism), based on expropriating workers' knowledge, codifying it and transferring it to capital, and then assign-ing tasks existing of specific standardised times and methods of completion. The second starts from accepting the impossibility of completely capturing the cognitive dimension of labour and eliminating the margin of workers' autonomy. Faced with this dilemma, the manager promotes the voluntary engagement of the workers' knowledge and time in the manager's interests. The third consists of the implementation of various techniques to evade the wage relation and the responsibility for managing the time and activities of the workers. Among these techniques are: the piecework distinctive of mercantile capitalism and early industrial capitalism, and today's use of the figure of self-employment.

In the organisation of platform work, these three attempts to more effec-tively capture labour power to the benefit of capital appear in a mixed form. They are adapted and redesigned according to the particular characteristics of the different platforms. Concerning the first attempt, we observe a revival of the technical division of labour in an emerging 'neo-Taylorism' or 'digital Taylorism', a useful concept with which to describe not only new modes of workplace surveillance, control and deskilling, but also '… how a variety of forms and combinations of software and hardware as a whole allow for new modes of the measurement, standardisation and quantification, decomposition and surveillance of labour – often through forms of (semi-) automated management and control' (Altenried 2020: 149). This concept applies to some extent to all platform work, but it is particularly relevant when considering microtask labour performed on online platforms. As with classic Taylorism, workers perform repetitive microtasks which are part of a larger process they are unaware of and disengaged from, like identifying images, symbols, sounds, or transcribing fragments of conversations which contribute to developing artificial intelligence. Amazon Mechanical Turk (AMT) explains it in this way: 'MTurk enables companies to harness the collective intelligence, skills, and insights from a global workforce to streamline business processes, augment data collection and analysis, and accelerate machine learning development'.[2] While digital Taylorism does not represent an entirely new form of control, it does have some unique digital characteristics. Contrary to classic Taylorism, microtask platforms do not necessarily determine when a worker works or how much time is spent on a task. They rather rely on the extensive reserve army to permanently maintain a sufficient supply of labour for the tasks at hand. By virtue of the technology, the labour is performed by thousands of crowd workers who cooperate 24 hours a day around the world, while the monitoring techniques characteristic of Taylorism are obscured by algorithmic management. Therefore, as the 'mechanical Turk' metaphor suggests, the platform is designed to sell living labour as if it were machinic labour (Altenried 2020).

The second historical attempt, i.e. the promotion of the voluntary engagement of the workers, is expressed in platform capitalism by invoking the figure of the entrepreneurial self (see the following section for a more detailed analysis). The platforms project an image of the autonomous entrepreneurial self, unencumbered by bosses, who freely manages her choices concerning what work she performs, when she does it and how much time she spends on it. Workers do often enjoy these sides of platform work (even though autonomy is largely fictitious in many cases). This is particularly so in the case of macrotasks, where the platforms and their clients require the highest degree of involvement of the worker and all her knowledge and skills, which results in an appeal to the worker's interest in learning and developing skills and knowledge.

However, some argue that real learning opportunities are limited as digital workers are,

(...) in many cases kept at arm's length, unable to access information about the wider chain their labour forms part of. Those digital workers are unsure of what function their tasks serve; what the meaning of tasks are, or how their work is put into use by end-clients. Furthermore, only some digital workers were able to articulate or make qualified guesses as to how their clients derive value from the labour they performed. (Graham et al. 2017: 152)

The latter view, combined with the ever-present control and evaluation by platforms, enables us to identify a certain 'Taylorisation of cognitive labour' which limits skills upgrading.

Finally, the third attempt to control labour power is expressed through the evasion of the wage relation by appealing to the figure of self-employment and the incorporation of systems of payment uncoupled from working hours. Through the figure of self-employment and the terms and conditions that the workers are obliged to accept each time they connect to the app, the platform companies make efforts to conceal the existence of employment relations, and at the same time they avoid and allow their clients to elude business risks.

For online macrotasks this is realised in the form of payment per project, in which workers engage their knowledge and affects. In the case of online microtasks and a majority of work on offline platforms (e.g. food delivery and passenger transport), the intensification of the appropriation of labour power is produced through piecework payments. Along these lines, what Marx recognised towards the end of the 19th century is reasserted:

> Given piece-wage, it is naturally the personal interest of the labourer to strain his labour-power as intensely as possible; this enables the capitalist to raise more easily the normal degree of intensity of labour. It is moreover now the personal interest of the labourer to lengthen the working-day, since with it his daily or weekly wages rise. (Marx 2018: 390)

Our second characteristic of the way in which labour platforms organise and control the labour process is that the above-discussed attempts to maximise the capturing of labour power are modernised and permeated by algorithmic management. This is a new mode of managing labour power, in which surveillance, supervision and, ultimately, control are carried out by algorithms. The uniqueness of this type of management in the era of digital technology consists in the fact that the monitoring and evaluation of the workers is performed in an individualised, continuous and remote way. Furthermore, the algorithmic technology enables a refinement and concealment of the processes of standardisation, codification and appropriation of knowledge in its diverse forms.

As we noted in the first section, one of the distinctive elements which characterises platform capitalism is the gathering and systematisation of enormous volumes of data. With regards to workers, this implies a continuous surveillance and manipulation of the information on their profiles and performances. This is achieved through the use of biopolitical technologies, such as GPS tracking, the periodic capture of identities by requesting 'selfies' (for offline platforms), or through information about the private sphere such as data related to civil status, illness, photos and videos of the workers' faces and bodies (for online platforms). This, as is mapped out by Lehdonvirta et al.

(in this volume), grants the platforms the power to reintroduce discriminatory practices along the lines of class, gender and ethnicity.

This data gathering also enables the companies to supervise and assess the workers' performance, making use of a large volume of evaluations completed both by the companies themselves and by customers, clients and providers. Some online platforms include tests and other qualification measures or, in the case of more complex tasks, allow clients to control workers via random screenshots or keystroke counters (Altenried 2020). In the case of offline platforms, customers and providers produce evaluations and in some cases publish comments online about the workers' performance.

As has been amply documented (Rosenblat & Stark 2016; Shapiro 2018; Haidar 2020), such evaluations, materialised in points and rankings, are converted into complex systems of rewards and punishments. While this is more widely documented for the offline platforms, where the workers can suffer temporary or permanent 'deactivations' (euphemisms for suspensions and dismissals) this also occurs on the online platforms. In effect, microtask workers depend on positive ratings from the task requesters in order to receive more work in the future, so a rejected task means not only potential loss of payment, but potentially restricted access to further work (Altenried 2020). The continuous monitoring and ratings are designed to control the labour process, and therefore the process of valorisation: the algorithms establish tariffs, bonuses, commissions, regulations and procedures to follow. In some cases the platforms attain control through strict rules and regulations. In others this is achieved in an indirect or induced way through the 'gamification of work'; in other words the generation and monitoring of conduct through gaming mechanisms, using images with a strong visual impact which set targets and offer rewards to the participants with the aim of maximising their performance.

Likewise, the almost complete digitalisation of the relationships between platforms and workers, and the high versatility and low transparency characterising the algorithms, express the asymmetry of power between the two. This disparity is intrinsic to the relations between capital and labour; the unique quality that the platforms contribute is the digitalisation of existing asymmetries as a mode of concealing their existence. The metaphors of the 'black box' (Pasquale 2015; Moore & Joyce 2020) and the 'shadow employer' (Gandini 2019) imply that the notion of control or directive power is concealed and transferred to the impersonal authority of the system.

Finally, the third characteristic of the way in which labour platforms organise and control the labour process is that they blur the boundaries between working hours and free time. This happens in different ways. Several of the offline platforms offer bonuses for those who work during certain hours (in delivery and transport), while online platforms encourage working during the waking hours of clients in the global North which do not coincide with the normal working day of those living in the southern hemisphere.

Likewise, the particular dynamics of the platforms cause workers to be in a constant state of attention in order to snap up new job offers and to dedicate hours of their free time to engaging in unpaid work constructing their public profiles and searching for the next job. Also, and more significantly, they use their time, energy and emotions to become entrepreneurial and productive subjects, attuned to the demands of clients and the figure of the entrepreneurial self. In this way, the division between work and life, or between working hours and free time, is effaced, intensifying the tendency towards the real subsumption of society under capital. This tendency draws us closer to the dystopia pursued by the capitalist political project: a worker wholly dedicated to capital.

4   THE ARTIFACTUALITY OF THE PLATFORM WORKER: THE ENTREPRENEURIAL SELF

Just as we identified algorithmic management as a historic form of controlling the labour process and subordinating knowledge to the processes of valorisation of capital, it is possible to identify in the construction of the platform worker a compounded form of the entrepreneurial self; that is, the aspirational figure par excellence of hegemonic neoliberal governmentality in contemporary capitalism.

The ideal of the entrepreneurial self started to develop with the discontent of workers after the rebellions of May 1968 in France, and the rejection of the discipline of labour under the Taylorist-Fordist type of organisation. Along these lines, Bröckling (2013; see also Foucault 1997) maps out a genealogy of entrepreneurialism and observes that it constitutes an offshoot of the varied manifestations of the post-1968 counterculture which, in spite of their anti-capitalist impulse, can be seen in hindsight as laboratories for the gestation of an entrepreneurial attitudinal orientation. Outlining a genealogy of entrepreneurialism by tracing its roots to the counterculture of independence enables us to understand its success: the entrepreneurial self could only become a hegemonic figure because it reflected a collective desire for greater autonomy, personal realisation and non-alienated labour (Bröckling 2013).

The management literature of the 1990s radicalised this programme, both inside and outside companies, with self-management manuals and methodical, success-oriented lifestyles, aimed at self-optimisation. In the sphere of production this translated into new participatory models of organising work as forms of building consent, or in Burawoy's (1979) terminology, 'voluntary submission' in the workplace. In the development of platform work this ideal was strengthened by an array of techniques of government through which, as Foucauldian approaches to neoliberal governmentality point out, individual liberty is constructed (i.e. is not natural) and recharacterised as autonomy (Dean 1999; Rose 1999).

The platforms in all their diversity are permeated by this conception. They discursively present themselves as an opportunity for workers to increase their autonomy, organise their own time, earn income and obtain other benefits (learning, self-development, meeting people, constructing networks), without bosses or restrictions, and according to the individual investment that each worker-entrepreneur makes of her time, skills, efforts, motivations and emotional commitment. This individualisation has resulted in the radical responsibilisation of the workforce, based upon an extreme version of self-interested individualism (Fleming 2017).

This discourse is accompanied by a heterogeneous group of performance technologies (monitoring and surveillance, rewards and penalties, etc.), which contribute to fabricating and enhancing autonomous subjects and promoting highly individualised and demanding working practices: self-discipline, self-realisation, and competition with oneself and other workers. Therefore, as suggested in the previous section, the reconciliation between life and work proclaimed by the movement which challenged alienation in the 1960s has materialised for platform workers as the subsumption of all aspects of their life under work.

The complexity of this phenomenon derives from the fact that the platforms' discourses and technologies of performance constitute practices of government as well as the promotion of workers' self-government, which in this articulation combine notions of liberty and submission (Dean 1999). In the figure of the entrepreneurial self this is expressed as an extremely powerful 'real fiction' (Realfiktion), which sets and keeps in motion a continuous process of modification and self-modification of subjects (Bröckling 2013).

These constructions of subjectivity, with all their ambivalences and tensions, have particular characteristics according to the geographical specificities in which the online and offline platforms are embedded and operate. This involves the incorporation of other determinations and subjects of government that transcend the platform companies: political-juridical interventions (whether direct or indirect) that establish the conditions of free, entrepreneurial and economically rational conduct of individuals; and the cultural constructions that are associated with a process of neoliberalisation structured according to class, gender and racial interests.

With regards to this situated configuration, we can empirically observe that online platform workers emphasise the benefits of working from home, without bosses, and above all being able to autonomously organise their working hours and free time. This is, as mentioned earlier, especially valued by women, which seems to indicate a reproduction of patriarchal models of unequal distribution of domestic labour and care work between men and women.

The geographically embedded character of the configuration of platform work is expressed clearly by Leung et al. (in this volume), who note how in China and India the entrepreneurial spirit and individualism promoted by the platforms represent relatively novel values imported from the West that are enthusiastically embraced by the middle classes, particularly young recent graduates. In India, the authors observe, the platforms represent a movement away from the feudalist ethos which permeates most workplaces in that country, fostering exploitative and sycophantic conduct and practices.

These brief considerations about how platform work and workers' subjectivities are constructed in harmony with the ideal of the entrepreneurial self, with its returns and advantages, both real and imaginary, enable us to spotlight the ambivalent and conflictual character of labour platforms. In this section we have chosen to emphasise how the idea of the autonomous worker is constructed from a positive axiology. However, the 'real fiction' of the entrepreneurial self also produces contradictory feelings. Feelings of self-realisation, autonomy and satisfaction are accompanied by feelings of frustration, impotence, discontent and injustice. These representations are informed by the physical, mental and emotional fatigue provoked by the gamification, the technological dehumanisation, and the unilateral, shifting and opaque nature of algorithmic decisions.

Although, as Bröckling (2013) points out, simulation and stimulation intermingle until they can no longer be differentiated. What remains unclear is how far individuals maintain the fiction, how difficult it is for them to sustain it, and what counteracting experiences they can endure. Along these lines, it now remains for us to analyse how these ambivalences and tensions impact on the construction of organisational responses from workers.

5   WORKERS' ORGANISATION AS A FIELD OF TENSION

The question of platform workers' organisation and resistance has been studied from a variety of perspectives. One is labour process theory, which takes on a dual dynamic in which control always sparks resistance (in a latent or active form). Along these lines, Joyce and Stuart (in this volume) show how three broad categories of platform management methods (algorithmic management, pay and wider forms of regulation) each include dimensions of control, which are associated with three types of resistance: micro-level fiddles and individual resistance, informal collective actions, and actions organised by unions or other worker representation and advocacy groups, on a more formal basis.

Others analyse resistance from the perspective of the challenges that platform work poses for workers' representation, placing special emphasis on trade union responses. For example, Vandaele (in this volume) reasserts the categories of power resource theory (structural, associational, institutional and societal power) and two ideal type representation approaches: the logic-of-membership, if efforts are concentrated on worker organisation, and the logic-of-influence, if the responses are rooted in the institutional logic of national systems of industrial relations. Similarly, Arias et al. (in this volume) study workers' organisation and strategies from the perspective of trade union traditions: rank and file type organisation, with horizontal and combative features, on the one hand, and hierarchical, vertical, bargaining-oriented organisation, on the other.

These interpretations make important contributions towards analytically arranging the repertoires of collective action, demands and forms in which the workers organise in the context of platforms. However, besides this, it is necessary to develop an approach which gives an account of the ambivalent character of platform work. Epistemologically this involves incorporating an analysis of feelings of injustice and discontent, as well as the libidinal component, i.e. satisfaction and benefits.

Indeed, the tensions around platform work constitute a necessary component with which to understand workers' organisation: how are the tensions between subjection and freedom expressed in their forms of organisation? To what extent do these tensions affect workers' demands and repertoires of action? How far do they permeate political meanings and projections? The hypothesis animating these questions is that organisational responses are an expression of the particular tensions between subjection and freedom that characterise platform work.

By organisational responses we understand forms of organisation, repertoires of collective action, along with the demands and political projections that the workers construct. We can hypothesise that the construction of organisational responses depends on varying articulations between multiple determinations: the forms of control exercised by the platforms, the power resources of workers and unions, union traditions and strategies, and governmental interventions, all corresponding to specific geographical configurations of the labour market, culture and institutions. Here we want to draw particular attention to the connections established between the tensions around the subjection/ freedom dyad and the organisational responses that are constructed along with their claims, forms of collective action and perspectives.

To this effect, we distinguish four organisational responses as inductively constructed Weberian ideal types, which reflect varying combinations of satisfaction and defence of the autonomist ideal, and feelings of injustice and recognition of the existence of relations of subordination and dependence.

These ideal types, by definition, are not expressed in practice in a pure form, but in a variety of combinations.

First, we can identify the responses we describe as 'pro-status quo', which most tightly cleave to the ideal of the entrepreneurial self and which defend the full development of autonomy. Constructed on the basis of the satisfactions and benefits provided by the platforms, the workers engage in limited actions with the sole aim of improving the conditions in which they operate on the labour market.

Here we find the participation of workers in different forms of digital associativism, social networks and forums where they share information and tips about how to earn a higher income and avoid sanctions. Examples are online clickworkers who warn other workers about clients who pay badly or fail to pay; app-based taxi drivers who report on changes in the algorithms and ways of circumventing them; food delivery workers who share information about which neighbourhoods have higher demand, etc. Sharing information and tips can also be accompanied by coordinated action, as is the case with clickworkers who act together to manipulate the configuration of algorithmic preferences or who develop browser plugins (e.g. Turkopticon) which help workers to increase their access to better-paying tasks (Joyce and Stuart, in this volume).

While these actions are collective, no questioning of the founding logic of the platforms arises, no demands or claims are presented to the platforms, and there is no construction of a political subject, but rather an interest in improving their conditions without disrupting the status quo. However, that does not detract from the construction of solidarities tending to equalise, in a partial and limited way, the asymmetries of information and power between workers and platforms. These solidarities also counteract the relationship of competition that exists between the participants who, from the representation of the entrepreneurial self, are conceived of as rivals competing for the market.

A second set of responses can be described as 'reformist' and are the paroxysmal expression of the tensions which permeate the organisation of work and the workers in their subjectivity, for whom satisfaction, desire for autonomy, discontent and rejection of arbitrary algorithmic practices are enmeshed. This set of responses is diverse; it includes a wide repertoire of action, with varying demands, organisational forms and meanings. The main objective is to partially reform the functioning of and relationship with the platforms, without abandoning the vindication of sovereignty over their use of time and organisation of their own lives.

To illustrate these expressions, we can refer to the diversity of responses from food delivery workers. Although these workers often joined the platforms having been seduced by promises of freedom in their activities, expectations turn to discontent when faced with what are viewed as abusive practices that violate the contract of trust between parties. In many cases, workers coordinate actions and jointly oppose the company that takes advantage of them. How and with what meanings these demands and actions develop from the experience of these contradictions is uncertain, sinuous and heterogeneous.

In some experiences the workers organise into associations which demand that the established terms and conditions be respected or improved, a demand which reframes the relationships between workers and platforms in terms of a commercial contract between equal parties. Other demands are often added to these which are aimed at improving income and working conditions on the platforms: rate increases, minimum payment for working hours, health coverage and insurance, etc. The demand for recognition of an employment relationship does not take precedence, nor do attempts to sign collective bargaining agreements, which for many workers represent a threat to the benefits of platform work.

The repertoires of action and institutional forms that their organisation take are as heterogeneous as the demands that motivate them. Here, although not exclusively, the logic of membership takes precedence: in some cases the workers are self-organised (such as 'Riders for Rights' in Spain), while in other cases they are organised by rank and file trade unions, or are supported and absorbed by larger unions (for a detailed analysis of the European case see Vandaele's chapter). Therefore, both self-organisation (as a priority) and trade unions can channel demands which strive to win improvements and labour rights, while maintaining the status of independence.

Similarly, the demands are expressed through a variety of repertoires of action, many of them associated with digital technology. These include twitter hashtag campaigns, virtual boycotts and campaigns ('Justice4Couriers' in Finland, #BrequeNosApps in Brazil, #EnTuPedidoVaMiVida in Mexico) through which they aim to build solidarity with customers, as well as demonstrations and strikes by disconnecting or logging off. Emblematic of this type of response are the wave of food delivery worker strikes which began in London in the summer of 2016 and which spread to the rest of the UK and other cities in continental Europe (Joyce and Stuart in this volume), the global Uber strikes that took place in May 2019 with heightened levels of coordination across the United States and other countries (Johnston 2020), and more recently the international wave of food delivery worker strikes protesting the lack of protection they have suffered in the context of the pandemic. These strikes are dissociated from the routine mechanisms of conflict which are characteristic of the classic dynamics of strike/negotiation. Given the low levels of workplace bargaining power resources, the log-offs are more an expression of dissatisfaction and a demonstration of latent power than part of a strategy aimed at achieving more thorough transformations. However, it is possible to infer that the strikes, with the commitments, solidarities and proposals they mobilise, contribute substantively to the construction of a worker identity in the context of the platforms.

A third type of response can be characterised as 'standardisation', in which workers organise on the basis of a recognition of the asymmetry of power in relation to the platforms, their exploitative character, and the search for a resolution which would minimise the tension between freedom and subjection, in favour of a recognition of the standard employment relationship. Here the idea of autonomy is called into question, it is experienced as a deception which generates more disadvantages than benefits, since the platforms control and discipline the workers without granting them any type of labour rights or social protection.

On this basis, the main demand raised is to change the status of the workers from independent contractors to employees, and for bargaining over collective labour agreements. The repertoires of action include demonstrations and strikes, but also the use of legal channels through which the workers seek a legal recognition of their status. Here, the construction of links with political authorities and local businesses takes on a greater role, as they can contribute towards constructing social dialogue or regulating labour relations.

As might be expected, the institutional forms which better adapt to these demands are the unions, and the logic which prevails is that of influence. However, self-organisation can also direct demands along this path, generally with the support of trade unions. One expression of this phenomenon is the establishment of works councils with trade union support in cities in Austria and Germany (Vandaele in this volume; Johnston 2020).

It is perhaps for this type of response that geographical characteristics occupy a more important position, given that the characteristics of the labour markets, actors and labour relations institutions are more decisive. Thus, it is not surprising that it is in the Scandinavian countries, with more cooperative labour relations and strong unions, where collective bargaining about platform work is more advanced (ibid.).

Finally, a fourth type of organisational response can be described as a 'disruption'. Here, as with the previous type, there is a recognition of asymmetrical and exploitative relations, but unlike the previous type it does not translate into renouncing the idea of autonomy and a demand for regulation. Instead, the vindication of autonomy along with the workers' ability to organise their labour process independently of the companies predominates, thus disrupting the prevailing platform model.

Along these lines, rather than taking action and presenting demands to the platforms, the workers maximise their cooperative efforts. Therefore, the organisational form *par excellence* is cooperative platforms. Swiftly constituted and with an uncertain future, Vandaele (in this volume) identifies at least ten cooperatives in different European countries which use the software developed by the federation of bike delivery workers' cooperatives 'Coopcycle'. This association defines itself as a mutualist, solidary and autonomous strategy inspired by the solidarity model of social security in which one contributes according to capabilities and receives according to needs. The political horizons in this sense are presented as more radical, not seeking to negotiate with platforms but rather to transcend them with forms that combine autonomism and mutualism.

It remains unclear whether the organisational responses will tend to converge in the same way that the business models of platforms companies have done in recent years. Neither is it clear which are the most appropriate alternatives to effectively confront the enormous power imbalances that characterise the relations between workers and platforms. What emerges however, as a noteworthy feature, is that the demands, actions, forms and projections are complex and permeated by the same contradictions that characterise platform work and platform workers. Taking an optimistic view of the ambivalences, tensions and quasi-aporetic character of platform work, rather than acting as a constraint they can be seen as fertile territory for action and transformation.

CONCLUSIONS

Labour platforms constitute a dynamic and growing global phenomenon that accelerated after the 2008 crisis and has been further speeded up by the COVID-19 pandemic, given the increase in the demand for platform services and the unemployment-fuelled supply of labour. They raise a series of questions about capitalism, work and labour relations which we have discussed in a concise form in this introduction, and which will be examined in more detail throughout the rest of this volume. The following conclusions emerge from our discussion.

One is that the expansion of labour platforms is not an isolated, technology-driven process but one that can only be understood as part of the broader process of capitalist development and change. It represents an intensification of earlier trends of optimisation, (re)commodification and global fragmentation of labour processes and has been dependent on the ongoing financialisation and neoliberalisation of capitalism. Related to this, labour platforms are global phenomena but geography continues to matter, both in the relationships of dependence and inequality they create between the global North and South and in the way they affect local labour markets.

Furthermore, labour platforms constitute a hybridisation of different historical attempts to close the gap between the productive capacity of labour power and its effective application in the service of capital. The main instrument of control here is algorithmic management: the control exercised by the platforms leads to the obliteration of the distinction between working time and free time, intensifying the tendency towards the real subsumption of society under capital. This is further strengthened by the construction of the platform worker as a form of the entrepreneurial self, autonomous and free. However, the 'real fiction' of the entrepreneurial self produces contradictions between feelings of self-realisation, autonomy and satisfaction on the one hand and feelings of frustration, impotence and injustice on the other.

Indeed, labour platforms create continuous ambivalences and tensions which impact on the construction of organisational responses from workers, reflecting varying combinations of satisfaction and defence of the autonomist ideal, and feelings of injustice and recognition of the existence of relations of subordination and dependence. We distinguish four ideal-typical organisational responses that can be used to depict workers' responses: pro-status quo, reformist, standardisation, and disruption, each representing a particular combination.

As this introduction has shown, the algorithmic technology, the construction of competitive individualised subjectivities and the insistence on the figure of the self-employed worker allow the platform companies to deploy their business model and to reinforce power asymmetries in relation to the workers. Taking into account the magnitude of these asymmetries and the complexity and versatility of the platform model, the recurrent question is how to protect platform workers? Much of the corresponding debate focuses on the question of whether the figure of self-employment fits the actual situation of platform workers and how to better regulate platform work.

These are important issues as protective regulations can reduce power asymmetries and employee status may confer a range of employment and social rights to platform workers. However, considering the widespread (or growing) presence of precarious work in the labour market in general, bringing platform work within the scope of protective legislation will not by itself be sufficient to tackle the disadvantageous position of platform workers. From a regulatory perspective, this requires a broader debate around how to guarantee the effective application of existing regulations and the possible need for supplementary norms in general or for platform workers in particular.

To improve the position of platform workers, apart from the question of regulation, additional attention should be given to the even more complex but important challenges related to algorithmic management, workers' subjectivities and inequalities: how to get a grip on the unilateral, ever-changing and opaque digital management mechanisms? How to deal with gender inequality in labour platforms, including unequal responsibilities for unpaid domestic and care tasks? How to construct a collective workers' identity? And, most importantly, how to construct sufficient power resources to counteract the power of the platforms? Responding to these questions requires a profound debate among scholars, platform workers as well as in the broader working-class and labour movement. With this book we hope to make our contribution to this debate.

NOTES

1. According to a PwC report, among the top ten of the largest companies by market capitalisation in mid-2020, seven were predominantly platform companies: Apple, Microsoft, Amazon, Alphabet, Facebook, Tencent and Alibaba. See https://www.pwc.com/gx/en/audit-services/publications/assets/global-top-100-companies-june-2020-update.pdf
2. See www.mturk.com

BIBLIOGRAPHY

Aloisi, A. (2015), 'Commoditized Workers: Case Study Research on Labor Law Issues Arising from a Set of on-Demand/Gig Economy Platforms', *Comparative Labor Law & Policy Journal*, **37** (3), 653–690.

Altenried, M. (2020), 'The Platform as Factory: Crowdwork and the Hidden Labour behind Artificial Intelligence', *Capital & Class*, **44** (2), 145–158.

Bensusán, G., Eichhorst, W. & Rodríguez, J. M. (2017), *Las transformaciones tecnológicas y sus desafíos para el empleo, las relaciones laborales y la identificación de la demanda de cualificaciones*. Santiago de Chile: CEPAL.

Boyer, R. & Durand, J.-P. (1997), *After Fordism*. London: Macmillan Press.

Brenner, N., Peck, J. & Theodore, N. (2010), 'Variegated Neoliberalization: Geographies, Modalities, Pathways', *Global Networks*, **10** (2), 182–222.

Bröckling, U. (2013), *El self emprendedor*. Santiago de Chile: Universidad Alberto Hurtado.

Burawoy, M. (1979), *Manufacturing Consent: Changes in the Labor Process under Monopoly Capitalism*. Chicago: The University of Chicago Press.

Castells, M. (1996), *The Rise of the Network Society. Vol. I of The Information Age: Economy, Society and Culture*. Malden, MA and Oxford, UK: Blackwell.

Crouch, C. (2004), *Post-democracy*. Cambridge: Polity Press.

Crouch, C. (2016), 'The March Towards Post-Democracy, Ten Years On', *The Political Quarterly*, **87** (1), 71–75.

De Stefano, V. (2015), 'The Rise of the Just-In-Time Workforce: On-Demand Work, Crowdwork, and Labour Protection in the Gig-Economy', *Comparative Labour Law & Policy Journal*, **37**, 471–503.

Dean, M. (1999), *Governmentality. Power and Rule in Modern Society*. London: Sage.

Degryse, C. (2019), 'Introduction', in I. Daugareilh, C. Degryse & P. Pochet (eds), *The Platform Economy and Social Law: Key Issues in Comparative Perspective*. Brussels: European Trade Union Institute (ETUI).

Deutschmann, C. (2011), 'Limits to Financialization: Sociological Analyses of the Financial Crisis', *European Journal of Sociology*, **52** (3), 347–389.

Doellgast, V., Lillie. N. & Pulignano, V. (2018), *Reconstructing Solidarity: Labour Unions, Precarious Work, and the Politics of Institutional Change in Europe*. Oxford: Oxford University Press.

Drahokoupil, J. & Piasna, A. (2017), 'Work in the Platform Economy: Beyond Lower Transaction Costs', *Intereconomics*, **52** (6), 335–340.

Esping-Andersen, G. (1990), *The Three Worlds of Welfare Capitalism*. Princeton, NJ: Princeton University Press.

Fleming, P. (2017), 'The Human Capital Hoax: Work, Debt and Insecurity in the Era of Uberization', *Organization Studies*. Accessed at https://doi.org/10.1177/0170840616686129

Foucault, M. (1997), *Ethics: Subjectivity and Truth. (Essential Works of Michel Foucault, 1954–1984. Vol. 1)*. New York: New Press.

Fuchs, C. (2014), *Digital Labour and Karl Marx*. New York: Routledge.

Fuchs, C. (2016), 'Digital Labor and Imperialism', *Monthly Review*, **67** (8), 14.

Gandini, A. (2019), 'Labour Process Theory and the Gig Economy', *Human Relations*, **72** (6), 1039–1056.

Gereffi, G. (2011), 'Global Value Chains and International Competition', *The Antitrust Bulletin*, **56** (1), 37–56.

Gereffi, G. (2014), 'Global Value Chains in a Post-Washington Consensus World', *Review of International Political Economy*, **21** (1), 9–37.

Graham, M., Hjorth, I. & Lehdonvirta, V. (2017), 'Digital Labour and Development: Impacts of Global Digital Labour Platforms and the Gig Economy on Worker Livelihoods', *Transfer*, **23** (2), 135–162.

Haidar, J. (2020), *La configuración del proceso de trabajo en las plataformas de reparto en la Ciudad de Buenos Aires. Un abordaje multidimensional y multi-método (julio/agosto de 2020)*, Informe de coyuntura No. 11, octubre 2020. Buenos Aires: IIGG.

Harvey, D. (2005), *A Brief History of Neoliberalism*. Oxford: Oxford University Press.

Huws, U. (2013), 'Working Online, Living Offline: Labour in the Internet Age', *Work Organization, Labour and Globalization*, **7** (1), 1–11.

ILO (2018), *Women and Men in the Informal Economy: A Statistical Picture*. Third Edition. Geneva: International Labour Office.

Johnston, H. (2020), 'Labour Geographies of the Platform Economy: Understanding Collective Organizing Strategies in the Context of Digitally Mediated Work', *International Labour Review*, **159** (1), 25–45.

Kalleberg, A. (2009), 'Precarious Work, Insecure Workers: Employment Relations in Transition', *American Sociological Review*, **74** (1), 1–22.

Kenney, M. & Zysman, J. (2016), 'The Rise of the Platform Economy', *Issues in Science and Technology*, **32** (3), 61–69.

Keune, M. & Pedaci, M. (2020), 'Trade Union Strategies Against Precarious Work: Common Trends and Sectoral Divergence in the EU', *European Journal of Industrial Relations*, **26** (2), 139–155.

Langley, P. & Leyshon, A. (2017), 'Platform Capitalism: The Intermediation and Capitalisation of Digital Economic Circulation', *Finance and Society*, **3** (1), 11–31.

Lepadatu, D. & Janoski, T. (2020), *Framing and Managing Lean Organizations in the New Economy*. London: Routledge.

Marx, K. (2018), *Capital. A Critique of Political Economy, Volume I, Book I*. Champaign, IL: Modern Barbarian Press.

Möhlmann, M. & Zalmanson, L. (2017), 'Hands on the Wheel: Navigating Algorithmic Management and Uber Drivers' Autonomy'. International Conference on Information Systems (ICIS 2017), Seoul. Available at: https://www.researchgate.net/publication/319965259_Hands_on_the_wheel_Navigating_algorithmic_management_and_Uber_drivers%27_autonomy

Moore, P. V. & Joyce, S. (2020), 'Black Box or Hidden Abode? The Expansion and Exposure of Platform Work Managerialism', *Review of International Political Economy*, **27** (4), 926–948.

Pasquale, F. (2015), *The Black Box Society: The Secret Algorithms That Control Money and Information*. Cambridge, MA: Harvard University Press.

Peck, J. (2013), 'Explaining (with) Neoliberalism', *Territory, Politics, Governance*, **1** (2), 132–157.

Rose, N. (1999), *Powers of Freedom. Reframing Political Thought*. Cambridge: Cambridge University Press.

Rosenblat, A. & Stark, L. (2016), 'Algorithmic Labor and Information Asymmetries: A Case Study of Uber's Drivers', *International Journal of Communication*, **10**, 3758–3784.

Shapiro, A. (2018), 'Between Autonomy and Control: Strategies of Arbitrage in the "On-Demand" Economy', *New Media & Society*, **20** (8), 2954–2971.

Silver, B. (2003), *Forces of Labor: Workers' Movements and Globalization Since 1870*. Cambridge: Cambridge University Press.

Soriano, C. & Cabañes, J. (2020), 'Entrepreneurial Solidarities: Social Media Collectives and Filipino Digital Platform Workers', *Social Media + Society*. DOI: 10.1177/2056305120926484

Srnicek, N. (2016), *Platform Capitalism*. Cambridge: Polity Press.

Standing, G. (2011), *The Precariat: The New Dangerous Class*. London: Bloomsbury.

Standing, G. (2016), *The Corruption of Capitalism: Why Rentiers Thrive and Work Does Not Pay*. Hull: Biteback Publishing.

Streeck, W. (2017), *How Will Capitalism End?* London and New York: Verso.

van der Zwan, N. (2014), 'Making Sense of Financialization', *Socio-Economic Review*, **12** (1), 99–129.

van Doorn, N. (2017), 'Platform Labor: On the Gendered and Racialized Exploitation of Low-Income Service Work in the "On-Demand" Economy', *Information, Communication & Society*, **20** (6), 898–914.

van Doorn, N. & Badger, A. (2020), 'Platform Capitalism's Hidden Abode: Producing Data Assets in the Gig Economy', *Antipode*. DOI: 10.1111/anti.12641

van Doorn, N., Ferrari, F. & Graham, M. (2020), 'Migration and Migrant Labour in the Gig Economy: An Intervention (June 8, 2020)'. Available at SSRN: https://ssrn.com/abstract=3622589

Vercellone, C. (2020), 'Prólogo. Tiempos y destiempos de la ley del valor/plusvalía', in P. Miguez (ed.), *Trabajo y valor en el capitalismo contemporáneo. Reflexiones sobre la valorización del conocimiento*. Los Polvorines: Universidad Nacional de General Sarmiento, pp. 11–22.

Xia, H., Wang, Y., Huang, Y. & Shah, A. (2017), '"Our Privacy Needs to be Protected at All Costs": Crowd Workers' Privacy Experiences on Amazon Mechanical Turk', *Proceedings of the ACM on Human-Computer Interaction*, **1** (2), article 113.

PART I

Platform labour in contemporary capitalism

1. Value, rent and platform capitalism

Nick Srnicek

INTRODUCTION

As data have become central to the modern economy, reflections on its value and contribution have proliferated.[1] The aim of this chapter is to try and cut through the various accounts of value in the digital economy, highlighting inconsistencies and misunderstandings where needed, as well as extracting useful mechanisms and concepts where possible. In particular, this chapter will critique the currently dominant approach to data's value: the free labour thesis which argues that our online activities are productive of surplus-value. While this account of how value is produced, circulated, and captured offers intuitive (and sometimes comforting) analyses, I will argue that it nonetheless relies upon mistaken assumptions and inferences. In its place, I will offer an account that focuses on rent and value appropriation, rather than value creation. This approach will draw upon a Marxist analysis of the economy for its utility in understanding economic dynamics beyond the surface-level flow of prices, as well as its emphasis on medium- and long-term trends within a historical mode of production. The ultimate goal here will be, at a high level of abstraction, to set out where and how platforms are situated within the value-theoretic circuits of contemporary capitalism.[2] This macro-level picture will help to frame later chapters in this book, focused on the more detailed elements of work and labour relations.

While much of the ensuing discussion will be pitched at a high level of abstraction, these arguments are not merely scholarly. They touch upon some of the key issues today for understanding the systemic dynamics of global capital. Most notably, the question of whether the free labour thesis is true or not has an enormous bearing on how capitalism is doing. If true, the incorporation of billions of users into an unwaged digital system of capital accumulation should indicate that we are – or soon will be – in a new period of solid economic growth.[3] If false, we should instead expect that capitalism is and will continue to be sluggish and prone to all sorts of emergency measures to ward off imminent crisis. One look at the rise of negative interest rates, the ballooning balance sheets of central banks, and the protracted recovery from the 2008 crisis, would all suggest that the free labour thesis should be held with some suspicion. The contrasting approaches also have different implications for the world of work and labour relations. The free labour thesis would claim that work is extending across the social factory, and that more and more of our activities are being directly incorporated into the circuits of capital. For this approach, it ultimately matters little whether it is waged or unwaged work that is expanding. The alternative approach would, instead, argue that wage-labour remains the focus of the accumulation process and that efforts to constrain the power of these workers continue to take precedence. The debate over where and how value is created in the digital economy has political implications as well. If the free labour thesis is correct, then there is a persuasive case to be made that users deserve Wages for Facebook (modelled after the original Wages for/against Housework campaign)[4] (Toupin 2018). If the thesis is mistaken, then our strategic resources would be better turned else-where. Likewise, there are implications for any strategic analysis of capitalists' power. A free labour approach might see less antagonism between platform firms and non-platform firms, whereas the approach we will elaborate here sees a growing source of antagonism between these two capitalist fractions. To get a better sense of which approach better approximates the conditions of contemporary capitalism, we will now turn to a more in-depth analysis of their arguments.

1   A CRITIQUE OF THE FREE LABOUR THESIS

Originating in the wake of the dot.com boom with Tiziana Terranova's path-breaking work, the 'free labour thesis' has gone on to become what is arguably the dominant Marxist approach to the data-driven economy of today (Andrejevic 2014; Brown 2014; Cohen 2008; Coté and Pybus 2007; Fuchs 2017; Greene and Joseph 2015; Jarrett 2014; Terranova 2000). Though not without its critics, the free labour thesis has become entrenched as both a dom-inant common sense in critical writing around the digital economy, as well as a more widely circulated intuition that is increasingly appearing in mainstream media discussions (Posner and Weyl 2018; *The Economist* 2018). While there is a strong autonomist Marxist strand, the most sophisticated versions of this argument often draw upon the work of Dallas Smythe and his unique approach to the role of advertising within capitalism (Smythe 1977). We will here take Christian Fuchs' work as the most developed version of this approach.

For Fuchs, time spent by users on social media platforms is time that pro-duces value in the form of data commodities that are sold to advertisers (Fuchs 2014, pp. 89–90). This includes both the active creation of online content as well as the more passive 'data exhaust' created by simply being online. This data commodity then has its value realised when users interact[5] with the subsequent ads and the advertiser pays the platform (Fuchs 2014, pp. 117–18). This online activity is deemed to be exploited and therefore value-producing.[6] This labour is also deemed to be ideologically coerced – one can leave Facebook, but only by withdrawing oneself from a key means of sociality (Fuchs 2014, pp. 90–1). This aspect is important because a key element of wage-labour is that it is coerced: if the proletariat had access to their own means of subsistence, they would not need to enter into and compete on a labour market and capitalism would lose its value generator. An element of coercion is therefore an essential condition for value-producing labour. Lastly, Fuchs also argues that, like wage-labour, this online labour is alienated in that the workers do not own the data and content that they produce online.

There are a number of arguments that can be laid against this position. We will begin by taking the argument at its strongest and assume that its claims are true. In this case, let us fully accept the free labour thesis – our online activities are value-producing. Yet immediately we can raise suspicions about how significant this added source of value creation is to the digital economy.[7] Looking at the top-tier Western platforms,[8] only Facebook and Google are dependent on advertising.[9] Amazon is increasing its share of advertising but remains much more dependent on cloud computing and its North American ecommerce platform. Apple and Microsoft also have small advertising segments, but their businesses are dominated by other elements. And even among the two advertising oligopolies, Google is shifting towards new revenue sources in the form of cloud computing, gaming, and general consumer hardware. This is part of a broader turn towards enterprise-facing businesses – with Amazon's Web Services (AWS) perhaps the clearest indicator of this, as the company's operating income largely comes from this enterprise service, rather than from more consumer-facing ecommerce. So even if the free labour argument is entirely correct, it appears to only explain a small – and dwindling – portion of the digital economy.

More fundamentally, we can question whether these activities are in fact generative of surplus-value. The Marxist framework offers a very stringent set of conditions that have to be met in order for surplus-value to be created by a production process. In particular, value-producing work is waged labour that operates in the context of a production process with markets for inputs (labour, in particular) and markets for output, where the overall aim is an expansion of value. (Importantly, this does not mean that value-producing labour is only industrial labour or physical labour – every economic sector, as well as immaterial labour, can be considered to produce value *under the right conditions*.) Do our online activities meet these criteria? First of all, personal data is not typically sold by these firms. While data brokers do commodify data in some sense, this is not the business model of the advertising platforms (Christl and Spiekermann 2016; Federal Trade Commission 2014). Instead, what companies like Facebook and Google do is use data to create and offer finely targeted advertising spaces that companies can then bid over. This is not the sale of data to another entity in any meaningful sense. Yet even if data *was* commodified and sold, the data is not produced in a competitive market with the aim of increasing value. Put simply, just because something has been commodified and sold in market does not make it a *capitalist* commodity. For that to take place, the production process of the commodity needs – at a minimum – to be oriented towards the market, the creation of surplus-value, and the reinvestment of that value back into a new production cycle. For a number of commodities, these conditions simply do not hold: for instance, informal petty commodity production in developing economies, most artistic products, and most online activities (Sanyal 2013; Beech 2016).

Perhaps more to the point, there is no notion of socially necessary labour time – and therefore no notion of abstract (value-producing) labour – within the unpaid 'work' of online activities. There is no market mediation of this 'work', which would render inefficient work as uncompetitive, and which would drive the competitive systemic search for greater productivity. There is, in other words, no implicit standard against which any given production process could be measured as either efficient or inefficient. For example, if a data commodity is produced by our online activities, what quantity of socially necessary labour time (SNLT) does it embody? Fundamentally, this is impossible to determine. SNLT requires competition between different producers, mediated by the market and validated by exchange, in order to exist. Absent these sorts of conditions, all we have is concrete labour time and use values. It is telling, therefore, that when Fuchs goes to calculate the value created by unpaid Facebook users, he relies upon concrete labour time (Fuchs 2014, p. 105). There is no notion of abstract labour time that could be used to carry out the same calculations. In fact, arguably, the very nature of personal data means that it cannot be subjected to a capitalist production process without destroying the very characteristics which make it useful in the first place – its (relatively) spontaneous, unmanaged expression of someone's behaviour. If the processes which generate authentic personal data were to be really subsumed, that data would become an expression (predictable and pointless) of that rationalised production process, rather than an expression of a self.

All of this is not to say that online activities *can't* be value-producing. The social media manager for a firm may spend part of their time producing content to be shared online – and this would be value-producing work. The difference is the social relations into which the same activity is placed: waged and guided by capitalist imperatives, or not?

2   RISE OF THE RENTIER

A major part of the reason for the dominance of the free labour thesis is that it appears to parsimoniously explain a key intuition of the platform economy: that our personal data *is* incredibly valuable for the technology giants. And yet, as we have argued here, the free labour explanation relies on illegitimately applying the concept of productive labour beyond its remit. So how else can we explain the utility of data extraction while simultaneously explaining the vast wealth and resources of the largest platforms?

To begin with, we need to recall that within a Marxist approach, the *distribution* of value is not necessarily in direct correspondence with the *production* of value. In the simplest model of how this asymmetry emerges, we might imagine the production processes of capitalism as creating a vast and growing pool of surplus-value, which is then appropriated afterwards and distributed amongst a variety of capitalist and non-capitalist actors. Crucially, this entails that there is no direct or necessary relationship between the surplus-value created by a capitalist and the surplus-value appropriated by that same capitalist. With respect to the platform giants, this means that their obvious capacity to capture value need not be matched by their immanent capacity to produce value.

The first way in which this divergence between production and appropriation occurs is through the equalisation of the profit rate across industries.[10] As a result of the tendency for capital to seek after the highest rate of profit, producers will move into sectors with abnormally high rates of profit. This leads to more supply (as existing firms invest more to take advantage of high profits), more competition (as new entrants move in to take advantage of high profits), and the ensuing dynamics eventually create a lower rate of profit for that sector. The opposite process happens in industries with a low rate of profit, until the (tendential) point at which the rates are equalised across industries. Significantly, for our purposes, the rates of profit will thereby diverge from the sources of the profit. Industries with low organic composition will create most of the surplus-value, but as a result of the equalisation process will tend to receive less value back than they created. By contrast, industries with high organic composition will create less surplus-value but will appropriate more of it in the end.

The second way in which the location of value production diverges from the location of value appropriation is through the use of economic and political power to capture surplus-value created elsewhere. For example, a capitalist financed with a large debt may produce a significant amount of surplus-value, but interest and tax payments will require that a cut of that surplus-value be distributed to finance capital and government. The latter two actors have not necessarily created any value, yet they have provided services which are necessary for the reproduction and realisation of the initial productive capital. Their roles and positions within the overall accumulation process therefore enable them to appropriate surplus-value despite not necessarily producing any surplus-value. As a result, the initial capitalist ends up with less surplus-value than they produced. This is a general process throughout the capitalist system:

> There are many other modes of appropriation of surplus value, such as monopolization of sectors of the market, marketing and advertising, establishment of intellectual property rights through patents, copyrights, and trademarks, ownership of scarce energy or other natural resources, superior cleverness in arranging financial transactions or structuring financial property rights, controlling medical treatment, and so forth. (Foley 2013, p. 260)

Through a variety of means, therefore, economic actors (whether capitalist or not) will tend to use their powers to capture as much value from the aggregate pool of surplus-value as possible.

It is this second process which is particularly significant in explaining the contemporary dominance of the platform giants.[11] The argument in the remainder of this chapter will be that 'rent' is the most appropriate category for understanding the location of platforms in the capital accumulation process.[12] This argument will build on, though diverge from at points, a number of recent works on the topic (Christophers 2019; Fine 2019; Mazzucato 2019; Rigi and Prey 2015; Sadowski 2019, 2020; Zeller 2007). What then do we mean by rent? First of all, we do not mean the neoclassical idea of rent-seeking, which refers to government interference in markets that enables a firm to extract higher profits than would otherwise be possible (Birch 2019, p. 10). This concept of rent remains beholden to a neoclassical image of markets and states and postulates perfectly competitive markets as the natural state of things. We will instead draw upon Marx's notion of rent which, while focused on the ownership of land, can be usefully generalised for a broader understanding of how rents operate today. While Marx differentiates between a number of different types of rent (differential, absolute, and monopoly), the common element is that rent is income which accrues from the ownership, control, and/or possession of a scarce asset[13] (Birch 2019, p. 2; Christophers 2019, p. 2; Foley 2013).

The notion of rent is useful here for a few reasons. First, as argued above, it helps us to situate platforms in relation to the productive economy. Second, it helps us to understand that much of the value of the digital giants is the result of ownership and/or control over scarce assets. This is most obviously (personal) data, but it is also a matter of infrastructure and intellectual properties as well. Lastly, this more general notion of rent leads us to an important point: that while Marx wrote about rent as something stemming from a natural asset (i.e. land), the idea of rent as ownership and/or control over a scarce asset ultimately does not distinguish between natural and non-natural assets. The concept of rent can apply to any asset, which allows us to extend the idea – and the mechanism of value capture – to a much broader range of economic phenomena than is traditionally the case. In Christophers' work, for instance, eight different types of assets are outlined, each with their own particular dynamics, and each with their own history of prominence and occlusion (Christophers 2019). The distinctions between natural and non-natural assets, in turn, give rise to different discursive apparatuses surrounding their production, maintenance, and justification. The ownership of land, for example, is more readily deemed 'unproductive', whereas ownership of non-natural property contains the vestiges of productive activity which are often mobilised when it comes to arguments around the validity of intellectual property.

With these basic characteristics of rent in mind, the remainder of this section will argue that we can distinguish between three prominent mechanisms of rent in the contemporary digital economy: intellectual property rents, advertising rents, and infrastructure rents. Each of these is in play, to varying degrees, in all the major platforms – though some have obvious affinities with the types of platforms I have outlined in *Platform Capitalism*. Advertising rents are obviously most closely associated with advertising platforms as their primary source of revenue. Infrastructure rents are, in turn, more closely associated with the cloud platforms and lean platforms.[14] Platforms, in general, are much more about the capture of value from elsewhere in the economy. Data, in this reading, rather than being a source of all digital value, are instead a means to achieving the capture of rents. It is a valuable input (i.e. raw material) which enables, for example, the creation of personalised ad spaces, the production of new proprietary goods and services (such as a search engine), and the optimising of existing goods and services (such as cloud provision). While there are presently limited cases where data function as a commodity exchanged on the market, more often than not data act as an input that differentiates companies from their competitors. Instead of seeing data as the result of exploitation therefore, it is perhaps more useful to see them as the result of appropriation.

3   INTELLECTUAL PROPERTY RENTS

The first major source of rents for the digital platforms – intellectual property (IP) – has been covered quite extensively in the existing literature (Foley 2013; Frase 2016; Perelman 2003; Stalder 2018). In this case, companies create – or today, more often purchase – valuable knowledge, information, technologies, and other immaterial products. Unlike traditional physical assets, there is no a priori reason that these immaterial assets could not be replicated and spread around to anyone who might find a use for them. Except, crucially, the state then applies and enforces IP rights which enable companies to exclude others from using these immaterial assets. In other words, the state extends the property-form to intellectual products, and thereby grants a monopoly over this IP.[15] With monopoly ownership of a scarce asset, firms are then able to extract a rent from other economic actors who want access to that resource.[16]

Such rents play a large role in numerous industries today, such as the pharmaceutical, biotechnology, consumer products, or entertainment industries (Christophers 2019). With their emphasis on information, they also play a large role in high-tech industries as well. In terms of the major platforms, all rely quite significantly on IP for their respective power, but many also generate significant revenues from the strategic licensing of IP. Microsoft is perhaps the leader amongst the top platforms, boasting of having more than 61,000 patents (with a further 26,000 pending) and listing US$17.3 billion of intangible assets (pre-amortisation) in its financial statements for 2019 (Microsoft 2019). Such is their importance that absent the IP surrounding Microsoft Windows, for instance, it is difficult to see how the company would be in the market-leading position that it is right now.

This highlights another point about IP: that it can be used in a variety of ways to create market power, with rents existing in a number of direct and indirect forms (Christophers 2019; Zeller 2007). The most obvious rent is the income that accrues from charging others for access to the IP. Microsoft Windows, for example, charges users a fee to download and use the operating system; and Microsoft's more recent shift to cloud software means that access is something which is constantly threatened by repeal. More generally, licensing fees and royalty payments are all examples of this type of rent. A second form of IP rent emerges when a company uses IP to create a product or service that, because of IP exclusion, others cannot copy. The company can then sell that product and reap the rewards from having monopoly rights over the IP at the heart of it. Many of Google's platforms are examples of this, with proprietary knowledge lying behind the services that draw in users, extract their data, and attract advertisers. Lastly, IP rent can also occur when a company directly sells its IP rights to another company, effectively turning the IP into a financial asset that can be used to reap an income stream immediately. For example, in 2011 Google spent more than US$12 billion to acquire a smartphone company, Motorola Mobility (Taylor and Waters 2011). While Motorola was deemed a lagging company at the time, it did have access to more than 17,000 patents that were crucial for Google's struggle with Apple – and therefore Motorola's owners were able to turn them directly into commodities to be sold.

As with the other rents, their existence is often premised on a foundational kernel of surplus-value production. In this case, for instance, the initial production of IP is (typically) a value-producing activity. The wages, fixed capital, and production process for generating immaterial products are no different in value terms than the production processes for creating material products. Both of them can generate surplus-value in the process. The difference arises after the production of the product, when the potentially widespread cheap replication of IP is instead locked up by monopoly rights and an income stream of rent is generated. Moreover, because intellectual property is non-rivalrous, it means the potential rent is not constrained in the same ways that land might be, reducing the significance of the initial production process.[17]

Advertising Rents

The most obvious rent, one which has a large and direct impact on the user-facing levels of the internet, is advertising. Here, monopoly ownership over personal data – and the network effects that draw in user data – combines with the creation and control of targeted online advertising spaces. The more data one has, the more targeted an ad can become, meaning that the handful of companies with massive amounts of personal data are able to effectively dominate the market. Advertisers, eager to spread word of their products, then rely upon these scarce assets and pay a rent to their owners in order to post their ads in the most valuable spaces. In traditional Marxist terms, it is a flow of surplus-value from the productive sectors of the economy towards a non-productive sector – one which is oriented towards the realisation and validation of surplus-value, but which has no direct role in the production of surplus-value. In effect, the handful of firms who control the data which enable targeted advertising build an online environment which they then rent to others for a fee.

Two of the largest Western platforms, Facebook and Google, are almost entirely indebted to the extraction of advertising rents. In their most recent financial statements, Facebook received 98.5 per cent of its revenue from advertising, while Google received 85.8 per cent of its revenue from advertising.[18] A third major platform, Amazon, is also seeing rapid growth in this area (Weise 2019). The source of these firms' particular power in the digital advertising market, however, stems from their control over massive collections of personal data. Here, personal data are used to reduce costs (of finding out information about individuals) and to create targeting systems that ostensibly offer prime real estate for those who want to market their products.

Nothing of this is to say that advertising does not play a value-theoretic role in capitalism. For instance, the production of ad platforms can, itself, be surplus-value generating as a firm employs constant and variable capital in order to produce market research commodities, technological platforms, and other outputs. But in general advertising's role is heavily circumscribed and almost entirely related to the distribution of value rather than the production of value. Advertising may shift demand from one firm to another, or one sector to another – but both are redistributions of demand. Advertising may also create new demand, but in this case it, at best, decreases the turnover time of the production process[19] (Lebowitz 1986, p. 168). With targeted advertising, the promise is that the data collected can enable advertisers to more quickly – and cheaply – find consumers, thereby reducing their turnover time and enabling the capital tied up in the process to be channelled instead towards production. As Bruce Robinson says, 'Functionally, it may be seen to play a role analogous to traditional market research in aiming to provide the basis for a more precise relationship between the seller and the market' (Robinson 2015, pp. 46–7). Advertising can enable, in other words, individual capitalists to more rapidly create surplus-value, but advertising does not, in itself, create surplus-value (Caraway 2016, p. 77).

Infrastructure Rents

While intellectual property rents and advertising rents have been covered quite extensively in the existing literature, the third primary form of rent has been much less discussed. Infrastructure rents emerge from the fees paid for access to the use of a platform. As Christophers points out, such rents are neither natural (like land) nor state-created (like intellectual property), but instead emerge from the network effects that drive platforms towards monopolistic positions (Christophers 2019, p. 11). As a result, their scarcity is a product of these dynamics, and as the economy becomes increasingly digitised the owners of these platforms gain more control over the fees that can be charged to access them.

Cloud computing is perhaps the clearest example, with businesses renting access to hardware and software that, in an earlier era, they would have owned. But infrastructure rents also emerge to a less obvious degree from the rise of the 'as-a-service' business model whereby others retain ownership over a particular asset (cars, homes, bikes, etc.) and then charge users a fee to access them for a period of time. As Jathan Sadowski has put it, through this 'platforms have [...] been able to expand rentier relations in ways that *enclose* everyday things' (Sadowski 2019). Infrastructural rents also exist in the form of intermediary platforms that others come to rely upon. Uber and Airbnb, for instance, appropriate a part of the economic transaction that their platform makes possible (Christophers 2019, p. 11). The economic actors who use these platforms are, in effect, paying a tithe to the platform owners in order to use their scarce asset.

While part of infrastructure rents emerges from control over key intellectual property, fixed capital is an essential aspect for their existence. AWS is the exemplar here, with vast amounts spent on building a planetary-sized comput-ing infrastructure – a scale that precludes all but a few competitors (currently, Microsoft, Google, and Alibaba) from ever standing a chance in the market.

This infrastructure also manages to appropriate a vast amount of income for Amazon. In 2017, for instance, more than 100 per cent of Amazon's operating income came from AWS.[20] In effect, the rest of Amazon was losing money, while the cloud computing unit was bringing in more than US$4 billion of operating income. Such is the influence of infrastructural rents in our contemporary era.

As with the other forms of rent though, it is not all unproductive activity, and cloud computing does have other impacts on value. Most obviously, cloud computing is desirable for businesses because it enables the rapid expansion of resources, often at levels of technical expertise that are far beyond what the businesses themselves can provide, effectively increasing productivity and the extraction of relative surplus-value in many cases. Similarly, the pure intermediary platforms have rapidly expanded in part because they reduce transaction costs and thereby (at least potentially) raise the rate of profit for firms that rely on them. Their impact on value creation also extends to their ability to reduce turnover times, enabling less capital to be tied up in the circulation process and more of it to be devoted to productive activities (Dantas 2019, p. 142).

CONCLUSION

Given these three forms of rent, the primary conclusion to be drawn is that much of platform capitalism is based on the appropriation of value that is produced elsewhere in the global economy. As we have been at pains to point out, this is not to say that these platforms have no impact on value accumulation, as, for instance, platforms can reduce transaction costs for other businesses and thereby impact the rate of surplus-value creation for those businesses. Nor is it to say that these platforms have not created what mainstream economists call 'consumer surplus' that goes unmeasured by metrics based upon monetary forms (Brynjolfsson et al. 2019). Yet what is ultimately determinant for capitalism qua system is capital accumulation as expressed in monetary form. And in those terms, platforms are more impediments than accelerants.

This presents a number of direct consequences. If platforms are predominantly rentiers, then capitalism not only does not have a new source of value, in fact it has a new obstruction to accumulation – a conclusion which is diametrically opposed to the free labour thesis. The growth of this rentier sector is doubly damaging for capital. It means, first, a reduction in the average rate of profit because these non-productive capitalists must receive the same rate of profit as other sectors – yet they generate no new surplus-value themselves, and instead act to thin out the total surplus amongst more capitalists. Second, since these tech rentiers are monopolists, they also prevent the equalisation of the profit rate by impeding the flow of capital into direct competitors. As a result, not only do they appropriate surplus-value from productive firms, they also appropriate *more* than the average firm receives.[21] All of this also entails that there is an emerging antagonism between fractions of capital: between the platform owners and the non-platform companies that increasingly depend on them and pay them rents. As Marx and others have long noted, rentiers have different class interests than productive capitalists or workers. (Neocosmos 1986). But unlike various accounts of digital feudalism or an emergent new mode of production, this struggle takes place *within* the structural imperatives defined by capitalism – a struggle over the distribution of surplus-value rather than its overcoming (Wark 2019).

However, this obstructive function of rent is moderated by another characteristic of many of these companies. On one level, they appear as monopolies dominating their particular industries (search engines, ecommerce, social media, etc.). Yet many of the orthodox characteristics of monopolies do not appear here: lowered output, for instance, or reduced innovation. If anything – and this brings us to a key contemporary mystery – these monopolistic firms appear instead to be one of the prime innovators and investors in the global economy. In the US economy, for instance, the tech giants are some of the biggest spenders on capital expenditures and research and development (Meeker 2018). This is not the usual activity of standard rentiers, which are typically presented as obstructions to capital accumulation. This investment is all the more striking given that, in general, the post-2008 period has been one of the weakest periods in the US for growth in investment.[22] Yet the technology giants have been a notable exception to this trend. So we have productive capitalists who are *not* investing, and non-productive rentiers who *are* investing. What to make of this?

While it is not entirely clear, two hypotheses present themselves. The first hypothesis has to do with the disaggregation of capital accumulation functions. For instance, Marx noted that, at times, different types of capital (production, commercial, financial) could converge into one firm, while at other times, specialised firms might concentrate on particular functions. While not a distinct type of capital, perhaps today we are seeing a case where the investment function of the accumulation process is being displaced to particular firms? A second hypothesis builds on the debates in economic geography in the 1970s and 1980s around the standard interpretation of rentiers (as obstructions to accumulation) and a new interpretation of rentiers (which argued they had important distributive functions for capital) (Haila 1988). As David Harvey and others argued, land was becoming a financial asset through which landowners took on an economic interest in attracting the most productive uses of capital in an effort to generate higher returns both now and in the future (Haila 1988, pp. 83–4; Harvey 2006). Insofar as advertising and IP rents both rely on the price mechanism to distribute finite supply to a far larger demand, we might see them as similarly operating a useful distribution function for capital.

(Infrastructural rents, by contrast, appear at the moment much less subject to this, since supply exceeds demand.) In turn, investment is a rational effort to seek to expand their rentier empires.

In either hypothesis, these are firms that, as we have seen, are growing their infrastructural empires across the economy. If their investment is largely pouring into the further expansion of this rentier apparatus (an open question), then we truly are seeing a significant shift in intra-capitalist power. When we turn to the world of work, we can see that these macroeconomic shifts have other significant impacts as well. Broadly speaking, the capturing of global value by a handful of planetary platforms should be expected to exacerbate inequalities between workers: with those working for the constrained non-platform companies facing increasing squeezes, while workers for the major platforms instead having the potential – though not always the actuality – of better working conditions. This is particularly the case for high-skill workers in advertising and cloud platforms, which continue to reap significant profits from their positions. On the other hand, lean platforms – despite their ability to monopolise infrastructural rents – remain beset by low margins, with their workers facing the brunt of these challenging economic conditions. In any case, any given conjuncture of capitalism is a unique mixture of the continuous and the discontinuous, and while we can use continuities to shed much light on the digital platform giants, it is clear that there nevertheless remain significant novelties that have yet to be fully understood.

NOTES

1. My thanks to Matt Cole, Julieta Haidar, Maarten Keune, Michal Rozworski, and Jathan Sadowski for their comments on an earlier draft of this chapter.
2. This chapter will make explicit some of the arguments that were only implicit – or unfinished – in my earlier book *Platform Capitalism* (Srnicek 2016).
3. Christian Fuchs, for example, calculates that Facebook received 64 billion hours of unpaid work in 2011 (Fuchs 2014, p. 105). By any reasonable standard, this would suggest a vast expansion of surplus-value and a significant increase in the rate of profit. A critic of my argument could, however, claim that absent this new source of surplus-value, capitalism would be in an even more dire situation than what it currently finds itself in. This could admittedly be true, though the critic would then have to show the timings and ways in which this new source has gradually expanded and impacted the global pool of surplus-value.
4. It is worth noting though that the most prominent advocate of the free labour thesis, Christian Fuchs, rejects the idea of Wages for Facebook, instead preferring universal basic income as a better response.
5. The relevant interaction depends on what pricing model is being used for the advertising – whether cost-per-click or cost-per-impression.
6. While a detailed textual exegesis of the source of Fuchs' error goes beyond the scope of this chapter, we would argue that it stems from conflating a moral idea of exploitation with a political economy idea of exploitation here. For instance, when

responding to critics and when attempting to justify a broad image of value production, Fuchs typically relies on the intuition that a particular activity is (morally) exploited and then claims that since the activity is (economically) exploited it is therefore value-producing.

7. With its focus on advertising and personal data, the following critiques also broadly apply to the notion of 'surveillance capitalism' (Zuboff 2019).

8. We focus on Western platforms in this chapter, but the major Chinese platforms tend to be even less dependent on advertising revenues. Alibaba, on a generous reading, only makes 6 per cent of its revenues from advertising, Tencent makes 18 per cent, and even Baidu remains significantly less dependent on advertising with 73 per cent of its revenue from that segment (source: 2019Q3 financial statements).

9. The following discussion relies on revenue breakdowns found in the 10-K and 10-Q filings of these companies.

10. Note that this equalisation is under the assumption of the free flow of capital, with no barriers. As we will see later, absent this free flow of capital, some areas can maintain unusually high rates of profit.

11. The first process also has an important role to play, particularly in the ways in which it generates hierarchical global value chains through which surplus-value is produced in developing nations and then transferred to leading firms in the developed world (Caffentzis 2013; Dedrick et al. 2010). This process, however, has more relevance to goods-producing firms with extensive supply chains, like Apple, than to the rent-appropriating platform firms like Google and Amazon.

12. Much of the following discussion will rely implicitly upon Marx's analysis of rent (Marx 1991, pp. 751–950).

13. Brett Christophers argues for adding a second condition on to this definition: namely, 'market conditions of limited or no competition' (Christophers 2019, p. 2). This latter condition he draws from the mainstream understanding of rent, which takes into account the market conditions of an asset. Christophers' argument here is that monopoly control of an asset is insufficient to guarantee that a rent is accrued – e.g. monopoly ownership of an asset for which substitute goods are easily procurable means that buyers will simply tend towards the substitute good rather than paying the rent. However, this latter condition seems more akin to a characteristic that (partially) determines the quantity of rent rather than determining whether a rent exists or not. For this reason, we will stick with the more traditional Marxist and heterodox definition of rent.

14. In *Platform Capitalism* I distinguished between cloud and industrial platforms, though I no longer believe this distinction points to more than a surface-level difference. At best, there is a distinction between the general and the particular.

15. With respect to Marx's terminology, IP rents are a type of monopoly rent rather than a differential rent. Broadly speaking, the former rent accrues to a rentier by virtue of monopoly control over an asset (e.g. land-in-general). By contrast, the differential rent accrues first to a capitalist who has access to a rentier's asset (e.g. particularly productive land) which enables a cheaper production process. The surplus profits that are generated by virtue of access to the higher quality asset are then appropriated by the rentier.

16. The exact quantity of rent depends on a number of factors. As Christian Zeller notes, 'The amount of the monopoly rent depends on the concrete demand and supply conditions. The more inelastic the demand reacts to price increases, the larger the rent. If substitution goods exist, the demand is more elastic and thus

the monopoly rent smaller. The more strategically a patent is localized in a technological development path, or the broader the field covered by the patent, the more numerous and the higher the licensing revenues the owner can call in from all those who want to use the patent for the development of technologies and products. In contrast to the differential rent, which arises due to differently favorably located or fertile pieces of land, no information differential rent can emerge, because every enclosed information is unique and is normally used in each case for the production of specific products' (Zeller 2007, p. 98).

17. Strictly speaking, there remain some limits to access and replication of immaterial assets, and so we therefore should be careful not to assume that these costs are zero. Making the latter assumption often tends towards overly optimistic conclusions and mistaken beliefs in a 'break' from capitalism.
18. Based on calculations from 10-Q statements for 2019Q3.
19. As Brett Caraway argues, 'the activities of unwaged content producers allow firms to decrease costs (c+v) of new media commodities (content and market research), thus raising the rate of profit (s / c+v) and the rate of surplus value (s / v). To the extent that free labor contributes to this process, it should inform our analysis of value' (Caraway 2016, p. 77).
20. Calculation based on Amazon's 10-K financial statement for FY2017.
21. It is worth emphasising here that by productive and unproductive we do not intend any moral judgement, nor do we intend that the unproductive is without utility for society. Instead we simply mean what is productive of value *for* capitalism, a category which all too often in fact excludes activities we would deem useful for society.
22. See https://fred.stlouisfed.org/series/PNFI

REFERENCES

Andrejevic, M. (2014), 'Surveillance in the Big Data Era', in K. D. Pimple (ed.), *Emerging Pervasive Information and Communication Technologies (PICT)*, Springer Netherlands, 55–69.

Beech, D. (2016), *Art and Value: Art's Economic Exceptionalism in Classical, Neoclassical and Marxist Economics*, Chicago: Haymarket Books.

Birch, K. (2019), 'Technoscience Rent: Toward a Theory of Rentiership for Technoscientific Capitalism', *Science, Technology, & Human Values*. https://doi.org/10.1177/0162243919829567

Brown, B. (2014), 'Will Work For Free: The Biopolitics of Unwaged Digital Labour', *TripleC: Communication, Capitalism & Critique*, **12** (2), 694–712.

Brynjolfsson, E., A. Collis, W. E. Diewert, F. Eggers and K. J. Fox (2019), *GDP-B: Accounting for the Value of New and Free Goods in the Digital Economy*, Working Paper 25695, National Bureau of Economic Research.

Caffentzis, G. (2013), *In Letters of Blood and Fire: Work, Machines, and the Crisis of Capitalism*, Oakland, CA: PM Press.

Caraway, B. (2016), 'Crisis of Command: Theorizing Value in New Media', *Communication Theory*, **26** (1), 64–81.

Christl, W. and S. Spiekermann (2016), *Networks of Control: A Report on Corporate Surveillance, Digital Tracking, Big Data & Privacy*, Wien: Facultas.

Christophers, B. (2019), 'The Rentierization of the United Kingdom Economy', *Environment and Planning A: Economy and Space.* https://doi.org/10.1177/0308518X19873007

Cohen, N. (2008), 'The Valorization of Surveillance: Towards a Political Economy of Facebook', *Democratic Communiqué*, **22** (1). Accessed 5 October 2019 at https://journals.flvc.org/demcom/article/view/76495

Coté, M. and J. Pybus (2007), 'Learning to Immaterial Labour 2.0', *Ephemera*, **7** (1), 88–106.

Dantas, M. (2019), 'The Financial Logic of Internet Platforms: The Turnover Time of Money at the Limit of Zero', *TripleC: Communication, Capitalism & Critique. Open Access Journal for a Global Sustainable Information Society*, **17** (1), 132–58.

Dedrick, J., K. L. Kraemer and G. Linden (2010), 'Who Profits from Innovation in Global Value Chains?: A Study of the iPod and Notebook PCs', *Industrial and Corporate Change*, **19** (1), 81–116.

Federal Trade Commission (2014), *Data Brokers: A Call for Transparency and Accountability.*

Fine, B. (2019), 'Marx's Rent Theory Revisited? Landed Property, Nature and Value', *Economy and Society*, **48** (3), 1–12.

Foley, D. (2013), 'Rethinking Financial Capitalism and the "Information" Economy', *Review of Radical Political Economics*, **45** (3), 257–68.

Frase, P. (2016), *Four Futures: Life after Capitalism*, London: Verso.

Fuchs, C. (2014), *Digital Labour and Karl Marx*, New York: Routledge.

Fuchs, C. (2017), 'The Information Economy and the Labor Theory of Value', *International Journal of Political Economy*, **46** (1), 65–89.

Greene, D. M. and D. Joseph (2015), 'The Digital Spatial Fix', *TripleC: Communication, Capitalism & Critique*, **13** (2), 223–47.

Haila, A. (1988), 'Land as a Financial Asset: The Theory of Urban Rent as a Mirror of Economic Transformation', *Antipode*, **20** (2), 79–101.

Harvey, D. (2006), *The Limits to Capital*, London: Verso Books.

Jarrett, K. (2014), 'The Relevance of "Women's Work": Social Reproduction and Immaterial Labor in Digital Media', *Television & New Media*, **15** (1), 14–29.

Lebowitz, M. A. (1986), 'Too Many Blindspots on the Media', *Studies in Political Economy*, **21** (1), 165–73.

Marx, K. (1991), *Capital: A Critique of Political Economy, Volume III*, London: Penguin Classics.

Mazzucato, M. (2019), *The Value of Everything: Making and Taking in the Global Economy*, Penguin.

Meeker, M. (2018), *Internet Trends Report 2018*, TechCrunch. Accessed 13 November 2019 at https://www.slideshare.net/joshsc/techcrunch-mary-meeker-2018-internet-trends-report

Microsoft (2019), *Annual Report 2019*. Accessed 12 November 2019 at https://www.microsoft.com/investor/reports/ar19/index.html

Neocosmos, M. (1986), 'Marx's Third Class: Capitalist Landed Property and Capitalist Development', *The Journal of Peasant Studies*, **13** (3), 5–44.

Perelman, M. (2003), 'Intellectual Property Rights and the Commodity Form: New Dimensions in the Legislated Transfer of Surplus Value', *Review of Radical Political Economics*, **35** (3), 304–11.

Posner, E. A. and E. G. Weyl (2018), 'Want Our Personal Data? Pay for It', *The Wall Street Journal*, 20 April. Accessed 25 April 2018 at https://www.wsj.com/articles/want-our-personal-data-pay-for-it-1524237577

Rigi, J. and R. Prey (2015), 'Value, Rent, and the Political Economy of Social Media', *The Information Society*, **31** (5), 392–406.

Robinson, B. (2015), 'With a Different Marx: Value and the Contradictions of Web 2.0 Capitalism', *The Information Society*, **31** (1), 44–51.

Sadowski, J. (2019), 'Landlord 2.0: Tech's New Rentier Capitalism'. Accessed 11 October 2019 at https://onezero.medium.com/landlord-2–0-techs-new-rentier -capitalism-a0bfe491b463

Sadowski, J. (2020), 'The Internet of Landlords: Digital Platforms and New Mechanisms of Rentier Capitalism', *Antipode*, **52** (2), 562–80.

Sanyal, K. (2013), *Rethinking Capitalist Development: Primitive Accumulation, Governmentality and Post-Colonial Capitalism*, New Delhi: Routledge India.

Smythe, D. (1977), 'Communications: Blindspot of Western Marxism', *Canadian Journal of Political and Social Theory*, **1** (3), 1–27.

Srnicek, N. (2016), *Platform Capitalism*, Cambridge: Polity Press.

Stalder, F. (2018), 'Intellectual Property', *Krisis*, **2**, 83–5.

Taylor, P. and R. Waters (2011), 'Google Snaps up Motorola Mobility', *Financial Times*, 15 August. Accessed 12 November 2019 at https://www.ft.com/content/ e906bedc-c734–11e0-a9ef-00144feabdc0

Terranova, T. (2000), 'Free Labor: Producing Culture for the Digital Economy', *Social Text*, **18** (2 63), 33–58.

The Economist (2018), 'Should Internet Firms Pay for the Data Users Currently Give Away?', 11 January. Accessed 25 April 2018 at https://www.economist.com/news/ finance-and-economics/21734390-and-new-paper-proposes-should-data-providers -unionise-should-internet

Toupin, L. (2018), *Wages for Housework: A History of an International Feminist Movement, 1972–77*, London: Pluto Press.

Wark, M. (2019), *Capital Is Dead*, London: Verso.

Weise, K. (2019), 'Amazon Knows What You Buy. And It's Building a Big Ad Business From It', *The New York Times*, 20 January. Accessed 12 November 2019 at https://www.nytimes.com/2019/01/20/technology/amazon-ads-advertising.html, https://www.nytimes.com/subscription

Zeller, C. (2007), 'From the Gene to the Globe: Extracting Rents Based on Intellectual Property Monopolies', *Review of International Political Economy*, **15** (1), 86–115.

Zuboff, S. (2019), *The Age of Surveillance Capitalism: The Fight for a Human Future at the New Frontier of Power*, London: Profile Books.

2. Platforms and exploitation in informational capitalism

Mariano Zukerfeld

INTRODUCTION

Platforms are increasingly shaping work and labour relations all over the world. Various insightful analyses of this apparent tendency have been published, and most of them mention the exploitative nature of these relations. However, they tend to leave aside what kinds of exploitation exist and how they are related to different types of platforms and, more generally, to the present stage of capitalism. Thus, regarding this issue, there are three connected vacancies.

First and foremost, a theory of capitalist exploitation that is capable of (but not limited to) framing the variety of exploitative relations that take place between capitalist platforms and exploited subjects, whether they are workers or not. Exploitation became a ticklish subject for many progressives and left-wing academics, as informational capitalism brought some anomalies to textbook Marxism. Marxist theory of exploitation focuses on waged, 'productive' labour and depends ultimately on time as a universal measure. Now, how to frame relations in which capital obtains a surplus value at the expense of exploited actors, but which do not occur in the context of labour relations? 'Prosumers' on Internet platforms are a typical example: they produce content (software, audiovisuals, texts), data, and pay attention to advertising, etc., but they are not, *prima facie*, "productive" workers who are capable of producing surplus value according to standard Marxism. Furthermore, how to conceptualize the production processes in which the creation of wealth is not directly related to the notion of *working time*? This is what happens with the so-called 'knowledge-intensive activities', in which once the knowledge has been created in a certain amount of time, its subsequent uses become dissociated from that initial time amount. Production and reproduction divorce, and this has even more pronounced consequences regarding the production of informational goods, made of digital information and, therefore, having close to zero marginal or reproduction costs.

This situation has led to two alternatives. On the one hand, the most frequent one among critical scholars consists in resorting only occasionally and vaguely to the notion of exploitation. Their critical vocation is exercised upon other relevant topics as surveillance, precarization, or inequalities instead.

On the other hand, there are scholars who will not give up either Marxism or its concept of exploitation. Among them, the usual responses consist of treating the anomalies that informational capitalism brings up with old Marxist recipes. In turn, it results in two equally unsatisfying options: while some academics try to silence the anomalies by constraining them into the Procrustean bed of a rigid ahistorical theory, others end up forcing Marxist theory with painful contortions to tackle informational capitalism.

It is within this context that this chapter aims to briefly present a theory of exploitation which is capable of dealing with different kinds of exploitation that take place in informational capitalism and particularly in capitalist platforms.

Secondly, platformization is rarely framed by a narrative that clearly distinguishes stages of capitalism and periods within these stages. But even if stages and periods are distinguished, this is usually done by resorting to technological or economic determinisms. However, platform work and especially capitalist exploitation are inextricably related to other traits of informational capitalism.

Thirdly, although sound typologies have been developed on the relation among capitalist platforms, work, and labour, they have been usually focused on a particular subset of platforms, i.e. platforms where the activities carried out by workers easily accommodate to the traditional notion of work. Nonetheless, other platforms where neglected or contested forms of exploitation are emerging are barely looked upon as such.

Therefore, the main objective of this chapter is to relate *different types of platforms* with different kinds of *capitalist exploitation* within *informational capitalism*. In order to reach this goal, we need first to discuss each concept separately and only then put the pieces of the puzzle together.

The second section characterizes the transition from industrial capitalism to informational or cognitive capitalism. Although it is indisputable that digital technologies and the Internet played a major role in that transition, other aspects must be discussed as well. Transformations in the organization of productive processes, regulations (particularly in property law) and business models are obviously crucial and would allow me to distinguish two phases within informational capitalism. But also shifts in axiological beliefs and identities are linchpins of platforms' exploitative side.

The third section is devoted to exploitation. Drawing on a cognitive materialist approach where capitalist exploitation depends ultimately on unremunerated knowledge, it begins by recuperating contributions of previous theories of capitalist exploitation. Then it moves towards providing a definition of capitalist exploitation and presenting three kinds that are crucial to give an account of platform work: exploitation through alienation, exploitation through reproduction, and exploitation through attention. Finally, these three kinds of exploitation are related to different business models of industrial and informational capitalism, and to the phases of the latter.

The fourth section discusses what types of work, labour, and productive activities are subsumed under capitalist platforms. On the one hand, there are three types of *through-the-platform* workers: gig labour, prosumers, and self-employed owners. Gig labour is epitomized by those who work through Uber, Freelancer, Zolvers, and other platforms. The platformization of pro-sumption brings into tension the distinction between working time and leisure time, and even the traditional concept of work itself. Those who produce and consume content, data, and attention through YouTube or Facebook embody this tendency. In turn, there is commercial work carried out by self-employed owners through platforms (the renting and selling of physical goods) which arguably configures new tendencies in work processes, such as those of Airbnb or Amazon. On the other hand, there are several types of *work behind the plat-forms*: in-house or outsourced development of software and hardware, infra-structure, human resources, marketing, logistics, and warehouse work. The fifth section builds on previous sections to present a typology of exploitation of platform work in informational capitalism. Thus, I discuss which of the three types of exploitation proposed in section 3 prevails in each kind of productive activity. Additionally, some comments regarding ideology, ownership of means of production, and the relation between time and value are introduced. The sixth section provides concluding remarks.

1 INFORMATIONAL CAPITALISM AND ITS DISTINCTIVE FEATURES[1]

Capitalism can be analytically divided into three stages: mercantile capitalism, which ranges approximately from the mid-15th century to the end of the 18th century; industrial capitalism, which covers the period from the end of the 18th century up to the third quarter of the 20th century, and informational capitalism, whose beginnings can be approximately dated to the 1970s and which continues to this day (Castells 1996; Boutang 2011; Zukerfeld 2017). Platforms and platformization of work, as we shall see, are archetypical from the present phase of informational capitalism. But how can we characterize this stage? We aim to answer this question below as briefly as possible while avoiding reductionisms.

1.1   Digital Technology and Informational Goods

Industrial capitalism's most apparent aspect is the development of energy technologies in the form of machines. Informational capitalism, in turn, is strongly associated with information and specifically digital technologies (Castells 1996; Vercellone 2011; Boutang 2011; Fuchs 2010). Understanding its technological underpinnings thus becomes a necessary but not sufficient condition to grasp informational capitalism. Four of these technological underpinnings are summarized below.

Although information technology has existed at least since the origins of writing, informational capitalism is characterized by the fact that digital technologies tend to subsume most information technologies (i.e. analogue information technologies). This advance is due to the particular evolution of productive forces in the branch of hardware production, described by the self-fulfilling prophecy known as Moore's Law. It refers to the exponential progress and cost reduction of the most varied types of digital technologies.

Digital information can be defined as all forms of knowledge codified in binary form through on-off electrical signals. A distinctive feature of digital information is that it has marginal production costs close to zero or, in other words, negligible reproduction costs (Varian 1995; Cafassi 1998; Boutang 2011; Rullani 2000). We refer to all goods composed purely or mainly of digital information as informational goods (software, music, videos, texts, data, etc.). Software is an especially significant type of informational good. It is the most important means of production of our era, as it is a necessary ingredient in all digital technologies.

Informational capitalism is usually characterized as a networked society (Castells 1996). Network properties usually include: high flexibility, the lack of a central node, and the so-called Metcalfe Law: the usefulness of a network increases exponentially with the number of connected nodes. Of course, the relevance of networks in informational capitalism is firmly tied to the boom of networks of digital technologies, the Internet being the main one.

The consumption of superabundant information requires human attention, which is finite and scarce, in order to be meaningful, for humans as well as capitalist enterprise. This divergence between superabundant information and scarce human attention is the material basis that explains why attention has become such a particularly important commodity today (Davenport and Prusack 2001; Simon 1996; Celis Bueno 2016). Despite the fact that the scarcity of attention was important along informational capitalism, it became particularly poignant in its later phase, with the proliferation of broadband and streaming. It is no mystery that the platform economy is built on all of these features.

1.2   Organization of Productive Processes

Informational capitalism radically departs from industrial capitalism regarding the organization of productive processes. Although this transformation is boosted by the technological tendencies mentioned above, it is not in any way determined by them. Organizational features of informational capitalism might be summarized around three interdependent axes: networks, flexibilization, and polarization.

Along with digital networks, two types of well-known but rarely coupled together organizational networks shaped productive processes during the take-off of informational capitalism. On the one hand, the well-known *network enterprise*, in their interior and exterior: the company as a group of islands, projects articulated in a relatively flexible way, the company as a network reaching towards the exterior, outsourcing anything that exceeds its core business (Castells 1996). In this organizational modality power tends to be exercised as *control* (complementing or replacing the *discipline* of the industrial period). On the other hand, *collaborative production* (production of informational goods among peers over the Internet, usually during free time).

Networks are related to the bunch of organizational trends grouped under the concept of *flexibilization*. Indeed, it stems from just-in-time, and other organizational features of Toyotism (Coriat 1990; Piore and Sabel 1984), and also from the deregulation of markets championed by neoliberal governments (which are the archetypical political form of informational capitalism). Flexibilization typically includes higher labour turnover, outsourcing and homeworking, unpredictable working hours, variable and individualized wages, the erosion of collective labour, and the relocalization of the production process (Eyck 2003; Standing 2002), all of which tend to result in a precarization of work (Armano and Murgia 2014). Flexibilization is also related to the blurring of the boundary between leisure time and working hours (originally pointed out by Italian Autonomism – e.g. Lazzaratto and Negri 2001), which is boosted by digital technology.

In turn, capitalist metabolism includes a trend towards an increase in the polarization of the workforce. The decomposition of industrial labour results in a split: while some become highly skilled global informational workers, others end up as low-skilled, local, precarious services providers. Not only are these groups linked by their origins, but it is their current dynamics which ties them together. Indeed, informational productive processes in some developed countries depend on legal or illegal precarious labour (Iñigo Carrera 2003; Fuchs and Sevignani 2013).

The platformization of work relies on the aforementioned tendencies. However, platforms add a specific organizational layer which is not in-built in network organizations: they operate as gatekeepers and middle-men, perverting the allegedly horizontal and immanent flow of goods and services that characterize networks. More importantly, the governance of the productive process is increasingly performed by algorithms, i.e. algorithmic management. As a consequence, the so-called platform economy represents a new organizational form that signals the beginning of a second phase within informational capitalism.

1.3 Subjectification, Recognition and Axiology

Informational capitalism also means profound changes vis-à-vis industrial capitalism in the way subjects perceive themselves and bond with others; that is, in their identity, subjectification, and recognition (Ricoeur 2005). While in industrial capitalism subjects were built as individuals interacting with a society, in the first phase of informational capitalism, the society as a totality began to fall apart, turning into ever-changing *networks*. Disaffiliated and vulnerable subjects became more individualistic (Castel 2002). In the second phase, individuals tend to become *dividuals* (as announced by Deleuze 1992), attention-seeking nodes defined by fragile connections to digital networks.

As opposed to individuals and societies, dividuals and networks are increasingly dependent on capitalist social networking platforms. Thus, and remarkably, identity, subjectivity, and recognition are subsumed under the commercial objectives of those companies.

Regarding the topic of this chapter, the main axiological trait of informational capitalism is the ideology of the *entrepreneur of the self* (Foucault 2010; Boltanski and Chiapello 2005). From the first decade of the new millennium, that is to say the second phase of the current stage, 'communities' are cheered and, moreover, openness moves from the margins to the centre of capitalist axiology.

1.4 Regulations and Business Models

In the transition from industrial to informational capitalism, the capitalist system needed to deal with a very concrete menace: informational goods could escape the commodity form as they had close to zero marginal costs. The first, adaptive, and still extremely relevant attempt of the capitalist system to deal with informational goods was to dramatically expand intellectual property rights (May and Sell 2006; Drahos 2004; Zukerfeld 2017b). This is how a *profit-from-enclosures* model was deployed, with firms such as Microsoft, Pfizer, and Universal as its flagships.

However, this model increasingly revealed its limits and in the first decade of the new millennium it became clear that it was simply not good enough for capitalist business to prosper. Profit from enclosures is hardly compatible with the technological (once the informational good is distributed, it is very difficult to stop its massive circulation) as well as organizational, subjective, and axiological (which favour openness and free flows of informational goods) features of informational capitalism. Indeed, two complementary business models emerged.

As a reaction to the expansion of private intellectual property rights, a movement advocating for open knowledge, free culture, and non-commercial sharing practices spread and thrived (Benkler 2006; Bauwens 2006). At some point in the 2000s, companies started noticing that they might profit from openness and sharing practices: millions of people were willing to work for free. *Profit from openness* is based on the disguised exploitation of unpaid digital work, carried out mostly during leisure time, with non-commercial pur-poses, by individuals as part of fan cultures, peer communities, or in the role of being users of some service or platform (Fuchs 2013; Scholz 2013; Fisher 2012; Zukerfeld 2014; Lund and Zukerfeld 2020).

But yet another business model was developed to fight back against the perceived menaces of de-commodification brought by informational capital-ism. As informational goods could not be delivered as goods – because illegal copies cannot be controlled – some companies simply decided to *provide them as services*. Indeed, you do not download the audiovisual content, it is streamed by the platforms instead.

Now we can summarize the division of informational capitalism into two periods. The first one might be called the phase of *networks*; it lasts from the 1970s to the 2000s, and is characterized chiefly by the profit-from-enclosures model – backed by intellectual property rights expansion – the take-off of digital technologies and the Internet, and the slow decomposition of the cultural, political, and philosophical structures that shaped industrial capital-ism. The second one, the phase of *platforms*, extends from the 2000s to the present, and it is dominated by profit from openness and informational goods as services business models, the organizational, axiological, identity features described above, which are all related to the ubiquitous presence of Internet platforms and their algorithms.[2]

Bearing this in mind, we can associate concepts such as the post-industrial society (Bell 1973) or societies of control (Deleuze 1992) with the first period of informational capitalism. Even narratives by Castells (1996) or cognitive capitalism theorists (Rullani 2000; Boutang 2011; Vercellone 2011) tend to be focused on the features of this first period. At the other end of the spectrum, concepts such as platform capitalism (Srnicek 2017) and surveillance capital-ism (Zuboff 2019) place their emphasis on the second period of informational capitalism.

2   CAPITALIST EXPLOITATION[3]

Here I want to briefly introduce a theory of exploitation which draws on the contributions of various authors. On the one hand, a Marxian approach (Marx [1867] 1990, but also Hilferding [1910] 1981; Sweezy 1942), from which I maintain the necessity of exploitation, understood as a relationship of free and legal exchange of objectively asymmetrical magnitudes, to all stages of capitalism. On the other hand, Sraffian (Hodgson 1988; Garegnani 1979) and Analytic Marxist approaches (Roemer 1985; Cohen 1979; Elster 1985; Wright 1985) contributed to keep the emphasis on a theory of exploitation that is not necessarily based on Marx's labour theory of value. Also, they provided me with the vocation for systematic analysis. However, this perspective has not incorporated elements which help us to consider the exploitation that occurs in informational capitalism. Similarly, authors from autonomist and cognitive capitalism currents have touched on the subject (Fumagalli 2015; but especially Boutang 2011). From these and other authors I take the idea of the divorce between labour time and value production and the integration of intellectual property into the analysis. However, I reject the autonomist philosophical perspective and respectfully disagree with some traits of cognitive capitalism theory (for instance, its subsumption of knowledge to labour). Finally, from cultural materialism and associated perspectives (Fuchs 2010, 2012, 2015; Fisher 2012), the main contributions that I appropriate are, on the one hand, the idea that online platforms, in contrast to discourses about freedom and community, operate on the basis of the capitalist exploitation of users (although not only of them), and, on the other hand, the updating of Smythe's (2006) contribution which conceives of a type of exploitation of audiences through social media sites.

In this context, here I will concisely define capitalist exploitation and its three modalities. I understand capitalist exploitation to be a social relationship that fulfils the following requirements:

1. *Exchanges* inscribed into *productive processes* are generated between at least two classes of actors, *Exploiters (E)* – who receive or translate resources – and *exploited (e)* – who produce or bear them.
2. The exchanges between *E* and *e* are, in economic terms, objectively asymmetrical in relation to the value of the goods and services transacted, in such a way that *E* obtains a surplus value as regards *e*.[4] This occurs regardless of the subjective representations that these actors hold about said exchanges.[5]
3. The productive processes in question are orientated to the production of *commodities*. Specifically, the *E* actors involved in these processes act

(including in relation to the *e* actors) with the principal – if not the exclusive – goal of *making a profit*.

4.   The positions of *E* and *e* are also asymmetrical with regard to the perspective that they have about the productive process which they share: while the *E* actors tend to have an overarching view of the totality of the process, the *e* actors only perceive one or a few fragments of the process.
5.   These relationships take place, to a greater or lesser degree, in a *consensual* way and are *not illegal*: they do not imply any clear, evident, or indisputable violation of any current legislation.

Capitalist exploitation adopts three modalities:

Exploitation through alienation
This modality is the closest to the traditional Marxian concept of exploitation. It is characterized by the purchase, by capital, of a certain amount of working time; that is, the exclusive use of human energy and knowledge through its application to the object of work over a given period. This working time can be fixed or flexible, long or short, it does not matter at this point. Usually, the capitalist contributes the means of production while the goods and services produced by labour are by definition owned by the capitalist, all under the laws of physical private property. Thus, energies and knowledge are objectified in the goods (or consumed in the services provided) but, decisively, the product of the labour performed by the exploited turns out to be alienated from the worker. The capitalist realizes it as a commodity through its sale, obtaining the pursued surplus value. Nonetheless, to put the productive process into motion again, the exploiter must resort to labour power again and again.

This modality works very well to understand and measure exploitation where the application of productive knowledge (which generates value) tends to coincide with working time: energy-intensive tasks and/or those in which the knowledge used is relatively stable in time. This was the usual case during industrial capitalism and that is why this modality is characteristic of that period, although it remains in the present.

Exploitation through reproduction or copying
Exploitation through reproduction or copying refers to the situation in which the exploiters reproduce knowledge that had been created or was carried out by the exploited, usually by translating it into a new bearer. This knowledge becomes the property of the capitalist exploiter, due to the lines drawn by intellectual property law (patents, copyright, trademarks, and others).

Capital may proceed to the objectification of said knowledge in machinery (industrial or informational), its codification in manuals of procedures, or its inoculation into other workers.

Thus, even if the exploited continues to possess said knowledge materially, she might be dismissed and, in some cases, even banned from using the knowledge she stills carries.

Exploitation through reproduction encompasses various sub-modalities. Here it suffices to say that it can occur both inside and outside labour processes.

Exploitation through attention
In exploitation through attention, certain digital information is inoculated by the exploiting actors into the subjectivity of the exploited actors. This modality is based on the aforementioned fact that in the second phase of informational capitalism the flood of information results in scarcity of human attention. Thus, scarce human attention – whose consumption exhausts it – is exchanged for superabundant access to informational goods whose cost of reproduction tends to zero, shaping potentially asymmetrical exchanges of values.

In the guise of the exploiter actor giving away something, he actually gets something more valuable for free: human attention and the possibility of disembarking his ads and taking advantage of the cognitive, affective, and emotional networks of the exploited actors.

Exploitation through attention is of a different nature than the two previous modalities and is the most alien to the usual notion of exploitation. Of course, its distinctive feature is that the direction of knowledge flows is reversed: capital is looking for introducing knowledge bits into exploited subjects, as it profits from selling the cognitive storage capacity of them. In turn, it takes place mostly in leisure time and the exploited prosumers are external to the firms which profit from them. Furthermore, monetary exchanges are generally not involved in the relationship and, in fact, whether the activities that the exploited carries out might or might not be called 'labour' is a contested topic. In other words, labour is not a *sine qua non* condition for exploitation to take place. While even the most alienated workers are aware that they participate in a productive process, those exploited through attention perceive themselves as involved just in processes of idle consumption. Again, we come across a key point: here there are capitalist productive processes, and therefore exploitation, but there may be no work for the exploited.

It is crucial to point out that the three modalities are not mutually exclusive, but rather that two or three of them act (sometimes in consort) simultaneously in many productive processes. As mentioned above, an admittedly polemical but crucial tenet of this approach *is that exploitation implies the existence of a productive process, but not necessarily a labour process.*

Table 2.1   *Types of capitalist exploitation*

Through alienation	Through reproduction	Through attention
Capitalist buys a certain amount of labour time.	Capitalist copies knowledge created by exploited in labour or leisure time.	Capitalist gets attention time during exploited leisure time.
Energies and knowledge of the exploited are objectified and owned by the capitalist through private physical property law.	Knowledge is translated into information that the capitalist owns through intellectual property law.	Information managed by the capitalist is translated into subjective knowledge of the exploited.
Services of the exploited are required repeatedly.	A particular knowledge-bearer exploited subject is no longer needed.	Scarce attention of the exploited is needed repeatedly.
Traditional notion of exploitation during industrial capitalism.	Present throughout history, but widespread in informational capitalism.	Archetypical of the phase of the platforms of informational capitalism.

Source: Author's elaboration.

How are these types of exploitation related to different stages of capitalism and their distinctive features? Different types of exploitation are indeed related to the various stages of capitalism. However, those connections are not linear and should not be oversimplified. In a nutshell, exploitation through alienation was paramount during industrial capitalism but it is still quite relevant in informational capitalism. In turn, exploitation through reproduction always existed. It soared during industrial capitalism through the codification of workers' knowledge by Taylorist procedures and its objectification in machines. But the features of digital information and informational goods discussed in section 2 boosted exploitation through reproduction to a whole new level. In turn, the aforementioned polarization of the workforce in informational capitalism results in informational workers being mainly exploited by reproduction while precarious services providers tend to be exploited by alienation.

Regarding business models, exploitation through reproduction is easily related to profit from enclosures: companies making money on their knowledge-producing workers, paying once (or extremely modest royalties) and selling thousands of copies. On the other hand, exploitation through reproduction managed to take advantage of profit from openness as well, resorting not to waged workers, but to unwaged prosumers.

Exploitation through attention emerges prominently only towards the end of industrial capitalism, with mass media and broadcasting. But it is only during informational capitalism, and specifically its second phase, where it becomes profoundly relevant to grasp the dynamics of capitalism. This is so not only due to the generalization of Internet platforms based on advertising and data gathering, but also because of the subjectification, recognition, and identity traits of informational capitalism and especially those of its second phase: entrepreneurs themselves – who are ultimately dividuals seeking attention – are especially well-suited for being exploited through attention – and reproduction. This is why exploitation through attention is strongly associated with profit-from-openness business models.

3 PLATFORMIZATION: WORK BEHIND AND THROUGH CAPITALIST PLATFORMS[6]

Platformization affects all types of work and non-work-related activities. The separation is not clear-cut and there is a great variety of productive modalities which test the validity of the concepts of work and labour proper to industrial capitalism (Srnicek 2017; Scholz 2017; Langley and Leyshon 2017; Madariaga et al. 2019).

Types of platform work are discussed in several studies (De Groen et al. 2016; Howcroft and Bergvall-Kåreborn 2018; Graham and Woodcock 2018; Berg et al. 2018; Schmidt 2017; Vandaele 2018). In what follows I build on these insightful approaches to advance a typology capable of tackling not just work but, more precisely, capitalist exploitative relations, which exceed labour relations, as we shall see.

I provisionally define platform work as the productive activities of those subjects who are directly involved in generating profits for the platforms. Thus, what justifies grouping them together is that they are crucial to figure out how platforms make money. But how to distinguish the main types of platform work? Table 2.2 summarizes my proposal.

Table 2.2   *Types of exploited subjects and productive activities in for-profit platforms*

Type of activities	Sub-type of exploited subjects	Goods and Services produced	Examples
Behind the platform	Services' workers	Services	Warehouse and delivery workers in Amazon
	Industrial workers	Physical goods	Hardware builders in Amazon
	Informational workers	Informational goods	Software developers in Amazon

Type of activities	Sub-type of exploited subjects	Goods and Services produced	Examples
Through the platform	Self-employed owners	Physical goods and related services	Airbnb hosts, Amazon sellers
		Informational goods	Authors sharing music through Spotify App developers for Play Store or App Store
	Gig labour	Services	Delivery workers of Deliveroo Uber drivers TaskRabbit cleaning workers
		Informational goods	Software developers, writers, audiovisual content producers, and microtaskers on Upwork, and Freelancer Crowdworkers on Amazon Mechanical Turk
	Prosumers	Informational goods	Content creators for Facebook or YouTube Data producers for all platforms
		Attention services	Audiences paying attention to ads on Facebook or YouTube

Source: Author's elaboration.

There are four main types of platform work. The first distinction splits work behind and through the platform. While the latter refers to productive activities that are mediated by the platforms, the former alludes to the production and reproduction process of the platform company and the platform itself. Work through the platforms deserves a closer look and encompasses three varieties: self-employed owners, gig labour, and prosumers.

3.1   Behind-the-Platform Workers

Platforms, as productive units, are located in the fourth sector; that is, the information sector of the economy. As we discussed above, they employ informational workers but also industrial and services workers. Informational workers are unavoidable to run and maintain the platform itself: software developers and data scientists, audiovisual content designers, etc. As this is the core business, most of these workers are in-house. Some industrial workers are also needed, for instance to develop hardware. And platforms certainly require service workers, as warehouse and delivery workers. Industrial and services workers are to some extent outsourced.

Platforms are usually depicted as having a meagre workforce. This might be true for some platforms, but it is certainly not the case for others. Take Amazon, which nowadays (March 2020) employs 798,000 behind-the-platform workers. What do they do? Some 250,000 workers provide physical services in warehouses ('fulfilment centers' in Amazon jargon), but the rest of them work in a wide array of activities.

Thus, the fact that platform companies typically profit from underpaid 'independent-contractors' and unpaid prosumers should not obscure the fact that thousands of workers are under more or less formalized waged arrangements behind these platforms.

3.2   Through-the-Platforms Workers

Self-employed owners
Self-employed owners refer to platforms on which physical and informational goods are bought, sold, and rented. In this case, it is debatable whether the activities of asset-owners can be described as labour. However, in the case of *micro or small* businesses it is justified to label those activities as platform work if a certain threshold of production of goods and services is surpassed and their commercial activity *entirely depends* on Internet platforms.

There are two types of self-employed owners working through platforms. On the one hand, those providing *services*, renting, or selling *physical goods*. People selling stuff they produce through commerce platforms but also those who rent their houses through accommodation platforms. On the other hand, those producing informational goods. This includes musicians which upload their recordings to Spotify or similar platforms, or individual (or small firms of) software developers delivering apps through Play Store or App Store.

In this modality, the production of the goods and services – in other words, the productive process prior to their commercialization – takes place *outside* the platform. Thus, on the surface, it appears as if the platform enabled commerce, instead of production or consumption. However, the very reason why the productive process was set in place is, in reality, platforms. The production of an app or the rental of an apartment was conceived only as part of a platform-governed process. Indeed, small units of capital are increasingly subordinated to the control of platforms, their algorithms, and rankings, beyond specific legal forms.

Gig labour
Also, in gig labour a fundamental internal division arises from the materiality of the product of labour. Some workers offer physical services (transportation, food delivery, domestic services, and other manual labour), while others mediate the production of informational goods (i.e. software, audiovisual content). The means of production, the applicable regulations, public visibility, and political demands are accordingly divergent.

To distinguish varieties within the production of informational goods, I would resort to intellectual property and use the threshold of a *work* (a complete unit upon which copyright is bestowed automatically from its fixation on a tangible medium). While in 'crowdwork' or 'microtasking' workers develop *tasks* which fail to surpass that threshold, in other 'freelance' activities complete *works of authorship* are produced.

Physical gig labour is in all likelihood the category which brought public attention to platform work. It might be divided according to the spaces in which they are provided: public (transportation, delivery, and others) and private (cleaning, repairing) (Vandaele 2018). Not only are the platforms which intermediate in these types of labours specialized, but also regulations differ.

Prosumers

Prosumers perform the now well-known combination of the production and consumption of informational goods, mainly during leisure time and without any necessary monetary compensation. More precisely, there are three types of activities that might (or might not) be referred to as work.

Firstly, content production. For instance, some 50 million YouTubers upload 60 hours of video each minute. To engage prosumers in helping the platform to be profitable, YouTube successfully appeals to fantasies of enrichment, despite 97 per cent of 'creators' not earning enough to surpass the poverty line, payments per view having decreased in comparison to 2015, and the ratio between videos and views being on the fall (Bärtl 2018).

Secondly, prosumers also consume content and, more importantly, ads. Indeed, YouTube has 1.9 billion monthly active users worldwide, who watch some 5 billion videos daily, giving away not only their data, but also their valuable and scarce attention (Omnicore 2019). This has been stressed by Fuchs (2010) and his colleagues (e.g. Fisher 2012) who build on Dallas Smythe's (2006) notion of the audience commodity. According to this perspective, Internet users consuming ads are labouring and, therefore, creating value and being exploited (Fuchs 2010).

Thirdly, prosumers give away all types of data by 'sharing' personal preferences and location, liking videos, ranking drivers, and so forth. The relevance of these seemingly infinitesimal contributions has been underlined repeatedly and, as it was previously said, Srnicek (2017) even defines all capitalist platforms in relation to their profiting from these data. Therefore, prosumption as the main activity carried out on specific platforms (prosumption platforms such as YouTube or Instagram) must be added to the handing over of data that users (becoming prosumers) carry out on every single platform. But does the production of data qualify as work? The extent to which both ads consumption and data generation configure work is a contested topic (for instance Bolaño and Vieira, 2015 and Fuchs 2015). Here it is enough to stress that this kind of activity must not be swept under the carpet when exploitation in informational capitalism is discussed.

4   BEYOND WORK AND LABOUR: EXPLOITATION AND CAPITALIST PLATFORMS

To discuss exploitation in capitalism platforms' productive processes, it is important to distinguish between capitalist platforms themselves and specific productive activities carried out by different subjects. This allows us to better understand that most capitalist platforms draw on at least two modalities of exploitation, and many of them rely on the three of them. Indeed, there are various kinds of workers and prosumers involved in most platforms' productive processes and each one might be exploited in different ways. Therefore, in the same vein as Table 2.2, Table 2.3 intends not to focus on platforms but on the kinds of productive activities and exploitative relations that subjects are involved in.

Table 2.3   *Exploited subjects and type of exploitation*

Type of activities	Sub-type of exploited subjects	Goods and services produced	Type of exploitation
Behind the platform	Services workers	Services	Through alienation
	Industrial workers	Physical goods	Through alienation
	Informational workers	Informational goods	Through alienation and reproduction
Through the platform	Self-employed owners	Physical goods and Related services	Through alienation
		Informational goods	Through reproduction
	Gig labour	Services	Through alienation
		Informational goods	Through reproduction and alienation
	Prosumers	Informational goods	Through reproduction
		Attention services	Through attention

Source: Author's elaboration.

Thus, exploitation through alienation takes place mainly regarding service and industrial work behind and through the platforms – and to a lesser extent, to some informational work. This refers to workers whose payment is directly related to working time. Exploitation through reproduction is closely related to informational workers and prosumers – who produce informational goods which can be payed once, but copied and sold many times at close to zero marginal costs – but also to the production of massive amounts of data by all the subjects involved in these productive processes. Exploitation through attention, in turn, is largely concentrated in the attention services that audiences of prosumers provide to capitalist platforms.

An important caveat concerns the fact that there is no claim that exploitation necessarily exists in each type of productive activity. Table 2.3 only suggests, in each case, which kind of exploitation would take place if and only if the requisites for exploitative relations discussed in section 3 are met.[7]

As mentioned above, most platforms tend to resort to different kinds of exploitation, as they exploit different kinds of subjects in several productive processes. To illustrate how capitalist platforms take advantage of the different forms of exploitation, we can use again the example of YouTube.[8] YouTube generated US$15,150 million revenues in 2019 through its platform developed and supported by some 2,000 waged workers. Monetization is mainly explained by ads displayed on the 5 billion videos uploaded daily by YouTube's 50 million content creators or prosumers, watched by some 1,900 million users (Lund and Zukerfeld 2020, chapter 5).

But where are the revenues ultimately coming from? Marxian orthodoxy would emphasize exploitation of the 2,000 waged employees, this is, *exploitation through alienation*. The ratio between revenues and employees (known as RPE) is sometimes used as a measure of labour productivity or labour exploitation. In the case of YouTube, the company is making some US$10 million per employee per year. It turns out to be a colossal figure, not only if compared to McDonald's (US$66,000), Starbucks (US$84,000), or Accenture (US$87,000), but also to Facebook (US$1.6 million) and Alphabet itself (US$1.3 million) (Craft, 2017). Therefore, it becomes clear that either YouTube workers are incredibly productive and heavily exploited or there are other sources of value that the company profits from.

So, first of all, it must be distinguished that in addition to the exploitation through alienation of these workers, many of them are exploited through reproduction: they are paid for the development of software that is used repeatedly without additional compensation. But exploitation through reproduction is the key to understanding the contribution of the 50 million prosumers (of which only a tiny fraction receives some income at all, which even for them is quite modest, despite the platform's success in spreading the ideological discourse that 'YouTubers' get rich). These prosumers then give up their content (under the Terms of Service of the platform) that will attract users to the platform and, of course, to consume advertising. Here, then, the third modality is the one that helps to understand how YouTube earns money: the asymmetric exchange between the low commercial value provided by the firm for offering the videos and the value of the attention of the users who consume them, that is, the exploitation through attention.

So, YouTube, as many other platform companies, combines different modalities of exploitation of workers, prosumers, and users to shape a complex scheme of capital accumulation.

Exploitation through reproduction and *through attention* are helpful then not to replace but to complement exploitation through alienation. Indeed, exploitation through reproduction and through attention are especially useful to tackle situations where the production of use values that are crucial for the companies to generate profits are generated outside the factory, the worktime, and waged relations. This approach to exploitation might prove useful to counter discourses regarding topics where many Marxists perspectives fall short.

Capitalist platforms have put together a particular *ideological discourse,* whose main trait consists in referring to the workers as 'independent contractors' or 'partners', aiming at obscuring labour relations and exploitation (Howcroft and Bergvall-Kåreborn 2018). This could certainly not be detached from the ideological framework of the 'entrepreneur of the self' discussed in section 2.

In the same vein, ideological discourses from platforms include the so-called 'freedom': despite their differences, most – if not all – workers are said to choose their working hours. Of course, this is but negative freedom which neglects the material needs of workers and the fact that working time is ultimately governed by algorithms.

At the same time, most platforms flag up concepts usually associated with non-commercial spheres: communities (that are in reality instrumental networks), creativity (which YouTube understands as creating and expanding audiences), openness, affectivity, happiness, play, and enjoyment (all of which help to engage unpaid or underpaid producers) (Lund and Zukerfeld 2020, chapter 6).

Noticeably, in most of the through-the-platform work, payments and income are not necessarily measured in terms of labour time but on a piecework-based payment, (Vandaele 2018) or per-click in prosumption. This feature together with outsourcing resembles both the putting-out system and the piecework that Marx described (Marx [1867] 1990, chapter 13–14) and suggests a second 'formal subsumption of labour under capital' as Vercellone (2011) mentioned in another context.

Moreover, in activities performed through the platform, workers and prosumers are owners of the means of production. Although there are huge differences between owning houses, musical instruments, and bikes, all of them alleviate the platforms from providing these means. As mentioned above, in informational capitalism workers' ownership of important means of work is not enough for them to stop depending on the capitalist class, as platforms themselves (software, hardware, storage capacity, and, more importantly, attention flows of demand) become the mean means of production and are still controlled by capitalist firms.

Summing up, our approach allows us to focus on exploitation taking place in productive processes, instead of just work or labour. Exploitation might occur framed by work relations, during labour time, and be related with the owner-ship of the means of work. But, in the phase of platforms within informational capitalism, capitalist exploitation can also be located outside work relations, during leisure time, or, more accurately, in contexts where time and value are not straightforwardly related.

CONCLUDING REMARKS

In this chapter I have tried to combine a characterization of informational capitalism with a theory of exploitation and a typology of platform work to advance a proposal regarding how productive activities (work and pro-sumption) taking place on Internet platforms might be exploited by capitalist companies. At this point, it is worth introducing some caution and underlining some characteristics of the proposed approach.

There are two basic stands regarding exploitation. On the one hand, those that deny exploitation. Neoclassical theorists and the like assume that value is subjective and that exchanges in the market are due to the exercise of free will. Therefore, if parties agree on entering into certain relations, that means that the value exchanged in those relations is perceived as convenient for both said parties. Thus, exploitation only takes place in rare and anomalous situations. On the other hand, some Marxist approaches tend to assume that every single exchange under capitalist relations is exploitative. This stems from the confu-sion between the micro and the macro levels. Capitalism as a whole depends on exploitation (and also expropriation and regulation, by the way) to survive and grow. However, this should not obscure the fact that lots of capitalist busi-nesses fail in their exploitative aims, while others are extremely successful. The former might survive resorting to financial expropriations, rents, and other resources, or simply die. Therefore, to discuss whether exploitation takes place in a particular productive process, empirical evidence would be helpful.

Here we support an approach to exploitation which assumes that value is objective, that freedom does not dissolve exploitation, and that, in order to understand informational capitalism, we need to sublate Marx. Capitalism requires exploitation, but not all exploitation implies work and labour rela-tions. Our approach to exploitation – and specifically to capitalist platforms' exploitation of workers and prosumers – highlights the relevance of different types of knowledge in creating value. Moreover, as we focus on flows instead of individuals, it is a non-human-centred approach. This is closely related to one of the striking features of platforms as organizational devices. During industrial capitalism, there was a clear split among production, distribution, and consumption. Exploitation took place in the realm of production, as Marx emphasized. However, in informational capitalism, and particularly in its second phase, the division among production, distribution, and consumption became blurred partially because of the very existence of platforms – though the relation is dialectical, as platforms could only thrive in societies which already had faded away that division.

The key is that platforms, as firms, command productive processes but, at the same time, govern exchanges, and even consumption might take place on them. Platforms internalize markets. As many authors have pointed out, capitalist productive activities have expanded well beyond the traditional limits of production and labour. This is one of the reasons why some forms of exploitation (i.e. through reproduction and through attention) that already existed, but had rarely been noticed during industrial capitalism, became evident.

NOTES

1. Sections 2 and 4 are based on and summarize findings of a journal article which is currently under evaluation.
2. It is worth noting that the distinction between phases is dialectical – in a Hegelian sense. This implies that the arrival of the second phase does not mean the end or disappearance of the tendencies of the first one, but their sublation (negation, preservation, and up-lift).
3. This section is a summary and re-elaboration of Zukerfeld 2017, chapter 5, which provides an in-depth version.
4. Of course, this does not mean that in all cases gauging the magnitude of this asymmetry is easy or even possible. But the difficulty of numerically measuring something does not imply that it is impossible to grasp, or, still less, that it does not exist.
5. The fact that *e* actors consider these relationships to be legitimate or even useful does not prevent this characteristic from being present.
6. This section is based on and summarizes a journal article which is currently under evaluation.
7. Of course, we tend to believe that Deliveroo riders are much more likely to be exploited than Airbnb hosts. However, this chapter does not deal with this particular topic, and it would be a mistake to assume that some activities are inherently passible of exploitation where others are not. Special care must be taken regarding the relation between ownership of means of production and exploitation, as we will discuss below.
8. The figures in the main text refer specifically to YouTube (not to Google or Alphabet). For an in-depth discussion of YouTube's business model, see Lund and Zukerfeld 2020, chapter 5.

REFERENCES

Armano, E. and Murgia, A. (2014), 'The precariousnesses of young knowledge workers: A subject-oriented approach', *Global Discourse*, **3** (3–4), 486–501.

Bärtl, Mathias (2018), 'YouTube channels, uploads and views: A statistical analysis of the past 10 years', *Convergence: The International Journal of Research into New Media Technologies 2018*, **24** (1), 16–32.

Bauwens, M. (2006), 'The political economy of peer production', *Post-autistic Economics Review*, **37**, 33–44.

Benkler, Y. (2006), *The Wealth of Networks: How Social Production Transforms Markets and Freedom*, Boston, MA: Yale University Press.

Berg, J., Furrer, M., Harmon, E., Rani, U. and Silberman, S. (2018), *Digital Labour Platforms and the Future of Work. Towards Decent Work in the Online World*. Report. ILO.

Bolaño, C. R. S. and Vieira, E. (2015), 'The political economy of the internet: Social networking sites and a reply to Fuchs', *Television & New Media*, **16** (1), 52–61.

Boltanski, Luc and Chiapello, Eve (2005), *The New Spirit of Capitalism*, London: Verso Press.

Boutang, Y. M. (2011), *Cognitive Capitalism*, Cambridge: Polity Press.

Cafassi, E. (1998), Bits, moléculas y mercancías. En Finquelievich y Schiavo (comps.) *La ciudad y sus TICs: tecnologías de información y comunicación*. Buenos Aires: Universidad Nacional de Quilmes.

Castel, R. (2002), *From* Manual Workers *to* Wage Laborers*: Transformation of the* Social Question, New Brunswick, NJ: Transaction.

Castells, M. (1996), *The Rise of the Network Society.* Vol. I of *The Information Age: Economy, Society and Culture*, Malden, MA and Oxford: Blackwell.

Celis Bueno, C. (2016), *The Attention Economy: Labour, Time and Power in Cognitive Capitalism*, London: Rowman & Littlefield International.

Cohen, G. A. (1979), 'The labor theory of value and the concept of exploitation', *Philosophy & Public Affairs*, **8** (4), 338–360.

Coriat, B. (1990), *L'Atelier et lê robot: Essai sur lê fordisme et la production de masse à l'âge del'électronique*, Paris: Christian Bourgeois.

Craft (2017). Retrieved from https://craft.co/reports/s-p-500-revenue-per-employee-perspective

Davenport, T. and Prusak, L. (2001), *Conocimiento en acción*, Buenos Aires: Pearson Education.

De Groen, W. P., Maselli I. and Fabo B. (2016), 'The digital market for local services: A one night stand for workers? An example from the on-demand economy', CEPS Special Report 133, Brussels, European Centre for Political Studies. https://www.ceps.eu/ publications/digital-market-local-services-one-night-stand-workers-example-demandeconomy

Deleuze, G. (1992). 'Postscript on the societies of control', *October*, **59** (Winter), 3–7.

Drahos, P. (2004), 'Who owns the knowledge economy? Political organising behind the TRIPS' (Briefing 32), Newton, UK: The Corner House.

Elster, J. (1985), 'Roemer versus Roemer. Un comentario a *Nuevas direcciones en la teoría marxiana de la explotación*', *Mientras Tanto*, **22**, 115–127.

Eyck, K. (2003), 'Flexibilizing employment: An overview', ILO Working Papers 993597573402676. International Labour Organization.

Fisher, E. (2012), 'How less alienation creates more exploitation? Audience labour on social network sites', *TripleC: Communication, Capitalism & Critique*, **10** (2), 171–183.

Foucault, M. (2010), *The Birth of Biopolitics: Lectures at the Collége de France*, translated by Graham Burchill, Houndmills: Palgrave Macmillan.

Fuchs, C. (2010), 'Labour in informational capitalism', *The Information Society European Journal of Social Theory*, **26** (3), 179–196. DOI: 10.1080/01972241003712215.

Fuchs, C. (2012), 'Dallas Smythe today – The audience commodity, the digital labour debate, Marxist political economy and critical theory. Prolegomena to a digital labour theory of value', *TripleC: Communication, Capitalism & Critique*, **10** (2), 692–740. http://www.triple-c.at/index.php/tripleC/article/view/443

Fuchs, C. (2013), 'Class and exploitation on the internet', in T. Scholz (ed.), *Digital Labor: The Internet as Playground and Factory*, New York: Routledge, pp. 211–224.

Fuchs, C. (2015), 'Against divisiveness: Digital workers of the world unite! A rejoinder to César Bolaño and Eloy Vieira', *Television & New Media*, **16** (1), 62–71.

Fuchs, C. and Sevignani, S. (2013), 'What is digital labour? What is digital work? What's their difference? And why do these questions matter for understanding social media?' *TripleC: Communication, Capitalism & Critique*, **11** (2), 237–293.

Fumagalli, A. (2015), 'The concept of life subsumption of labour to capital: Towards the life subsumption in bio-cognitive capitalism', in E. Fisher and C. Fuchs (eds), *Reconsidering Value and Labour in the Digital Age*, London: Palgrave Macmillan, pp. 224–245.

Garegnani, P. (1979), *Debate sobre la teoría marxista del valor*, México: Pasado y Presente.

Graham, M. and Woodcock, J. (2018), 'Towards a fairer platform economy: Introducing the Fairwork Foundation', *Alternate Routes: A Journal of Critical Social Research*, **29**. Retrieved from http://www.alternateroutes.ca/index.php/ar/article/view/22455

Hilferding, Rudolf ([1910] 1981), *Finance Capital. A Study of the Latest Phase of Capitalist Development*, edited by Tom Bottomore and translated by Morris Watnick and Sam Gordon, London: Routledge & Kegan Paul.

Hodgson, G. (1988), 'Una teoria de la explotacion sin la teoria del valor-trabajo', *Economía Teoría y Práctica*, **12**, 141–153.

Howcroft, D. and Bergvall-Kåreborn, B. (2018), 'A typology of crowdwork platforms', *Work, Employment and Society*, **33** (1). https://doi.org/10.1177/0950017018760136

Iñigo Carrera, J. (2003), *El capital: razón histórica, sujeto revolucionario y conciencia*, Buenos Aires: Ediciones cooperativas.

Langley, P. and Leyshon, A. (2017), 'Platform capitalism: The intermediation and capitalisation of digital economic circulation', *Finance and Society*, **3** (1), 11–31.

Lazzaratto, M. and Negri, A. (2001), *Trabajo inmaterial. Formas de vida y producción de subjetividad*, Río de Janeiro: DPA Editora.

Lund, A. and Zukerfeld, M. (2020), *Corporate's Use of Openness: Profit for Free?* London: Palgrave Macmillan.

Madariaga, J., Buenadicha, C., Molina, E. and Ernst, C. (2019), *Economía de plataformas y empleo ¿Cómo es trabajar para una app en Argentina?*, Buenos Aires: CIPPEC-BID–OIT.

Marx, Karl ([1867] 1990), *The Process of Production of Capital*. Vol 1 of *Capital. A Critique of Political Economy*, translated by Ben Fowkes, New York: Penguin.

May, C. and Sell, S. K. (2006), *Intellectual Property Rights: A Critical History*, Boulder, CO: Lynne Rienner Publishers.

Omnicore (2019), 'YouTube by the numbers: Stats, demographics & fun facts'. Available at https://www.omnicoreagency.com/youtube-statistics/

Piore, M. and Sabel, C. (1984), *The Second Industrial Divide*, New York: Basic Books.

Ricoeur, P. (2005), *The Course of Recognition*, London and Cambridge, MA: Harvard University Press.

Roemer, John E. (1985), 'Should Marxists be interested in exploitation?', *Philosophy and Public Affairs*, **14** (1) Winter, 30–65.

Rullani, E. (2000), 'El capitalismo cognitivo ¿un déjà- vu?', in E. Rodríguez and R. Sánchez (eds), *Capitalismo cognitivo, propiedad intelectual y creación colectiva*, Madrid: Traficantes de Sueños.

Schmidt, F. A. (2017), *Digital Labour Markets in the Platform Economy: Mapping the Political Challenges of Crowd Work and Gig Work*, Bonn: Friedrich-Ebert-Stiftung.

Scholz, T. (ed.) (2013), *Digital Labor: The Internet as Playground and Factory*, New York: Routledge.

Scholz, T. (2017), 'Platform cooperativism vs. the sharing economy', *Big Data & Civic Engagement*, **47**.

Simon, H. (1996), *The Science of the Artificial*, Cambridge, MA: The MIT Press.

Smythe, D (2006), 'On the audience commodity and its work', in M. Durham and D. Kellner (eds), *Media and Cultural Studies*, Malden, MA: Blackwell, pp. 230–256.

Srnicek, N. (2017), *Platform Capitalism*, Cambridge: Polity Press.

Standing, G. (2002), *Beyond the New Paternalism: Basic Security as Equality*, London: Verso.

Sweezy, Paul M. (1942), *The Theory of Capitalist Development*, New York: Monthly Review Press.

Vandaele, K. (2018), 'Will trade unions survive in the platform economy? Emerging patterns of platform workers' collective voice and representation in Europe (June 19, 2018)'. ETUI Research Paper. Working Paper 2018.05. Available at SSRN: https://ssrn.com/abstract=3198546 or http://dx.doi.org/10.2139/ssrn.3198546

Varian, H. R. (1995), 'The information economy', *Scientific American*, **273** (3), 200–201.

Vercellone, C. (2011), *Capitalismo cognitivo. Renta, saber y valor en la época posfordista*, Buenos Aires: Prometeo.

Wright, E. O. (1985), *Classes*, London: Verso.

Zuboff, S. (2019), *The Age of Surveillance Capitalism: The Fight for a Human Future at the New Frontier of Power*, New York: PublicAffairs.

Zukerfeld, M. (2014), 'Inclusive appropriation and the double freedom of knowledge: On the capitalist exploitation of non-for-profit software, contents and data producers. Special Issue Free And Unpaid Work: Gratuity, Collaborative Activity And Precarioussnes', *Sociología del Lavoro*, **133**, 144–158.

Zukerfeld, M. (2017), *Knowledge in the Age of Digital Capitalism: An Introduction to Cognitive Materialism*, London: University of Westminster Press.

Zukerfeld, M. (2017b), 'The tale of the snake and the elephant: Intellectual property expansion under informational capitalism', *The Information Society*, **33** (5), 243–260. DOI: 10.1080/01972243.2017.1354107.

3. Platform capitalism – towards the neo-commodification of labour?

Petar Marčeta

INTRODUCTION

The aim of this chapter is to elaborate a theoretical reconceptualisation of platform capitalism, and specifically labour mediating platforms (Srnicek 2016), from the perspective of the commodification of labour. We will argue that this perspective, firstly, brings us closer to answering the often-posed question of what is old and what is new in the platform economy, and, secondly, helps us understand the implications of these developments as well as the potential futures they could usher in.

Previous research has identified the process of *platformisation* as a form of commodification of labour (Aloisi 2015; Bergvall-Kåreborn and Howcroft 2014; Boes et al. 2017; Wood et al. 2019). Early in the development of platform capitalism, legal scholars sounded the alarm, warning us that platform arrangements lead to a misclassification of workers, who, without the protections and rights afforded to employees, become 'commoditized' (Aloisi 2015). Pure online 'crowdwork' was also scrutinised early on, with some accounts showing how the physical separation of workers and the fragmentation of their tasks sets the stage for the commodification of labour (Bergvall-Kåreborn and Howcroft 2014). Looking at the wider picture of the technology used, there was also a discussion about how the emerging 'information space' becomes the launchpad for the expansion of capital into different spheres of life (Boes et al. 2017), hence the possibility of understanding the impact of platform technology across the board has opened up. Finally, in the most theoretically elaborate use of the concept of commodification, Wood et al. (2019) argue that despite the strong embeddedness in networks, platform work is essentially a hyper-commodified form of labour, exposing workers to insecurity and precarity.

We wish to build on these perspectives and their linkages, but in order to answer our questions, we ought to unpack the concept of commodification – stressing its importance for the process of accumulation and its relation to the concepts of *Landnahme* and the reserve army of labour. To this end, we will draw on theoretical insights from Marxism, the work of Karl Polanyi, and German critical sociology, articulating them with the booming literature on 'platform capitalism' (Srnicek 2016) and 'surveillance capitalism' (Zuboff 2019) which stresses the importance of data collection and analysis.

In order to form a comprehensive link between the theoretical conceptualisation of labour as a commodity and the observed realities of platform labour, in this chapter we will introduce the concept of *neo-commodification*, which we define here as the data technology-driven commodification of labour, which encompasses both the *recommodification* of labour through the undermining of the standard employment relationship (SER) and the expansive commodification of previously uncommodified labour.

Our argument will unfold as follows. Firstly, we examine the concept of commodification from both Marxist and Polanyian perspectives. We will try to show the relationship between the derived concepts of decommodification and recommodification and some critiques thereof. Secondly, we will develop the concept of neo-commodification, by investigating several of its elements: the negation of the SER, dismantling of social protection systems and, finally, the use of data and control mechanisms. Finally, in section 4, we will look into some of the implications of these trends, again engaging Marxist and Polanyian perspectives in a dialogue in order to better understand the institutional responses and struggles arising around the process of platformisation.

1   THE CONCEPT OF COMMODIFICATION

In this section we will look into the ways Marxist and Polanyian inspired ideas of commodification can be brought into dialogue, allowing us to study not only how institutions develop around and against the commodification of labour, but also how the process of capital accumulation seeks out new avenues, both within its current domains and beyond.

1.1   Labour as a Commodity

For the purposes of this chapter it is sufficient to trace the origins of the idea of commodification of labour to the work of Karl Marx as it offers a starting point from which to understand the systemic importance of the constitution of labour power as a commodity and opens up possibilities for a historical analysis of labour. While there is much more to be said about Marx's understanding of labour power as a commodity, here we are focusing on a particular interpretation which found its way to Polanyi, and later Esping-Andersen.

What looking back at the project of Marx reminds us of is the unique character of the capitalist mode of production (Harvey 2015, p. 41). Specifically, for the process of capital accumulation, the acquisition of the means of production and the purchase of a commodity which has the unique ability to create value are necessary (Marx 1976, p. 271). The only such commodity is labour power – i.e. human capacity to labour. In order for the purchase of labour power to be possible, a market must be in place in which capital and labour encounter each other as buyers and sellers, respectively. For this, Marx argues, two conditions need to be met. Firstly, 'labour-power can appear upon the market as a commodity, only if, and so far as, its possessor, the individual whose labour-power it is, offers it for sale, or sells it, as a commodity' (Marx 1976, p. 271). Secondly, the worker must be forced into such an exchange because he is not the owner of the means of production himself and has no other means of subsistence.[1] Hence, from a Marxist perspective, the commodification of labour power is a necessary precondition for the accumulation of capital, which in turn is the imperative of capitalist production (Burawoy 2010).

The other common source for the concept of commodification of labour is the work of Polanyi (2001). Initially working from a Marxist standpoint, his work has diverged, and the relation between the work of these two classical approaches remains disputed (Block 2003; Burawoy 2010). Polanyi's interest rests not in the process of capital accumulation as such, but in the development of the market economy which spreads through the process of commodification. Commodities are here defined simply as goods which are made in order to be sold on the market. However, the development of market society encounters a problem with commodifying labour, land and money, which Polanyi famously characterises as 'fictitious commodities' since they are in their essence not produced in order to be sold. Labour, he further argues, is 'another name for a human activity which goes with life itself', it is inseparable from its bearer and cannot be 'stored or mobilized' (Polanyi 2001, p. 75). Therefore, if the market was the 'sole director of fate' of human beings it would bring about the destruction of society (Polanyi 2001, p. 76). Hence the dual development of market society – on the one side expansion of markets and the commodity form, on the other the development of institutions counteracting this trend, protecting society from those very markets.

In conclusion, Marx sought to explain how capitalism is dependent on the commodification of labour power – a commodity which is peculiar in the sense that it is tied to the fortunes of those offering it for sale – the workers. Polanyi further develops this idea of labour as a fictious or false commodity, convincingly arguing how the drive to commodify that which cannot be commodified leads to a destruction of society. What is important to stress at this point, is that both Marx and Polanyi point towards the asymmetrical power relation at the heart of the commodification of labour. For Marxist theory this is a source of permanent struggle and crisis around the accumulation of labour (Harvey

2015), while Polanyi builds on this idea of an asymmetrical power relation and how it is altered by the countermovement of society and its institutions.

1.2   From Decommodification to Recommodification

Polanyi's work provides a foundation for understanding the early rise and spread of industrial capitalism, but also the ways in which society reacts, by embedding the market and preventing it from self-destruction. Building on this idea of a dual movement (marketisation on one side, and the countermovement on the other), the idea of decommodification, or reversing the trends of commodification has been developed in the study of institutions. It is widely accepted that the most developed form this process has taken are the post-war Western capitalist countries. Here we can identify two institutions through which decommodification is enacted: the labour contract and the welfare state.

The labour contract is seen as a specific institution based on the recognition of labour as a fictitious commodity – as such, it differs from a commercial contract. Crucially, labour contracts are supposed to guarantee a minimum level of autonomy to the bearers of labour power (Offe 1985, p. 20). Hence, it distorts the 'pure market' relationship, and forms the basis of what came to be known as the standard employment relation (SER). As Rubery et al. (2018, p. 510) summarise: 'the essence of the SER is found not in its habitual form of full-time permanent work but in its substantive protections against a pure market relationship, jointly provided by employers and the state through employment rights and social protection'. Finally, the structural importance of this institution is that it forms the basis of a system of industrial relations, which regulates the power balance between labour and capital (Offe 2011, p. 190).

The second important institution is the welfare state. Famously, Esping-Andersen (1990, p. 37) defined decommodification as the 'degree to which individuals, or families, can uphold a socially acceptable standard of living independently of market participation'. It is social protection, provided by the welfare state, in its various forms, from pensions, unemployment and sickness benefits to healthcare and housing, which enables individuals and families to uphold this living standard. If the labour contract emerges out of the fictitious character of labour as a commodity, and the SER regulates the struggle between labour and capital by defining responsibilities, the welfare state is the institutional embedding of these relationships. But the welfare state, as Fudge (2017) reminds us, does not appear naturally – it is a result of class struggle embedded in collective representation.

History has shown how fragile the compromise which emerged from this struggle has been. As Streeck argues, it didn't take long before it was challenged by the forces of capital, starting in the 1980s (Streeck 2017). This process is conventionally referred to as the age of neoliberalism (Harvey 2007), and while it is tempting to regard the ensuing process as that of deregulation of capitalism, analytically it is much more fruitful to think of this era as that of the re-regulation of capitalism (Standing 2007) in such a way to enable a stronger marketisation of societies. If welfare state capitalism was underpinned by the idea of decommodification, neoliberal capitalism unleashed its opposite, known as 'administrative recommodification' (Offe and Keane 1984, pp. 122–4). This term, introduced by Claus Offe, refers to government strategies aimed at bringing wider sectors of the population into a relationship of direct dependency on the market, therefore reversing the trend of decommodification. This term was then further elaborated by Greer who defines it as 'any institutional change that reinstates the discipline of labour market competition on workers, whether in or out of work and whether through reforms to welfare states, industrial relations, or labour markets' (Greer 2016, p. 165). The process of recommodification hence affects both the SER, which is loosened or bypassed in different ways, and the welfare state, which is increasingly being re-regulated into different forms of workfare states through activation policies (Crouch 2019; Greer 2016; Rubery et al. 2018). The latter refers to a shift in the basic logic of the welfare state, from universality to greater conditionality of benefits. In other words, instead of limiting the dependence of individuals on market mechanisms, workfare and activation policies are supposed to encourage better integration of individuals into labour markets.

Finally, this process has unravelled through the destruction of the system of collective representation and industrial relations, either through the direct destruction of trade unions (Harvey 2007), or through the abandonment of institutions which were set up to limit the power of capital (Baccaro and Howell 2017).

1.3   Critique of the Decommodification/Recommodification Perspective

Various critiques of the perspective discussed above have been developed over time, but for the purposes of this chapter it is sufficient to focus on how the Polanyian perspective can be revised. One critical reinterpretation of Polanyi's theory comes from the feminist perspective of Nancy Fraser (2014). Her argument, simply put, is that the protective mechanism that society develops against commodification is itself riddled with domination, namely the domination of women by men. The fictitious commodification of labour rests on the non-commodified labour that sustains it, this labour being done in the context of the sexual division of labour. However, as the market expands it commodifies this labour as well. On the one hand this has an emancipatory character because it undermines the gendered relations of domination, but on the other hand it commodifies the life chances of those performing it (Fraser 2014, pp. 546–9). The importance of this theoretical intervention lies in the way Fraser attempts to encompass forms of labour which have traditionally been unpaid (thus not commodified and 'invisible') but which are enforced through domination. This helps us theoretically explain the constraints and incentives which commodify new types of labour, thus effectively expanding the market dependency of certain categories of population (women, youth, elderly, etc.).

Indeed, as Standing (2007, p. 70) has argued, the era of welfare state capitalism 'involved the decommodification of *male* labour' and the advancement of a system of entitlements based on the norm of SER. This means that the process of decommodification was never complete and, hence, the concept of recommodification is only partially relevant. The shortcoming of focusing on this 'pendulum like' (Wood et al. 2019) movement between re- and decommodification can be seen as a sort of 'false optimism' (Burawoy 2010). As Burawoy argues, the illusion of the Polanyian perspective that society can completely fight back and embed the market is a consequence of forgetting the capitalist imperative of accumulation. This does not mean that we should forgo the study of decommodification – rather, it means that we should include in our perspective the way in which commodification persists and seeks out new avenues. For this, we will examine the concepts of *Landnahme* and the *reserve army of labour*.

Returning to Marx, we have seen how at the most basic level, commodification is a necessary prerequisite for the accumulation of capital. In order to put this issue into a more dynamic perspective, we will engage with the concept of *Landnahme* (Boes et al. 2017; Dörre et al. 2015; Harvey 2015), defined here as process of expanding commodification to decommodified as well previously uncommodified aspects of life in order to sustain the accumulation of capital. Importantly, the process of *Landnahme* has two dimensions (Boes et al. 2017). Firstly, internal *Landnahme* refers to reinstating or accelerating the logic of commodification further. A good example would be the previously discussed developments of recommodification, such as the workfare policies which force further labour market discipline. In a European context this could be illustrated by the increased conditionality of benefits, which forces job seekers to accept any kind of job, even if it involves unsatisfactory working conditions.

The second dimension is external *Landnahme*, which refers to the subsumption of labour outside of the mode of production (including those whose labour was not commodified before, and building up a reserve army of labour). This basic logic of expansion has been theorised and researched in different ways, but here we might invoke the work of Beverly Silver (2003) who looked into the ways by which capitalism tries to overcome its crises by moving production geographically (spatial fix), or through the discovery of new technology. Hence, an example of the external dimension is the migration of production to areas previously 'outside' of the capitalist system. Again, in a European context, this could be illustrated with the example of moving production from Western to Eastern Europe, where labour costs are lower and organised labour is weaker, during the 'transition' of the 1990s. These two dimensions are interrelated, and present different strategic options for capital, hence different combinations of the two can be observed at any given historical moment (Dörre et al. 2015).

Marxist theory offers another related term which can be helpful for under-standing the labour market dynamics we wish to study; namely, the mechanism of the reserve army of labour. This refers to the '"relative surplus population" generated by and needed by capitalism, whose standard of living is below that of the working class and whose members are available for exploitation in expanding areas of the economy' (Greer 2016, p. 165). Hence, the mechanism of the reserve army of labour serves to lower the costs of labour in new areas of capitalist expansion and can thus be seen as an accompanying process of *Landnahme.*

In conclusion, if used carefully, the concept of the commodification of labour can help us understand not only the changes that the SER and welfare states have been experiencing (internal *Landnahme*), but also the drive for further accumulation beyond embedded labour (external *Landnahme*). In the following section we will argue that the development of platform capitalism accelerates and opens up possibilities for both of these aspects, thus leading to what we shall refer to as the *neo-commodification* of labour.

2　　TOWARDS THE NEO-COMMODIFICATION OF LABOUR

In order to understand the historical embeddedness of platform capitalism, it is useful to briefly look into the historical context in which it first appears. Pinpointing the emergence of platforms usually begins with the post-crisis period of recovery – the period after 2008 (van Doorn 2017). It is argued that the financial crisis and subsequent recovery created a pool of unemployed ready to engage in any kind of work – fertile terrain for the development of hyper-flexible work offered by platforms (Schor and Attwood-Charles 2017, p. 7). Coupled with that were certain business trends, such as making high risk-high yield investments into the tech sector (Srnicek 2016, pp. 32–3). Our analysis shouldn't stop there, as the existing literature also stresses the importance of situating platforms in certain longer-term trends. Both Srnicek and van Doorn start their analysis in the period which begins at the turn of the 1980s (Srnicek 2016; van Doorn 2017) which in the previous section we saw as the period in which post-war settlements in Western capitalist democ-racies were dismantled through the process of recommodification. Platform capitalism is thus often seen as an extreme manifestation of the ideology and practice of neoliberalism (Murillo et al. 2017). In this section we will further develop this idea, by delving into the ways platformisation can be understood as neo-commodification. We will start by exploring what can conceptualised as the internal *Landnahme* of platform capitalism, the negation of the SER and social protection. Next, we will consider the external *Landnahme* of platform capitalism, enabled by data collection and connected control mechanisms. These two processes together form the specific combination of old and new processes which we will denominate the neo-commodification of platform capitalism.

2.1   Platforms and the Negation of the SER

The existing literature overwhelmingly argues that one of the key issues surrounding labour organized through platforms is the misclassification of workers as self-employed (Donini et al. 2017; Fabo et al. 2017; Garben 2017; Kilhoffer et al. 2017; Scholz 2017; Sprague 2015; Todolí-Signes 2017). This question, however, has several layers, and in light of the theoretical considerations from the previous sections, we can approach this issue as a question of the degradation of SER.

From a legal perspective this turned out to be a challenging question of applying 'tests' to decide the nature of the relationship between platforms and contractors, i.e. deciding whether a person working through an online platform is an employee or not. The application of these tests however, proved to be rather controversial, with diverse and sometimes contradictory rulings in different countries (Cherry 2016; Zekic 2019). Some cases, particularly when involving *Uber* or food delivery platforms, as the quintessential and highly visible platform companies, have attracted considerable media attention – as was the case when workers for Foodora in Australia (Zhou 2018), Deliveroo in the Netherlands (Andersen 2019) and Uber in the UK (Osborne 2016), in France (ETUI 2020) and somewhat symbolically, in the birthplace of platform capitalism, the state of California (Paul 2019) were all declared to be employees. Nevertheless, academic debates have questioned the adequacy of existing regulation and whether new categories of workers should be devised (Garben 2017; Sprague 2015; Todolí-Signes 2017). But as some have noted before (Cherry 2016), beneath the surface of these legal intricacies are very important questions about the contemporary state of labour, hence the discussion should not stop there.

Some researchers have noted how labour contracts in the platform economy have been substituted with Terms of Service agreements, which grant platforms immunity and relieve them of employer responsibilities (van Doorn 2017, p. 902). As Crouch notes about gig-work companies: 'they speak as though the gig turns the employment relationship into a truly equal contract, on shorn of the hierarchical implications of the employment relationship and therefore not requiring the balancing provisions of labour law to protect workers' (2019, p. 15). In other words, this sort of 'take-it-or-leave-it' arrangement reflects precisely those unequal power relations between seemingly 'free' agents on the marketplace, which Marx described long ago.

Furthermore, the platform economy is plagued by another, one might say, discursive element which could be rather unique. Namely, platform companies are known to have often mystified their role as employers, describing themselves instead simply as 'intermediaries' on the market. This is also recognisable in the official discourse[2] of the platforms, when they refer to themselves as 'tech companies' (Sundararajan 2016, p. 157) rather than transport, courier, rental, etc., companies. In line with this strategy is the lack of participation of platform companies in representative business organisations (in some cases there is even a conflictual relationship between platforms and organisations representing businesses in danger of being 'disrupted') which might engage in collective bargaining (Kilhoffer et al. 2017). Platform companies, nevertheless, can be organised in a different way – focusing attention on lobbying activities to influence regulation in their favour (Scholz 2017, p. 46), rather than taking up their role as a negotiation partner vis-à-vis their workers.

2.2   Challenging Social Protection Systems

Closely linked with the issue of SER is the platform workers' social protection coverage. Since, as mentioned, the connection between SER and social protection is in most cases rather strong, misclassified platform workers will often miss out on different kinds of protection, most notably unemployment and sickness benefits (Cherry 2016). In Europe, for example, workers in non-standard working arrangements and self-employed workers are rarely covered by any contributions-based benefit (Bouget et al. 2017). It is clear how the logic of labour platforms fits this trend: shifting the risks and responsibilities from employers to workers,[3] who are seen as supposedly free actors, engaging in a voluntary market exchange.

This lack of social protection coverage is clearly observable in data from the 2017 ILO survey, for example, which shows that only 35 per cent of platform workers worldwide had a pension plan, 37 per cent had some sort of social insurance and 29 per cent received government assistance (Berg et al. 2018, p. 60, see also Berg and Rani in this volume). A closer look at this data is even more revealing – for the majority of those covered by some protection, platforms are not the major source of income. Concurrently, the same survey reveals that the main motivation for participating in platform work is to supplement low income from the primary job (which might offer some social protection scheme).

Thus, we can conclude that while platform labour in its purest form bypasses or even erodes social protection systems which are not designed to cover solo[4] self-employed workers, it also presents a strategy to 'add up' a decent income through extra work – platform workers can thus be seen as a prime example of 'hybrid self-employed', where the boundaries between employment and self-employment are blurred – both in terms of their legal status and the discourse surrounding them (Murgia et al. 2020; Murgia and Pulignano 2019). Crucially for our topic, this sort of arrangement is not a system anomaly – it means that platform labour not only embodies the tendencies of recommodification but it also accelerates the workfare agenda, by imposing a market solution to market problems.

2.3   Data and Control

So far, we have shown how the tendency of platform companies to annul the SER, and subsequently also what is left of the decommodifying social protection institutions, fits perfectly with, and enhances, the recommodification agenda. In fact, one would be forgiven for observing that many of these issues fit the discussion on non-standard employment and labour recommodification so well, that they do not merit the status of a separate research topic. However, as explained earlier, there is a further element in the story about platforms, which showcases their novelty – that is, the use of technology which enables the commodification of labour.

Platform technology depends on the collection and analysis of data (Srnicek 2016). Naturally, the more data there is, the more successful the model is, as it rests on the principles of the economy of scale. This means that there is a natural tendency to monopolise data, but also to seek out new areas where it can expand. The development of smart technologies opened up these areas as never before, thanks to the data collection possibilities of devices such as the smartphone (Greenfield 2018). Crucially for labour, this principle holds for both on- and offline work – in both cases it is crucial to collect as much data as possible in order to assign and coordinate tasks, and manage and control the workforce. Commentators have noted how this information space opens up the area for this new external *Landnahme* of hyper-mobile capital and labour (Boes et al. 2017). What we then see is that, through the collection of data, the work and private spheres are merged into one – allowing the logic of the mode of production to expand from one to the other. Here lies the crucial aspect of platform capitalism which deserves attention and points towards its exceptionality. Through their reliance on expanding data, platforms present strong 'market making' possibilities (Drahokoupil and Piasna 2017), or, in line with our approach, strong commodification possibilities. If we return once more to Marx, we can see this digital data infrastructure as the perfect market-place where labour and capital can meet. But the workers themselves, with the above-described merging of work and leisure, can become fully available for work or, in other words, fully commodified.

Going further, we can argue that by means of internal *Landnahme*, platforms *recommodify* labour through the destruction of SER and social protection. However, critics have long argued that there are sectors of society performing work which has never been commodified, and, consequentially, could never have been recommodified or decommodified. Such is for example the care work predominantly performed by women, or various sorts of 'grey labour' performed by migrant workers who would otherwise face difficulties in the labour market.

This is fertile terrain for platforms to operate in: through external *Landnahme*, they also further the *commodification* of labour – by creating a fictious, global labour market. This principle can be applied to both on- and offline labour platforms. With the latter the competition is truly global, but with the former it similarly unleashes the potential for all unemployed or underemployed workers to become a sort of 'hybrid'. This is where we can once again evoke the concept of the reserve army of labour – if an internet connection is all it takes to gain access to a global labour market, the supply of labour can expand to levels never seen before, far outstripping the demand, as reported in research (see e.g. Berg and Rani in this volume).

Finally, some influential recent accounts of these trends argue that the commodification of data has a logic of its own, which is to predict and influence behaviour and find a way to monetise it (Zuboff 2019). When it comes to labour platforms, these behavioural nudges, coupled with tight metrics and the described immunity granted through Terms of Service agreements, allow platforms to wield unprecedented control over their workforce (Kalleberg and Dunn 2016; Moore and Joyce 2019; van Doorn 2017).

In conclusion, the combination of internal and external *Landnahme*, coupled with an algorithmic control system, expresses the *potential* of platforms to accomplish a *neo-commodification* of labour. However, Marxist and Polanyian accounts of commodification have certain implications – for Marxists they form the essence of the class struggle, by pointing us towards the essential con-tradictions underpinning labour relations. This is where a Polanyian perspec-tive is a useful next step, as it helps us understand the variety of institutional outcomes of these contradictory forces and processes. In the next section we will take a look at both of these approaches. In this manner, we can see what kinds of outcomes this neo-commodifying potential of platforms can have.

3   RESPONSES TO NEO-COMMODIFICATION

So far, our argument has unfolded in such a way as to balance out the claims of the novelty of platform capitalism and those which view it as 'old wine in new bottles'. We have argued how, despite fitting perfectly with some old commodification and recommodification trends, platforms open up spaces for a neo-commodification of labour on a global scale, thanks to their use of technology, data and elaborate control mechanisms.

In this section we will look into developments occurring in response to neo-commodification. As has been the case so far, we will do this by articulating Polanyian and Marxist perspectives. Firstly, we will take a look at how, rather than expecting a spontaneous stabilisation of the platform model, we ought to take into account the institutional re-embedding of platforms. However, as we will see shortly, there have been limited and very diverse responses to this problem. We will offer several potential explanations as to why these developments have been slow and varied, again focusing on the combination of novel and old practices in platform capitalism. Secondly, we will examine how the conflicts around neo-commodification elicit responses from both old and new actors.

3.1   Institutional Responses and Embedding Platform Capitalism

With the rapid expansion of platform capitalism, and given its reliance on venture capital and its short-term, high-risk, high-yield nature, questions have been raised about its stability and limits. For labour, the question is how much we can expect this neo-commodification to spread. Colin Crouch (2019, pp. 19–20) for example, while maintaining that the future of platforms is still open, argues that the specific balance of stability and flexibility offered by platforms might shift in favour of the workers, once a need arises for platform companies to guarantee more commitment from its labour force. Indeed, Crouch claims that certain companies are already offering certain fringe benefits to its 'self-employed' workers. We might further add that in the context of the pandemic crisis of 2020, this kind of countermovement on the part of capital might increase, as shown by some recent examples where platform companies have been offering forms of insurance to their workers (Marshall and Gregory 2020; Rana 2020).

But here, caution is advised: it is by no means unreasonable to question where the limits of the platform model lie; however, the limits to commodification are set by organised labour fighting back, holding ground and imposing standards, rather than capital's inherent need for stability. Thus, in order to better understand the future of platform labour and neo-commodification, we ought to look into the ways in which it has been incorporated into the institutional landscape, and also how these developments spark conflict.

The introduction of labour platforms in different contexts has mostly provoked a conflictual response. There is a notable diversity of approaches to regulating platform businesses, and labour issues have often been dealt with on a case-by-case basis, as shown earlier. Existing literature provides several examples of these developments.

The example of Uber is again paradigmatic. Thelen (2018) reports how the arrival of Uber always provokes a strong response from existing actors, yet the outcomes of these responses tend to diverge quite quickly. The regulatory approaches to taxi transport can be summarised in the following way: deregulation (USA), defence of existing regulation (Germany) and adaptation (Sweden). Interestingly, Thelen offers an explanation which focuses on how coalitions between different actors are formed to influence regulation, especially stressing the importance of consumers in the case of the USA. Here we can once again invoke the discursive power of platforms which, as Thelen argues, manage to present themselves as champions of innovation, making their regulation seem unpopular with the electorate.

An even stronger example of how governments promote the platform discourse is seen in Japan. As Shibata (2019) argues, the conservative government in Japan has framed the 'gig-economy' as an answer to some of the widely perceived societal problems, such as the lack of work-life balance and low participation rates of women in the labour market. Hence, the official government discourse promotes the gig economy as a way to bring more of the population into employment, and also promotes the familiar discourse of 'freedom' to perform paid work at any time (Shibata 2019, pp. 10–12).

In other cases, the aforementioned coalition between consumers and platforms is reversed, as Thelen (2018, p. 947) shows with the example of Germany, where a strong response from regulators (with a wide political consensus) and national-level taxi associations, managed to portray Uber as a threat to the public interest and safety. This response has been successful; as a result Uber offers a very limited service in Germany, while adhering to existing regulation.

Specific issues also arise around the questions of misclassification and social protection. Garben (2017) identifies four theoretical options to tackle this issue. First is the option of applying or extending existing regulation. Secondly, a new category can be devised, between employment and self-employment. Thirdly, social protection and employment status can be decoupled. And, finally, a special category can be devised just for platform workers. The actual applications of these categories are not yet so clearly distinguishable. The UK represents the closest example of the second approach. UK law recognises a category of 'worker' who has less protection than proper employees, but more than the self-employed. Even here, however, the application of this category to platform workers has not been straightforward, and court cases have been initiated (Garben 2017, p. 42).

With regard to the option of applying current regulation, a celebrated example of institutional embedding is the case of Nordic countries, where the problems of misclassification seem less salient, and there are even examples of collective agreement coverage (Dølvik and Jesnes 2018; Jesnes et al. 2019; Johnston 2020). According to research conducted by Jesnes (2019), some platforms in Norway have taken a distinctive approach, through the development of what she calls the 'hybrid' platform model. Here, platforms combine marginal part-time contracts and more stable employment relations, rather than self-employment. The explanation provided is that the existing regulation as well as pressure from the trade unions and regulators led to this outcome.

There are, however, two sides to this development. On the one hand, Jesnes argues that the hybrid model is a way to 'appease regulators and social partners' (2019, p. 70), but the actual outcomes are still far from the norm of SER and can lead to precarity, and as such can be detrimental to labour standards in general. On the other hand, one might argue that this is still a more favourable outcome than a complete disregarding of regulations and, since the platforms become a part of the industrial relations system, it could allow trade unions to exert more pressure in the future. In any case, it is telling that this example is an exception, rather than the rule, for the expansion of platforms. It is a rather specific context in which the institutions are strong enough to embed the platforms so quickly. Other examples point towards the difficulties of slowing down neo-commodification, where it more openly breaks out into disagreements between social actors, as we will see shortly. The important conclusion here should be that the disruptive effects of neo-commodification will not trigger a spontaneous re-embedding or the introduction of neutral policy but will be the subject of a power struggle between different actors.

Based on the discussion so far, we can conclude that there are several commonalities with regard to the impact of platforms on institutions and their ability to embed them. Nevertheless, these common pressures have resulted in a variety of outcomes.

Firstly, the platform business model itself is based on the idea of disruption or finding and taking advantage of grey zones of regulation (Söderqvist 2017; Thelen 2018). However, as we have seen, in some cases these grey zones have been eradicated quite quickly, with platforms being forced to adhere to existing regulation, or adapt their business to satisfy the social partners, as in the case of the Nordic countries.

Secondly, as mentioned earlier, a strong, and indeed unique, trait of the platform model is its discursive mystification. This mystification frames the debate around platform labour as a discussion between the technophiles and technophobes, and allows platforms to use their popularity with consumers, but, as we have seen, it can also be used by governments as part of a wider agenda of recommodifying policies. However, this is also a contested terrain – it is by no means unavoidable that the discussion is framed like this, as the example of Germany and Uber shows. In fact, the visibility of the platforms, and their responsibilities towards consumers, can focus public attention on these issues, and as we will see this opens up space for specific trade union strategies.

Finally, as the platform model challenges the positions of existing social actors, the response it incites will depend on the power resources and strategies of these actors. In this sense, while the first two sources of diversity in response, namely the capacity for disruption and mystification, are quite unique to platforms, the third one, its conflictual nature, is an ample illustration of how platformisation fits into the struggles around the development of non-standard employment relations.

It is worth noting that these developments are in a fairly early stage. As the disruptive effect of the apparent innovation of platforms fades, we might expect to see the consolidation of several distinguishable approaches. In any case, it is important to stress that there may arise a variety of institutional arrangements regarding platforms – there is not a single key to the impact of platforms, as it depends on contexts and actors. This point is worth keeping in mind, as it suggests that technology is not a force for the convergence of institutional systems around the world; rather, it highlights wider issues facing institutions of contemporary capitalism – in all its diversity.

3.2   Labour Organising: Old and New Actors

As mentioned earlier, from a Marxist perspective one could argue that the issues related to the commodification of labour form the basis of class struggle. The neo-commodification in platform capitalism, expressed in forms of technological and spatial fixes (Silver 2003), as well as tighter control over labour process (Gandini 2019; Moore and Joyce 2019), provoke growing resistance from workers. With neo-commodification being the novelty of platform capitalism, it remains an unknown quantity. However, as Moore and Joyce (2019) convincingly argue, labour studies can benefit from not viewing data and algorithm developments as a 'black box' (Pasquale 2015) – the fact that algorithms are skewed against the workers in a non-transparent way, with unilateral decisions about pay and conditions and the 'dropping' of workers from platforms, is one of the reasons why resistance is mounted against the platforms in the first place. In this way, the data technology is demystified and exposed as the 'structural antagonism' (Wood and Lehdonvirta 2019), or source of conflict.

The emergence of organised resistance to platform capitalism has been hampered from the offset, with unions facing both practical and legal difficulties. The previously discussed issues of misclassification mean that 'self-employed' workers might be prevented from unionising on the basis of anti-trust legislation (De Stefano 2017), and the mystification of the employers further means that workers can sometimes lack the adequate counterpart to whom to address their complaints (Johnston and Land-Kazlauskas 2018). Finally, the physical separation of workers on platforms can seriously hinder the possibilities of creating communities and networks.

Nevertheless, there is an ever-increasing number of worker- and union-led responses. Both established and grassroots unions have been addressing these issues for the past couple of years (Lenaerts et al. 2018; Vandaele 2018). Even the practical difficulties of organising have been addressed to some extent, with some reports of online networking proving to be an asset (Cant 2019; Maffie 2020). These practical issues have been less significant when it comes to 'offline' gig work, performed in physical space.

The most visible and often discussed example is that of delivery bike riders (Chesta et al. 2019; Marrone and Finotto 2019; Tassinari and Maccarrone 2017). One notable case is reported from Italy, where practical difficulties of organising have been overcome with industrial action organised in several cities. Chesta et al. (2019) argue that this is due to the riders' specific 'visibility in urban space', which translated into the ability to influence consumers and threaten the companies' public image. Added to that were the possibilities of using the technology to connect riders and create a social space, necessary for organising. While such cases should not be overstated, as their success has been limited, it is important to stress that both the technology and the discursive powers of platforms can be harnessed by the other side as well.

Finally, there are examples that show how successful organising can also deal with the difficulty of not having a viable partner for negotiations. Such was the case of Uber in France (Lenaerts et al. 2018, pp. 70–1), where in 2016 after a succession of strikes by Uber drivers, organised in a syndicate and supported by larger trade unions, the government invited Uber to join the negotiations.

It has been noted that these forms of unions are not so much a novelty as a return to the old days of activist unions, before their institutionalisation in Western capitalist countries. In line with this, it is claimed that platform workers are not a different category of worker, but that they are open to unionisation as a means to defend their interests (Vandaele et al. 2019). However, as a consequence of neo-commodification, platform workers include groups which might have been underrepresented in traditional trade unions. As such, this presents an opportunity for both sides to cooperate (Vandaele et al. 2019).

Such a bottom-up, grassroots response to neo-commodification could show that the existing actors and institutions have not adequately responded to the profound challenges of neo-commodification. Whether or not they adapt or get replaced will depend on contextual variables and power resources.

In conclusion, the neo-commodification of labour through platforms has provoked a response. Despite the difficulties, both traditional and new, grassroots forms of organising have been emerging. As we have argued that neo-commodification threatens not only the institutional systems around the SER but goes beyond it, commodifying labour even further, it is not surprising to see new actors and different types of struggles emerging. It is also reasonable to assume that the outcomes of these struggles will go beyond categories we are already familiar with. The labour of those who are failed by social protection, who are just entering the global labour market, and are forced to engage in hybrid forms of employment requires new representation and protection, a new social and political response to neo-commodification. This response, however, cannot be limited to preserving the status quo of SER and social protection, as we have argued that neo-commodification also goes beyond these categories. How far these new actors will go in their demands for decommodification is yet to be seen.

CONCLUSION

In this chapter we discussed two broad questions: the novelty of the process of platformisation and its consequences. We have attempted to frame this discussion within the theories of the commodification of labour. Taking as a starting point the historical specificity of labour under capitalism, we have explored the view of commodification as a dynamic and contradictory process, crucial for the accumulation of capital. Keeping this dynamic in mind, we have seen how the processes of *Landnahme* and the mechanism of the reserve army of labour push the further commodification of labour. While important insights into the nature of the welfare state and SER can be learned from a Polanyian perspective, we stressed how from a Marxist perspective commodification is a permanent source of struggle between labour and capital, and the decommodifying capacity of institutions – even if they are an outcome of a long struggle – can be overstated. This allows us to understand platform capitalism as a threat that goes beyond the current institutional embedding of labour.

The hallmarks of labour-mediating platforms that we explored in this chapter are the use of data technology and algorithmic management, coupled with exploiting legal grey zones and relying on strong discursive mystification. This combination not only undermines the foundations of the SER and social protection systems but also shapes the process of the *neo-commodification* of labour. The technological solutions offered by platforms enable a merging of the private and work spheres in such a way as to turn workers into a seemingly perfect (fictious) commodity. This is done on both a local level where labour markets are disrupted and regulation bypassed, pitching workers into intense competition, with little bargaining power or protection from existing institutions, and on a global level, where it creates a vast reserve army of labour competing for underpaid jobs. Thus, platform capitalism has an unprecedented potential for external and internal *Landnahme*, a disruption of existing labour relation systems, and a creation of novel areas of commodification and exploitation.

By looking at the consequences of the process of neo-commodification, we have seen how institutional systems have responded in a variety of ways. While these responses in some cases highlight existing conflicts, we have observed how they also generate novel responses from some new actors. Grassroots, activist unions around the globe have been tackling the issues of algorithmic control – showing that neo-commodification and the struggles around it have very real manifestations.

Therefore, our conclusion is that, while we can learn a lot about platforms through the application of 'old' concepts, they also present a novel development which brings to light new responses and new actors. While it is possible to endlessly draw comparisons between the aggressive commodification and grassroots resistance of old and current struggles, we have sought to provide a theoretical (re)conceptualisation which could inform further research.

Finally, with regard to the implications of neo-commodification, it is necessary to mention some limitations. Most importantly, the particular combination of old and new which we have explored so far does not lead us to propose a conclusion of a great discontinuity in the history of capitalism. Platform capitalism is better thought of as one of the trends within contemporary capitalism, whose longevity we are yet to discover, rather than a distinctive phase. Additionally, in this chapter we have investigated neo-commodification as a relentless drive towards turning human labour into a pure commodity; however, the underlying contradiction of capitalism means that this is never possible. Hence, this is by no means a prophetic argument about a future world of pure market relationships – these will always be embedded and contested at every step. But as neo-commodification seeks out new avenues, so does the class struggle. Organised labour requires new ideas to tackle new problems in order to turn the tide from neo-commodification to a new emancipatory future. Some glimpses of these potential futures are already visible.

NOTES

1. Marx calls this 'freedom' of the worker as freedom in the double sense – 'he can dispose of his labour-power as his own commodity, and that on the other hand he has no other commodity for sale, is short of everything necessary for the realisation of his labour-power' (Marx 1976, pp. 272–3). Hence, unlike a slave who is him-/herself a commodity bought and sold by slave owners, a worker in capitalism sells the labour power he/she owns. But since this labour power is his/her only commodity, their physical existence is dependent on selling this labour power, i.e. on commodification of labour. This 'freedom' of workers contains, as David Harvey put it, political and ideological ironies observable in many forms in contemporary society (Harvey 2010, p. 100).
2. A good illustration is the example of Deliveroo which was documented in the press – the company had devised an official vocabulary to be used in official communication in order to avoid suggesting the existence of any kind of employment relation (Butler 2017).
3. Some have called this an evasion of social responsibility, akin to tax evasion (Daugerild et al. 2019); another term used for this agenda is 'radical responsibilization' (Fleming 2017).
4. Self-employed without employees.

REFERENCES

Aloisi, A. (2015), 'Commoditized Workers: Case Study Research on Labor Law Issues Arising from a Set of on-Demand/Gig Economy Platforms', *Comparative Labor Law & Policy Journal*, **37** (3), 653–90.

Andersen, R. (2019), 'Rechtbank Amsterdam: Deliveroo-koeriers hebben recht op arbeidscontract', accessed 6 September 2019 at https://www.volkskrant.nl/gs-b0c65055

Baccaro, L. and C. Howell (2017), *Trajectories of Neoliberal Transformation: European Industrial Relations since the 1970s*, Cambridge, New York and Port Melbourne: Cambridge University Press.

Berg, J., M. Furrer, E. Harmon, U. Rani and M. S. Silberman (2018), *Digital Labour Platforms and the Future of Work: Towards Decent Pay in the Online World*, Geneva: ILO.

Bergvall-Kåreborn, B. and D. Howcroft (2014), 'Amazon Mechanical Turk and the Commodification of Labour', *New Technology, Work and Employment*, **29** (3), 213–23.

Block, F. (2003), 'Karl Polanyi and the Writing of The Great Transformation', *Theory and Society*, **32** (3), 275–306.

Boes, A., T. Kämpf, T. Lühr, B. Langes and A. Ziegler (2017), 'Cloud & Crowd: New Challenges for Labour in the Digital Society', *TripleC: Communication, Capitalism & Critique. Open Access Journal for a Global Sustainable Information Society*, **15** (1), 132–47.

Bouget, D., D. Ghailani, S. Spasova, B. Vanhercke, Liser, Ose, Applica, European Commission and S. A. and I. Directorate-General for Employment (2017), *Access to Social Protection for People Working on Non-Standard Contracts and as Self-Employed in Europe: A Study of National Policies 2017*, Brussels: European Commission.

Burawoy, M. (2010), 'From Polanyi to Pollyanna: The False Optimism of Global Labor Studies', *Global Labour Journal*, **1** (2), 301–13.

Butler, S. (2017), 'Deliveroo accused of "creating vocabulary" to avoid calling couriers employees', *The Guardian*, 5 April, accessed 9 December 2019 at https://www.theguardian.com/business/2017/apr/05/deliveroo-couriers-employees-managers

Cant, C. (2019), *Riding for Deliveroo: Resistance in the New Economy*, Chichester: Wiley.

Cherry, M. A. (2016), *Beyond Misclassification: The Digital Transformation of Work*, SSRN Scholarly Paper ID 2734288, Rochester, NY: Social Science Research Network, 18 February, accessed 5 April 2020 at https://papers.ssrn.com/abstract=2734288

Chesta, R. E., L. Zamponi and C. Caciagli (2019), 'Labour Activism and Social Movement Unionism in the Gig Economy. Food Delivery Workers Struggles in Italy', *PARTECIPAZIONE E CONFLITTO*, **12** (3), 819–44.

Crouch, C. (2019), *Will the Gig Economy Prevail?* Cambridge, UK and Medford, MA: Polity Press.

Daugerild, I., C. Degryse and P. Pochet (eds) (2019), *The Platform Economy and Social Law: Key Issues in Comparative Perspective*. Etui Working Paper 2019.10, Brussels: ETUI.

De Stefano, V. (2017), 'Non-Standard Work and Limits on Freedom of Association: A Human Rights-Based Approach', *Industrial Law Journal*, **46** (2), 185–207.

Dølvik, J. E. and K. Jesnes (2018), *Nordic Labour Markets and the Sharing Economy: Report from a Pilot Project*, Nordic Council of Ministers.

Donini, A., M. Forlivesi, A. Rota and P. Tullini (2017), 'Towards Collective Protections for Crowdworkers: Italy, Spain and France in the EU Context', *Transfer: European Review of Labour and Research*, **23** (2), 207–23.

Dörre, K., S. Lessenich and H. Rosa (2015), *Sociology – Capitalism – Critique*, London and New York: Verso.

Drahokoupil, J. and A. Piasna (2017), 'Work in the Platform Economy: Beyond Lower Transaction Costs', *Intereconomics*, **52** (6), 335–40.

Esping-Andersen, G. (1990), *The Three Worlds of Welfare Capitalism*, Princeton, NJ: Princeton University Press.

ETUI (2020), 'European Trade Union Institute (ETUI) – France: Uber Drivers Are Employees, Says the French Court of Cassation', accessed 7 April 2020 at https://www.etui.org/About-Etui/News/France-Uber-drivers-are-employees-says-the-French-Court-of-Cassation

Fabo, B., J. Karanovic and K. Dukova (2017), 'In Search of an Adequate European Policy Response to the Platform Economy', *Transfer: European Review of Labour and Research*, **23** (2), 163–75.

Fleming, P. (2017), 'The Human Capital Hoax: Work, Debt and Insecurity in the Era of Uberization', *Organization Studies*, accessed at https://doi.org/10.1177/0170840616686129

Fraser, N. (2014), 'Can Society be Commodities All the Way Down? Post-Polanyian Reflections on Capitalist Crisis', *Economy and Society*, **43** (4), 541–58.

Fudge, J. (2017), 'The Future of the Standard Employment Relationship: Labour Law, New Institutional Economics and Old Power Resource Theory', *Journal of Industrial Relations*, **59** (3), 374–92.

Gandini, A. (2019), 'Labour Process Theory and the Gig Economy', *Human Relations*, **72** (6), 1039–56.

Garben, S. (2017), *Protecting Workers in the Online Platform Economy: An Overview of Regulatory and Policy Developments in the EU – Safety and Health at Work*, accessed 9 December 2019 at https://osha.europa.eu/en/publications/protecting -workers-online-platform-economy-overview-regulatory-and-policy-developments/ view

Greenfield, A. (2018), *Radical Technologies: The Design of Everyday Life*, New York and London: Verso.

Greer, I. (2016), 'Welfare Reform, Precarity and the Re-commodification of Labour', *Work, Employment and Society*, **30** (1), 162–73.

Harvey, D. (2007), *A Brief History of Neoliberalism*, Oxford and New York: Oxford University Press.

Harvey, D. (2010), *A Companion to Marx's Capital*, New York and London: Verso Books.

Harvey, D. (2015), *Seventeen Contradictions and the End of Capitalism*, London: Profile Books.

Jesnes, K. (2019), 'Employment Models of Platform Companies in Norway: A Distinctive Approach?', *Nordic Journal of Working Life Studies*, **9**, accessed at https://doi.org/10.18291/njwls.v9iS6.114691

Jesnes, K., A. Ilsøe and M. J. Hotvedt (2019), 'Collective Agreements for Platform Workers? Examples from the Nordic Countries', *Nordic Future of Work, Brief*, **3**.

Johnston, H. (2020), 'Labour Geographies of the Platform Economy: Understanding Collective Organizing Strategies in the Context of Digitally Mediated Work', *International Labour Review*, **159** (1), accessed at https://doi.org/10.1111/ilr.12154

Johnston, H. and C. Land-Kazlauskas (2018), *Organizing On-Demand: Representation, Voice, and Collective Bargaining in the Gig Economy*, Working Paper, 29 March, accessed 9 December 2019 at http://www.ilo.org/travail/whatwedo/publications/ WCMS_624286/lang--en/index.htm

Kalleberg, A. L. and M. Dunn (2016), 'Good Jobs, Bad Jobs in the Gig Economy', *Members-Only Library*, **20** (1–2), accessed 9 December 2019 at http://www .lerachapters.org/OJS/ojs-2.4.4-1/index.php/LERAMR/article/view/3093

Kilhoffer, Z., K. Lenaerts and M. Beblavý (2017), *The Platform Economy and Industrial Relations: Applying the Old Framework to the New Reality*, SSRN Scholarly Paper ID 3053826, Rochester, NY: Social Science Research Network, 7 August, accessed 15 December 2019 at https://papers.ssrn.com/abstract=3053826

Lenaerts, K., Z. Kilhoffer and M. Akgüç (2018), 'Traditional and New Forms of Organisation and Representation in the Platform Economy', *Work Organisation, Labour & Globalisation*, **12** (2), 60–78.

Maffie, M. D. (2020), 'The Role of Digital Communities in Organizing Gig Workers', *Industrial Relations: A Journal of Economy and Society*, **59** (1), 123–49.

Marrone, M. and V. Finotto (2019), 'Challenging Goliath. Informal Unionism and Digital Platforms in the Food Delivery Sector. The Case of Riders Union Bologna', *PARTECIPAZIONE E CONFLITTO*, **12** (3), 691–716.

Marshall, A. and B. Gregory (2020), 'Coronavirus Exposes Workers to the Risks of the Gig Economy', *Wired*, accessed 13 April 2020 at https://www.wired.com/story/ coronavirus-exposes-workers-risks-gig-economy/

Marx, K. (1976), *Capital: A Critique of Political Economy*, London and New York: Penguin Books in association with New Left Review.

Moore, P. V. and S. Joyce (2019), 'Black Box or Hidden Abode? The Expansion and Exposure of Platform Work Managerialism', *Review of International Political Economy*, **27** (4), 1–23.

Murgia, A. and V. Pulignano (2019), 'Neither Precarious nor Entrepreneur: The Subjective Experience of Hybrid Self-employed Workers', *Economic and Industrial Democracy*, 1–27. DOI: 10.1177/0143831X19873966.

Murgia, A., R. Bozzon, P. Digennaro, P. Mezihorak, M. Mondon-Navazo and P. Borghi (2020), 'Hybrid Areas of Work Between Employment and Self-Employment: Emerging Challenges and Future Research Directions', *Frontiers in Sociology*, **4**, accessed at https://doi.org/10.3389/fsoc.2019.00086

Murillo, D., H. Buckland and E. Val (2017), 'When the Sharing Economy Becomes Neoliberalism on Steroids: Unravelling the Controversies', *Technological Forecasting and Social Change*, **125**, 66–76.

Offe, C. (1985), *Disorganized Capitalism: Contemporary Transformations of Work and Politics*, Cambridge, MA: The MIT Press.

Offe, C. (2011), 'Capitalism', in *International Encyclopedia of Political Science*, Thousand Oaks, CA: SAGE Publications, Inc., pp. 187–93.

Offe, C. and J. Keane (1984), *Contradictions of the Welfare State*, London: Hutchinson.

Osborne, H. (2016), 'Uber loses right to classify UK drivers as self-employed', *The Guardian*, 28 October, accessed 7 April 2020 at https://www.theguardian.com/technology/2016/oct/28/uber-uk-tribunal-self-employed-status

Pasquale, F. (2015), *The Black Box Society: The Secret Algorithms That Control Money and Information*, Cambridge, MA: Harvard University Press.

Paul, K. (2019), 'Gig economy: California bill granting employee status passes assembly', *The Guardian*, 30 May, accessed 5 April 2020 at https://www.theguardian.com/us-news/2019/may/29/california-bill-gives-employee-status-to-contract-workers

Polanyi, K. (2001), *The Great Transformation: The Political and Economic Origins of Our Time*, Boston, MA: Beacon Press.

Rana, P. (2020), 'WSJ News Exclusive | Uber, DoorDash and others discuss fund for drivers affected by coronavirus', *The Wall Street Journal*, 8 March, accessed 13 April 2020 at https://www.wsj.com/articles/uber-doordash-and-others-discuss-fund-for-sick-drivers-11583641022

Rubery, J., D. Grimshaw, A. Keizer and M. Johnson (2018), 'Challenges and Contradictions in the "Normalising" of Precarious Work', *Work, Employment and Society*, **32** (3), 509–27.

Scholz, T. (2017), *Uberworked and Underpaid: How Workers Are Disrupting the Digital Economy*, Cambridge: Polity Press.

Schor, J. B. and W. Attwood-Charles (2017), 'The "Sharing" Economy: Labor, Inequality, and Social Connection on For-Profit Platforms', *Sociology Compass*, **11** (8), e12493.

Shibata, S. (2019), 'Gig Work and the Discourse of Autonomy: Fictitious Freedom in Japan's Digital Economy', *New Political Economy*, **25** (3), 1–17.

Silver, B. J. (2003), *Forces of Labor: Workers' Movements and Globalization Since 1870*, Cambridge: Cambridge University Press.

Söderqvist, F. (2017), 'A Nordic Approach to Regulating Intermediary Online Labour Platforms', *Transfer: European Review of Labour and Research*, **23** (3), 349–52.

Sprague, R. (2015), 'Worker (Mis)Classification in the Sharing Economy: Trying to Fit Square Pegs into Round Holes', *ABA Journal of Labor & Employment Law*, **31** (1), 53–76.

Srnicek, N. (2016), *Platform Capitalism*, Cambridge and New York: Polity Press.

Standing, G. (2007), 'Labor Recommodification in the Global Transformation', in A. Buğra and K. Ağartan (eds), *Reading Karl Polanyi for the Twenty-First Century*, New York: Palgrave Macmillan.

Streeck, W. (2017), *Buying Time: The Delayed Crisis of Democratic Capitalism*, 2nd edition, with a new preface, London and New York: Verso.

Sundararajan, A. (2016), *The Sharing Economy: The End of Employment and the Rise of Crowd-Based Capitalism*, Cambridge, MA: The MIT Press.

Tassinari, A. and V. Maccarrone (2017), 'The Mobilisation of Gig Economy Couriers in Italy: Some Lessons for the Trade Union Movement', *Transfer: European Review of Labour and Research*, **23** (3), 353–7.

Thelen, K. (2018), 'Regulating Uber: The Politics of the Platform Economy in Europe and the United States', *Perspectives on Politics*, **16** (4), 938–53.

Todolí-Signes, A. (2017), 'The "Gig Economy": Employee, Self-employed or the Need for a Special Employment Regulation?', *Transfer: European Review of Labour and Research*, **23** (2), 193–205.

van Doorn, N. (2017), 'Platform Labor: On the Gendered and Racialized Exploitation of Low-Income Service Work in the "On-Demand" Economy', *Information, Communication & Society*, **20** (6), 898–914.

Vandaele, K. (2018), *Will Trade Unions Survive in the Platform Economy? Emerging Patterns of Platform Workers' Collective Voice and Representation in Europe*, Brussels: European Trade Union Institute.

Vandaele, K., A. Piasna and J. Drahokoupil (2019), '"Algorithm Breakers" are Not a Different "Species": Attitudes Towards Trade Unions of Deliveroo Riders in Belgium', ETUI Research Paper-Working Paper.

Wood, A. and V. Lehdonvirta (2019), *Platform Labour and Structured Antagonism: Understanding the Origins of Protest in the Gig Economy*, SSRN Scholarly Paper ID 3357804, Rochester, NY: Social Science Research Network, 5 March, accessed 5 November 2019 at https://papers.ssrn.com/abstract=3357804

Wood, A. J., M. Graham, V. Lehdonvirta and I. Hjorth (2019), 'Networked but Commodified: The (Dis)Embeddedness of Digital Labour in the Gig Economy', *Sociology*, **53** (5). https://doi.org/10.1177/0038038519828906

Zekic, N. (2019), *Contradictory Court Rulings on the Status of Deliveroo Workers in the Netherlands*, accessed 6 December 2019 at https://research.tilburguniversity.edu/en/publications/contradictory-court-rulings-on-the-status-of-deliveroo-workers-in

Zhou, N. (2018), 'Foodora rider classed as employee and wins unfair dismissal case', *The Guardian*, 16 November, accessed 5 April 2020 at https://www.theguardian.com/business/2018/nov/16/foodora-riders-ask-government-to-sue-german-parent-over-unpaid-wages

Zuboff, S. (2019), *The Age of Surveillance Capitalism: The Fight for the Future at the New Frontier of Power*, London: Profile Books.

PART II

Labour platforms between the global and the local

4. Working conditions, geography and gender in global crowdwork

Janine Berg and Uma Rani[1]

INTRODUCTION

Crowdwork is low paying and suffers from inefficiencies in design that hurt workers. But while the poor quality of the work is evident for workers in the Global North, many argue that these jobs are a boon for the Global South where wage levels are lower and job prospects are worse. Given more limited job opportunities and the possibility that remote work provides to remain in one's country of origin, it is not surprising that a number of developing country governments and some international agencies are providing assistance to support workers to pursue crowdwork. But is crowdwork the 'silver bullet' that some suggest and which the Global South hopes for? This chapter makes a comparison of working conditions of crowdworkers in the Global South and Global North drawing on findings from a survey undertaken by the International Labour Office (ILO).

In 2015 and 2017, the ILO conducted a survey on five leading, English-language microtask platforms: Amazon Mechanical Turk (AMT), Clickworker, Crowdflower (since renamed Appen), Microworker and Prolific to learn more about workers' experience. The survey was first posted in 2015 on the AMT and Crowdflower platforms for respondents to fill out and then reposted (with some adjustments) in 2017, on these two platforms as well as Clickworker, Microworker and Prolific.[2] The final clean sample included approximately 3,500 completed questionnaires from workers present in 75 countries, although this chapter's analysis is based on a sample of 3,189 workers.[3] The survey responses provide information on the socio-demographic characteristics of the workers, their reasons for performing crowdwork, their financial situation, their working conditions, as well as the different work experiences of the crowdworkers.

As the focus of the analysis is to explain job quality and work motivations among workers in the Global South and Global North, we disaggregate findings between the Global North and the Global South as well as by sex, when relevant. For the purpose of this chapter, we define workers in the Global North as workers from North America and Western Europe, and those from the Global South as workers living in Latin America, Africa, Asia, as well as the transition countries of Central and Eastern Europe.[4] In total, workers from the Global South comprised 30 per cent of the sample (970 individuals). Of the total sample, 38 per cent were women, and although among workers in the Global South the proportion of women dropped to one in five, it was nearly three in five in the Global North.

Digital labour platforms comprise an array of different work modalities that have the common feature of having work mediated through a digital platform, either a website or app. In addition, most work on digital labour platforms, whether it is an Uber driver in San Francisco, a computer programmer in Ukraine, or an audio transcriptor in the Philippines is subject to different sorts of algorithmic management, either regarding how the work is assigned, its monitoring or supervision, or how workers are disciplined. These algorithmic decision-making processes are nonetheless reliant on humans – initially in their design – but also in the data provided to the platforms, especially through client reviews.

Web-based digital labour platforms are cross-border – neither the client, customer nor the worker need to live in the same locality. The borderless nature of the internet means that workers from around the world can provide services through these platforms, so long as they have access to reliable internet connection and the terms of service of the platform, or the clients posting tasks, allow them to work. As such, digital work constitutes a 'planetary labour market' (Graham and Anwar 2018). However, as Mark Graham and Amir Anwar (2018) explain, the borderless nature of the work does not mean that geography disappears, but rather that the work is organized to take advantage of this global reach, allowing not only the possibility of getting work done at any time of the day, but also at a lower overall cost.

Though digital labour markets are the latest manifestation in a decades' long shift of outsourcing across borders, there are important differences with traditional business process outsourcing (BPO) as outsourcing is not to enterprises in the Global South, but rather to individuals (Berg et al. 2021). Digital platforms have, for the most part, classified these workers as independent contractors, thus they are not privy to the protections and benefits that an employee working in a BPO firm would receive, even if the work they are doing is for a client located abroad (James and Vira 2012). This poses problems in ensuring adequate social and labour protection for workers, but also in applying local regulations. Moreover, should a worker want to contest his/her classification in court, or should a dispute arise between the parties that would merit recourse to the courts, the parties are likely to face 'conflict of law' issues in deciding upon the proper jurisdiction to bring forth the case (Cherry 2019).

Crowdworking has become a global phenomenon, with workers represented from most countries of the world (Berg et al. 2018; Graham et al. 2017). Because of the ability to perform the work 'anytime, anywhere', crowdwork can create income and employment opportunities in regions where local economies are stagnant (Nickerson 2014; Roy et al. 2013; Narula et al. 2011), or for workers, who for personal circumstances are not able to access traditional employment opportunities. This attribute has led some commentators to refer to crowdwork as a 'silver bullet' in the fight against poverty (Schriner and Oerther 2014), and, indeed, several UN agencies, including the World Food Programme, have developed programmes to train refugees to perform 'lower-skilled, labor-intensive digital services, such as data entry, data cleaning, photo editing, and image annotation' with the hope of accessing income-generating opportunities on crowdworking platforms.[5]

Schriner and Oerther (2014), studying rural Kenya, document how workers engaged in crowdwork were able to utilize their incomes to set up small businesses and invest in education, likely improving their potential future earnings. Sundararajan (2016) advocates the development potential of crowdworking platforms as they create opportunities for non-specialists to access the labour market, while improving computer literacy. As a result, there is an underlying notion that crowdwork can provide gainful employment opportunities for developing country workers who have limited prospects. Given this, it is not surprising that policymakers from countries as diverse as the Philippines, Nigeria and Malaysia have sought to benefit from crowdwork by investing in digital infrastructure and programmes to train workers to perform tasks such as content access, search engine optimization and content creation on crowdworking platforms (King-Dejardin 2020; Graham et al. 2017; Kuek et al. 2015; Schriner and Oerther 2014). In pursuing such a strategy, it is necessary to ascertain both the quality of the jobs being created, but also the longer-term potential for growth of the individual workers' skill and career prospects as well as other possible linkages with the local economy.

This chapter assesses the working conditions of workers on five microtask platforms based on the results of the ILO survey discussed above, disaggregating by Global North and Global South as well as by sex. The section that follows provides background information on the socio-demographic characteristics of the survey respondents. This is followed by a section on working conditions, which reveals findings with respect to remuneration, the availability of work and the workers' access to social protection.

1 WORKING ON CROWDWORKING PLATFORMS: MOTIVATIONS AND WORK HISTORIES

In order to work on the microtask crowdworking sites, workers need to be digitally literate, have access to the internet, a computer to work on, and reasonable levels of English. It is thus not surprising that overall educational levels in our sample are high.

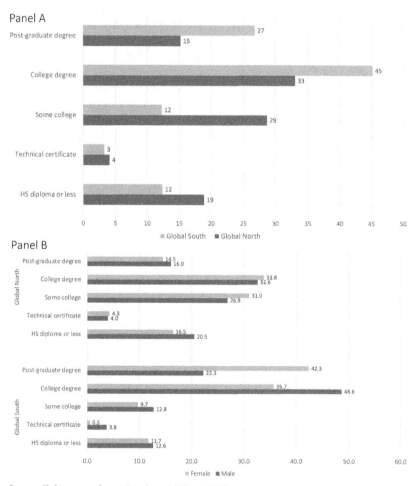

Source: ILO survey of crowdworkers, 2015 and 2017.

Figure 4.1   Levels of education, by Global North/Global South and sex

Among workers in the Global North, nearly half (48 per cent) have a college degree or higher, and 29 per cent have some college education. In the Global South, education levels are even higher, with 72 per cent holding a college or post-graduate degree (Figure 4.1, Panel A). The educational profiles in the Global South are even more impressive when the data are further disaggregated by discipline: about 57 per cent of the workers are specialized in science and technology (12 per cent in medicine and natural sciences, 23 per cent in engineering and 22 per cent in IT and computers). Across gender, a higher proportion of women workers had a college or post-graduate degree (78 per cent) compared to men (71 per cent) in the Global South, while there were no differences in the proportion of workers having higher education in the Global North (Figure 4.1, Panel B).

The survey asked workers about their reasons for undertaking crowdwork; if workers responded with several reasons, they were asked to identify the most important one. For one-third of the workers in 2017, the most important reason for performing crowdwork was to 'complement pay from other jobs', while for just over one-fifth it was because they 'prefer to work from home'. Disaggregating by Global North/Global South and male/female, we see that there is a four percentage-point difference between men and women both in the Global North and Global South, who state complementing pay as their primary reason (Global North: men, 39 per cent, women 35 per cent; Global South: men 22 per cent, women 18 per cent) (Figure 4.2). In both the Global North and the Global South, women reported more frequently than men that they crowdworked because they preferred to, or could only, work from home. In particular, the response 'can only work from home' had a ten percentage-point difference between women and men in the Global South (17 per cent for women versus 7 per cent for men) and an eight percentage-point difference in the Global North (13 per cent for women versus 5 per cent for men). This response can be attributed to the disproportionate shouldering of caregiving responsibilities by women across the world, regardless of the level of economic development.[6] When asked about main activity prior to beginning crowdwork, nearly 30 per cent of women reported caregiving as their main activity, compared with just 10 per cent of men.

Women and men from the Global South were also more likely to indicate that the pay was better than other jobs available. This response was particularly prominent among workers from Latin America, where 22 per cent of workers selected this reason as their principal motivation, many of whom were living in Venezuela.

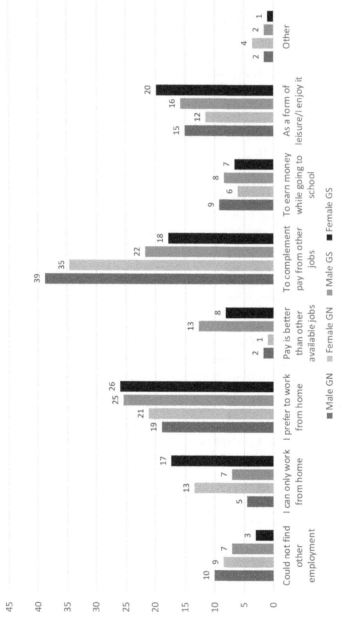

Source: ILO survey of crowdworkers, 2015 and 2017.

Figure 4.2   Most important reason for performing crowdwork, by Global North/Global South and sex

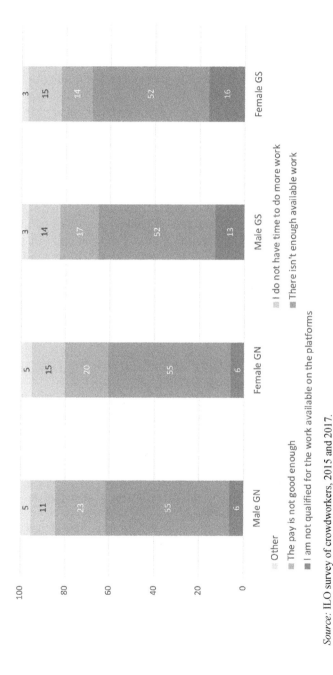

Source: ILO survey of crowdworkers, 2015 and 2017.

Figure 4.3 Reasons for not engaging in more crowdwork, by Global North/Global South and sex (percentage)

The survey asked about the financial situation of the workers and their households. Among workers in the Global North, 84 per cent reported that their household income was sufficient to cover their basic expenses compared with 75 per cent of workers in the Global South. While most workers could meet their basic needs, many were seeking additional sources of income either from crowdwork or non-crowdwork activities. About 86 per cent of workers from the Global North in our sample reported that they would like to do more crowdwork; in the Global South, the proportions were higher, with 93 per cent stating they would like to do more crowdwork. Roughly two-thirds (63 per cent in the Global North, 67 per cent in the Global South) stated that they would also like to engage in more non-crowdwork activities. When asked why they were not doing more crowdwork, over 50 per cent of the workers stated that it was because there was not enough work available. This points to an excess supply of labour on crowdworking sites, a finding documented in other studies of the platform economy. For example, Graham and Anwar (2018) estimated that only 7 per cent of workers registered on the Upwork platform have succeeded in securing a job on the platform. They calculate an 'oversupply of labour' percentage of over 90 per cent for most countries. This oversupply of labour is endemic to digital platform work given that most platforms do not limit the number of workers that can enrol. As more workers come to learn about crowdworking – especially if it is being advertised through government-sponsored training programmes – future income opportunities are likely to worsen.

2   WORKING CONDITIONS OF CROWDWORKERS: HOW WELL DO WORKERS FARE?

Crowdwork is appealing to workers as it allows the possibility to work from home as well as to combine the work with other work and non-work activities. It is also a new source of employment, which is of particular importance to countries that are experiencing economic and political crises, such as Venezuela, or where, in general, job and income-earning opportunities are scarce. But when assessing working conditions, it is important to keep in mind that the work on these platforms is, for the most part, being done by the well-educated of these societies, particularly in the Global South. Moreover, as mentioned previously, the workers are not hired as employees, but rather they work as independent contractors and thus do not receive benefits typically associated with the employment relationship, such as annual or sick leave, or social security protection. Given this, in this section we examine the working conditions of crowdworkers in the Global South and Global North across gender, focusing on remuneration, availability of work, working time and social protection.

2.1   Remuneration

The two ILO surveys conducted in 2015 and 2017 captured different aspects of the working conditions of the workers engaged on microtask platforms. To assess the remuneration of the workers, the surveys captured the time spent by crowdworkers doing paid work (i.e. actual work tasks that the crowdworker was paid for) and unpaid work (searching for tasks, taking unpaid qualification tests or screening tests in order to qualify for the work, communicating with requesters or clients, leaving reviews, etc.). It is important to consider unpaid work in the analysis as it constitutes approximately one-quarter of the workers' time, and the paid work cannot happen without it. In addition to revealing information on earnings from crowdwork, the survey also captured income earned from other jobs in a typical week, which permits an understanding of overall hourly earnings.

Table 4.1 presents the hourly earnings, for both paid work and paid and unpaid work, by gender, and across the Global South and Global North at nominal values and PPP (purchasing power parity) adjusted. Overall, the average hourly nominal earnings from crowdwork for the workers in the Global North for both paid (US$5.8), and paid and unpaid work (US$4.3), was higher than that of workers in the Global South (US$2.8 for paid work and US$2.1 for paid and unpaid work). Moreover, the distribution of earnings was skewed low, such that in both the Global North and South more than 60 per cent of the workers earned less than the mean earnings. In both the Global North and South, women earned less than men, which may at first appear surprising given that payment is by piece and most tasks are not allocated based on sex. Nevertheless, further analysis of the data reveals that the earnings gap between men and women can largely be explained by the individual characteristics of the worker (crowdworking experience and educational level) and the domestic responsibilities that women shoulder (Adams and Berg 2017).[7] The survey revealed how women choose to crowdwork as it allows them to earn an income yet still tend to unpaid care responsibilities.

In the Global North, the average hourly earnings of the workers from crowdwork were low, often below the local minimum wage. The federal minimum wage of the United States (US) is US$7.25, yet 48 per cent of the American workers on the Amazon Mechanical Turk (AMT) platform earned less than this minimum if just paid work is taken into consideration; increasing to 64 per cent when unpaid work is taken into account. This finding is further confirmed in a study by Hara et al. (2018), in which the activities of approximately 2,500 workers on the AMT platform were tracked via a plug-in over a two-year period. The study found that taking into account unpaid work, the median hourly wage was around US$2 per hour, and the average mean wages of workers was US$3.13 per hour. The study further found that only 4 per cent of the workers earned above US$7.25 per hour, raising concerns about sub-minimum wages (Hara et al. 2018).

Similarly, in Germany the minimum wage was set at Euros 8.84 in 2017, which is equivalent to US$9, which is advertised as the average earnings that a worker can earn on the German platform, Clickworker. However, the ILO findings show that the average hourly earnings among the survey respondents on Clickworker was US$4.6, which is roughly half that of the minimum wage; only 11 per cent of the survey respondents on this platform earned US$9 or more per hour for paid work, and the proportion fell to 7 per cent when both paid and unpaid work were accounted for.

Table 4.1   *Hourly earnings of crowdworkers, by sex and Global North and South (US$) (nominal and PPP adjusted rates)*

	Paid work						Paid and unpaid work					
	Nominal ($)			PPP adjusted ($)			Nominal ($)			PPP adjusted ($)		
	Male	Female	Total	Male	Female	Total	Male	Female	Total	Male	Female	Total
Global North	6.1	5.5	5.8	7.2	5.9	6.6	4.6	3.9	4.3	5.3	4.2	4.8
Global South	2.9	2.7	2.8	8.6	7.7	8.4	2.2	1.9	2.1	6.6	5.4	6.4

Note: Data trimmed at 1 and 99 per cent by region.
Source: ILO Survey of crowdworkers, 2015 and 2017.

Some of the differences in hourly earnings between the Global South and North are due to the nature of tasks and platforms that workers from different regions can access. Among the survey respondents, most of the workers in the Global North were performing tasks on AMT, Clickworker and Prolific which included the better-paid activities of content writing, content creation, and taking surveys and participating in experiments. In contrast, workers from the Global South (with the exception of Indians on the AMT platform) worked on the CrowdFlower (since renamed Appen) and Microworkers platforms, performing low-paying tasks such as data collection, categorization and content access. Prolific, which primarily posts surveys from the academic community, endorses 'ethical rewards', requesting researchers to reward participants with at least US$6.5 per hour; however, its pool of crowdworkers is primarily from Europe and North America.

In addition, many platforms offer design features that allow clients to restrict access to their task according to various criteria, including sex, or country of residence of the worker. As a result, platforms are able to exploit the geographies of space, and outsource different types of tasks to different regions, contributing to earning differentials among workers. For instance, on AMT the difference in the hourly earnings between American (US$6.90) and Indian (US$2.48) workers is substantial (Rani and Furrer 2019). This is largely because some of the better-paying tasks on the AMT platform, such as content writing, content creation and editing, are often only available to American workers, while low-paying tasks, such as data collection and content access, are left to Indian workers. Similar findings of restricting access to certain tasks based on nationality and gender were also observed in other platforms, such as oDesk (now Upwork) (Beerepoot and Lambregts 2015), Microworkers (Hirth et al. 2011) and Nubelo (now Freelancer) (Galperin and Greppi 2017). In addition, the amount received is often lower than what is stated on the platform, as the workers pay transaction fees for withdrawing the money or they lose money in exchange rate conversion.

Nevertheless, it is also true that when hourly earnings are adjusted for purchasing power parity (PPP), then the differences between regions reverses. Table 4.1 presents PPP-adjusted hourly earnings for both paid work and paid and unpaid work. Using PPP, the disparity in average hourly earnings is flipped, with workers in the Global South earning US$6.4 per hour compared to US$4.8 per hour in the Global North for both paid and unpaid work. Beerepoot and Lambregts (2015) find a similar trend when earnings were adjusted for PPP for workers in developing and advanced countries performing tasks on oDesk. As observed with nominal values, women in both the Global North and South earned less than men after PPP adjustments. The PPP differential works to the advantage of the platforms (and their clients), allowing them more easily to outsource tasks to lower-wage countries where low payment levels are more likely to be accepted.

While the PPP-adjusted higher earnings of Global South workers when compared with Global North workers may give the impression that these jobs are paying well, it is important to keep in mind that relative to the high education levels and local labour market earnings prospects, the wages are still relatively low, even in the Global South. In a related study, the earnings of Indian microtask workers with workers in the Indian local labour market is compared (ILO 2021). The study finds that offline workers who performed similar tasks in the local labour market (US$4.4) earned 1.5 times more than online microtask workers (US$2.6).

For many of the croworkers, both in the Global North (55 per cent) and the Global South (40 per cent), crowdwork is not their only job; rather they are dependent on crowdwork as a secondary source of income, often because they do not have sufficient earnings from their main job. In the overall sample, 16 per cent of the workers are engaged in regular employment, 31 per cent of the workers have temporary employment or work on a part-time basis and 16 per cent of the workers are self-employed. Overall, the hourly pay from other jobs was three times higher in the Global North (US$18.3) compared to the Global South (US$5.3). Male employees in 'regular' or standard employment in the Global North had higher average earnings in the Global North (US$27.3) compared to other work statuses, while female self-employed in the Global South had higher average earnings (US$9.7) (Table 4.2). For many of these workers, crowdwork provided additional incomes to support their livelihoods.

Table 4.2   *Hourly pay in other jobs, by work status, sex and Global North and South (US$)*

	Global North			Global South		
	Male	Female	Total	Male	Female	Total
All workers	20.9	15.1	18.3	5.2	5.7	5.3
Temporary employment	16.8	13.7	15.5	4.3	5.4	4.6
Self-employed	20.2	15.5	17.7	6.8	9.7	7.3
Regular employment	27.3	17.5	23.1	4.5	2.9	4.2

Note: Data trimmed at 1 and 99 per cent by region.
Source: ILO survey of crowdworkers, 2015 and 2017.

2.2   Availability of Work

A high proportion of workers in both the Global North and Global South expressed that they have the desire to do more crowdwork, but there is not sufficient work available to perform. This apart, it is also difficult for crowdworkers to secure a desirable and well-paying task due to high level of competition for tasks from the global labour force (Beerepoot and Lambregts 2015; Berg et al. 2018). This often leads to a situation whereby crowdworkers have to constantly search for tasks. On some platforms such as AMT, workers use scripts that enable them to sort tasks and more easily identify those that are well-paying, without losing time to reload their web browser. However, such strategies cannot be adopted on all platforms as many of the platforms block the use of such scripts. As a result, many crowdworkers also piece together work by working on multiple microtask platforms so that they have sufficient work and income. The proportion of workers working on multiple platforms was higher in the Global North (46 per cent) compared to the Global South (40 per cent).

On average, workers in the Global South worked for more hours per week when compared to the workers from the Global North. This was true of workers who did crowdwork as a secondary job (31.9 hours in the Global

South compared with 23.4 hours in the Global North), and those that did crowdwork as their main job (34.6 hours in the Global South compared with 23.4 hours in the Global North (see Table 4.3).

Table 4.3   Intensity of time spent on crowdwork, main job versus secondary job, Global North and South

	Global North		Global South	
	Crowdwork is main job	Crowdwork is secondary job	Crowdwork is main job	Crowdwork is secondary job
Number of hours/week				
... doing paid CW	20.0	17.2	28.0	25.2
... doing unpaid CW	7.8	6.4	7.2	7.1
Total CW	27.4	23.4	34.6	31.9
Share of individuals (%) doing CW ...				
... in the morning (5am–12pm)	61.8	59.8	58.1	54.1
... in the afternoon (12pm–6pm)	76.2	69.0	51.0	44.5
... in the evening (6pm–10am)	66.6	68.2	71.2	68.6
... in the night (10pm–5am)	37.3	36.4	55.6	54.7
... on 6 or 7 days per week	53.2	48.6	67.8	65.2

Source: ILO survey of crowdworkers, 2015 and 2017.

An important distinction in the working conditions between workers in the Global North and the Global South concerns working time arrangements and asocial hours. As workers accept tasks as they are posted, they are required to adapt to the temporal distribution of jobs (O'Neill 2018). Depending upon their location, tasks might be posted at different times of the day. The survey findings showed that a higher proportion of workers in the Global South (56 per cent) worked during the night (10 pm to 5 am) compared to only 37 per cent of the workers in the Global North (Table 4.3). This is because many clients on the platforms are located in the US, and post their tasks during their business hours, which is evening or night-time in some parts of the Global South (such as Asia or CEE). Similarly, a high proportion of crowdworkers worked for six or seven days a week in the Global South (68 per cent) compared to the Global North (53 per cent). The pressure to earn sufficient incomes through crowdwork forces many of these workers to be available during asocial hours, with negative consequences for work-life balance.

2.3   Social Protection

Another challenge that presents itself in the context of platform economy is access to social protection. The 2017 survey findings reveal that overall only one-third of the crowdworkers surveyed on microtask platforms were covered by any form of social insurance (Berg et al. 2018). In the Global North, about 60 per cent of the workers for which crowdwork was their main job were covered by health insurance and 20 per cent had a pension and retirement plan. Not surprisingly, workers for whom crowdwork was a secondary job had a higher proportion of insurance coverage, reflecting the likelihood that they received some of these benefits through their main job (Table 4.4). In the Global South, there is a similar pattern of higher coverage among those for whom crowdwork is a secondary job. There were no gender differences in the proportion of workers covered by health insurance in the Global North, whereas in the Global South women had greater health insurance coverage. More men than woman had a pension/retirement plan in the Global North; this pattern is not observed in the Global South. In both the Global South and North, it is likely that for those whom crowdwork was their main source of income, many are receiving insurance coverage from their spouses. In both cases, the work they are doing on crowdwork platforms is not directly contributing to social protection coverage, with important consequences for those workers who do not have access to coverage through other sources, be it another job, a spouse or a government-funded, non-contributory system. For these reasons, there are risks from crowdwork with respect to individual cover-age but also the long-term sustainability of social security systems, regardless of the place of work.

Table 4.4   *Access to various forms of social security benefits (share of crowdworkers covered), by sex and Global North/South*

	Health insurance		Pension/retirement plan	
	Crowdwork is main job	Crowdwork is secondary job	Crowdwork is main job	Crowdwork is secondary job
Global North				
Male	59.2	68.1	21.8	34.2
Female	60.1	65.1	18.4	29.7
Total	59.7	66.8	20.2	32.1
Global South				
Male	44.3	51.5	22.4	29.8

	Health insurance		Pension/retirement plan	
	Crowdwork is main job	Crowdwork is secondary job	Crowdwork is main job	Crowdwork is secondary job
Female	57.0	66.1	21.4	29.6
Total	47.0	54.6	22.2	29.8

Source: ILO survey of crowdworkers, 2015 and 2017.

CONCLUSIONS

The development of information and communication technologies has enabled the establishment of digital labour platforms as a business model that allows enterprises to outsource work to 'independent' workers located across the world. While this development has allowed workers to easily access income-earning tasks, and the flexibility to complete these tasks from their home, the design of the platforms, the competition among workers for the jobs and the lack of regulation translate into low earnings for what is a relatively well-educated labour force.

Our analysis of the ILO survey of nearly 3,200 crowdworkers reveals that while there are important similarities for workers across the world, there are also important differences depending on whether the worker is based in the Global North or Global South, as well as the sex of the worker. Women are equally represented on the microtask platforms in the Global North, but are less well-represented in the Global South. However, regardless of geography, many women engage in platform work as a means to earn income while they carry out unpaid care work in the home. This extra burden affects their earnings, resulting in lower pay when compared with men.

A higher proportion of workers from the Global South had education in science and technology fields, compared to those in the Global North, yet workers from the Global North had higher earnings compared to workers from the Global South, due to the nature of tasks they performed. Workers from the Global South faced certain restrictions in performing some well-paid tasks, leaving them with the more routine and less financially attractive jobs of data annotation and data cleaning. However, when the earnings were adjusted for PPP, the workers from the Global South had higher earnings compared to their counterparts in the Global North, though in some cases, such as India, the pay was still lower than similar jobs in the local labour market. Moreover, given their higher educational levels, the incomes earned, even once adjusted for PPP, are not commensurate with the level of education; moreover, it raises certain developmental questions about whether this is the best use of skilled labour.

The differentials in cost-of-living work to the advantage of the platforms (and their clients) who can outsource tasks to lower-wage countries, where there is an oversupply of labour and fierce competition among workers for the available tasks. Because of time differences, workers in the Global South were more likely to work asocial hours, and many workers worked seven days a week, affecting their work-life balance.

Currently, the platforms are not subject to labour and social security laws, or collective agreements, allowing an absence of minimum standards with respect to working hours, leave, minimum pay, social security and other benefits. And with an unfettered supply of labour, it is not surprising that earnings are low, or that workers spend substantial amounts of time searching for acceptable work. Given the problems of unemployment, underemployment and precarity in labour markets in the Global South (and increasingly in the Global North), it is understandable that governments, particularly in developing countries, might view platform work as a possible panacea. But in advocating such an approach it is important to appreciate the nature of the work, the benefits and risks to workers and the consequences of leaving this global labour market unregulated. As more workers learn of these platforms, the prospects of improving this situation, in the absence of regulation, are slim.

NOTES

1. Janine Berg and Uma Rani are senior economists in the International Labour Office, Geneva, Switzerland. The views expressed in this chapter are their own and do not necessarily reflect the views of the International Labour Organization. We would like to thank Marianne Furrer for excellent research assistance.
2. Workers were compensated for the task of completing the survey. For more details on the survey and the results see Berg (2016) and Berg et al. (2018).
3. This is because the 2015 survey was broken into two parts and we only include workers who filled out both parts of the survey.
4. For a list of countries included in the ILO survey see Berg et al. (2018).
5. See: https://innovation.wfp.org/project/empact
6. In 2018, women dedicated 4 hours and 25 minutes per day on unpaid care work compared with 1 hour and 23 minutes for men (3.2 times more hours than men). The unpaid care work gap exists in all countries of the world, though it is more pronounced in some regions than others (women spent 4.7 times more hours than men in the Arab States compared with 1.7 times more hours in the Americas) (ILO 2018).
7. Adams and Berg (2017) analyse the gender wage gap among American AMT workers and find a gap at the lower end of the wage distribution. The authors attribute this gap to the unpaid care responsibilities that women are doing as they crowdwork which cause interruptions in their work and lead them to favour short tasks that are less well-paid.

BIBLIOGRAPHY

Adams, A. and Berg, J. (2017), *When home affects pay: An analysis of the gender pay gap among crowdworkers*. Available at: https://ssrn.com/abstract=3048711 or http://dx.doi.org/10.2139/ssrn.3048711

Beerepoot, N. and Lambregts, B. (2015), 'Competition in online job marketplaces: Towards a Global labour market for outsourcing services', *Global Networks*, **15**(2), 236–255.

Berg, J. (2016), *Income security in the on-demand economy: Findings and policy lessons from a survey of crowdworkers*. Conditions of Work and Employment Series 74. Geneva: ILO.

Berg, J., Rani, U. and Gobel, N, (2021), 'From outsourcing to crowdsourcing: The shifting economic prospects of Indian platform workers', in J. Drahokoupil and K. Vandaele (eds), *Modern guide to labour and the platform economy*. Cheltenham, UK and Northampton, MA: Edward Elgar.

Berg, J., Furrer, M., Harmon, E., Rani, U. and Silberman, M. S. (2018), *Digital labour platforms and the future of work: Towards decent work in the online world*. Geneva: ILO.

Cherry, M. (2019), 'Regulatory options for conflicts of law and jurisdictional issues in the on-demand economy'. Conditions of Work and Employment Series No. 106. Geneva: ILO.

Corporaal, G. F. and Lehdonvrita, V. (2017), *Platform sourcing: How Fortune 500 firms are adopting online freelancing platforms*. Oxford: Oxford Internet Institute.

De Stefano, V. (2016), 'The rise of the "just-in-time workforce": On-demand work, crowdwork and labour protection in the "gig-economy"'. Conditions of Work and Employment Series No. 71. Geneva: ILO.

Galperin, H. and Greppi, C. (2017), 'Geographical discrimination in the gig economy'. Accessed on 10 May 2019, unpublished.

Graham, M. and Anwar, M. A. (2018), 'Digital labour', in J. Ash, R. Kitchin and A. Leszczynski (eds), *Digital Geographies*. London: Sage.

Graham, M. and Anwar, M. A. (2019), 'the global gig economy: towards a planetary labour market?' First Monday, **24**(4). doi.org/10.5210/fm.v24i4.9913.

Graham, M., Hjorth, I. and Lehdonvirta, V. (2017), 'Digital labour and development: Impacts of global digital labour platforms and the gig economy on workers livelihoods', *Transfer: European Review or Labour and Research*, **23**(2), 135–162.

Gray, M. L. and Suri, S. (2019), *Ghost work: How to stop Silicon Valley from creating a new global underclass*. Boston, MA: Houghton Mifflin Harcourt.

Hara, K., Adams, A., Milland, K., Savage, S., Callison-Burch, C. and Bigham, J. P. (2018), 'A data-driven analysis of workers' earning on Amazon Mechanical Turk', *Proceedings of the CHI Conference*, Paper No. 449, CHI '18, Montreal.

Hirth, M., Hossfeld, T. and Tran-Gia, P. (2011), 'Anatomy of a crowdsourcing platform – using the example of Microworkers.com', *Proceedings of the Fifth International Conference on Innovative Mobile and Internet Services in Ubiquitous Computing* (IMIS), IEEE, pp. 322–329.

ILO (2018), *Care jobs and the care economy: A challenge and an opportunity for the future of decent work*. Geneva: ILO.

ILO (2021). *World Employment and Social Outlook: The role of digital labour platforms in transforming the world of work*. Geneva: ILO

Irani, L. C. (2015), 'Difference and dependence among digital workers: The case of Amazon Mechanical Turk', *South Atlantic Quarterly*, **114**(1), 25–234.

James, A. and Vira, B. (2012), 'Labour geographies of India's new service economy', *Journal of Economic Geography*, **12**(4), 841–875. https://doi.org/10.1093/jeg/lbs008

Johnston, H. and Land-Kazlauskas, C. (2018), *Organizing on-demand: Representation, voice, and collective bargaining in the gig economy*. Conditions of Work and Employment Series No. 94. Geneva: ILO.

Kessler, S. (2018), 'The crazy hacks one woman used to make money on Mechanical Turk', *Wired*.

King-Dejardin, A. (2020), *Homeworking in the Philippines: Bad job? Good job?*. ILO Working Paper 25. Geneva: ILO

Kittur, A., Nickerson, J. V., Bernstein, M. S., Gerber, E. M., Shaw, A., Zimmerman, J., Lease, M. and Horton, J. J. (2013), 'The future of crowd work', *Proceedings of the CSCW '13 Conference*, San Antonio, Texas.

Kuek, S. C., Paradi-Guilford, C., Fayomi, T., Imaizumi, S., Ipeirotis, P., Pina, P. and Singh, M. (2015), *The global opportunity in online outsourcing*. Washington, DC: World Bank.

Narula, P., Gutheim, P., Rolnitzky, D., Kulkarni, A. and Hartman, B. (2011), 'MobileWorks: A mobile crowdsourcing platform for workers at the bottom of the pyramid'. Conference paper, January 2011. Available at: https://www.aaai.org/ocs/index.php/WS/AAAIW11/paper/download/3962/4263

Nickerson, J. V. (2014), 'Crowd work and collective learning', in A. Littlejohn and A. Margaryan (eds), *Technology-enhanced professional learning*. New York and London: Routledge, pp. 39–49. Available at: http://ssrn.com/abstract=2246203

O'Neill, J. (2018), 'From crowdwork to Ola Auto: Can platform economies improve livelihoods in emerging markets?', in H. Galperin and A. Alarcon (eds), *The Future of work in the Global South*. Ottawa, ON: International Development Research Centre, pp. 28–31.

Rani, U. and Furrer, M. (2019), 'On-demand digital economy: Can experience ensure work and income security for microtask workers?', *Journal of Economics and Statistics*, **239**, 565–597. https://doi.org/10.1515/jbnst-2018-0019

Roy, S., Balamurugan, C. and Gujar, S. (2013), 'Sustainable employment in India by crowdsourcing enterprise tasks', *Proceedings of the ACM DEV '13* Annual Symposium, Bangalore.

Schmidt, F. A. (2019), *Crowdsourced production of AI training data: How human workers teach self-driving cars how to see*. Working Paper Forschungsförderung, No. 155, August. Düsseldorf: Hans-Böckler-Stiftung.

Schriner, A. and Oerther, D. (2014), 'No really, (crowd) work is the silver bullet', *Procedia Engineering*, **78**, 224–228.

Sundararajan, A. (2016), *The sharing economy: The end of employment and the rise of crowd-based capitalism*. Cambridge and London: The MIT Press.

5. Global earnings disparities in remote platform work: liabilities of origin?[1]

Vili Lehdonvirta, Isis Hjorth, Helena Barnard and Mark Graham

---

It's much easier getting jobs when you're not from Kenya. If I could change anything, I'd change people's perceptions. It feels demoralizing that people think that
you're unskilled if you're from the third world. Third-world people are only offered
low-skilled jobs. [Male, 27, Nairobi]

Online labour platforms are websites and apps that mediate between buyers
and sellers of remotely deliverable knowledge work, such as software development, graphic design, writing, and data labeling (Horton, 2010). Online
labour platforms or different subsets of them are also referred to as online
gig platforms, freelancing platforms, outsourcing platforms, and microwork
platforms. Regardless of what we think about the job quality (Wood et al.,
2018) and income security (Lehdonvirta, 2018) of the kind of work that online
labour platforms often provide, they are clearly opening up new opportunities
for people in regions where other opportunities are scarce (Ghani et al., 2014).
The opportunities they open up are welcomed especially by people with skills
gained through experience or education, but with few avenues to apply those
skills locally (Braesemann et al., 2020). This has led to visions of a global
marketplace where geography no longer matters, and instead what counts is
the individual and their skills (Kuek et al., 2015). But such visions may be
going too far. Digital technologies can do much to bridge physical distance,
and at the same time be less effective in overcoming other gaps. In this chapter
we investigate ways in which location continues to matter for success even
in digitally mediated work, using statistical analysis of platform transaction
records supplemented with interview data.

To frame our investigation, let us start with the term "liabilities of
origin," a term used in international business scholarship to refer to the
special challenges that companies from emerging economies face as they
attempt to compete in international markets (Pant & Ramachandran, 2012;
Ramachandran & Pant, 2010). Thanks to the liberalization of international

trade, global markets in many industries are now in principle open for companies from almost any country. Yet certain challenges continue to hold back companies specifically from less economically developed countries. Some of these challenges stem from the companies' home country contexts. For instance, education systems in less developed countries can be weak and fragmentary, leading to a dearth of skilled graduates who could help the business produce high-quality outputs and be internationally competitive.

Other challenges stem from the host country context, that is, the customer's or client's side. In particular, international business scholars highlight "negative attributions" that customers in a particular country may attach to firms from emerging economies (Ramachandran & Pant, 2010). Studies in international marketing show that customers are often biased against products and services from marginalized countries, assuming them to be inferior in quality regardless of whether that is true in a particular instance or not (Verlegh & Steenkamp, 1999) and being less willing to pay for them (Koschate-Fischer et al., 2012). This has been found to apply also in electronic commerce (Bracamonte & Okada, 2015). Due to liabilities of origin such as these, firms originating in emerging economy countries are disadvantaged in international markets relative to their peers from other countries, even when they enjoy broadly the same level of market access in legal terms.

While the term liabilities of origin was originally coined to describe challenges faced by emerging-economy firms, similar liabilities linked with the country of origin also seem likely to hold back individual contractors offering services through online labour platforms. Platforms have done much to open up international market access for these contractors. Small emerging-economy firms rely mostly on personal networks to reach foreign clients (Ciravegna et al., 2014; Musteen et al., 2014), but few people in emerging economies have such international personal contacts. Platforms that bring together supply and demand across borders and provide tools for the two sides to communicate and to an extent trust each other are thus genuinely changing market access (Lehdonvirta et al., 2019; Braesemann et al., 2020). But this does not necessarily mean that they compete on an equal footing with contractors from high-income countries. Liabilities of origin stemming from both the home country context (e.g. poor-quality education) and the host country context (e.g. negative assumptions about quality) are possible. Moreover, when emerging economy firms struggle to navigate the global economy, they have a fairly substantial resource base that they can draw on for support and advice. Individuals engaging with a global marketplace via the Internet lack not only institutional protections but typically also the kind of resources that firms can draw on.

In the following sections, we analyze six months of transactions from a leading online freelancing platform to find out how the country of origin shapes online workers' experiences and earnings. The quantitative analyses are motivated and illustrated with salient quotes from face-to-face interviews conducted with online contractors in Southeast Asia (Philippines, Vietnam, Malaysia) and sub-Saharan Africa (Kenya, Nigeria, South Africa). Both data sets stem from a multi-year investigation of online labour platforms in emerging-economy countries. Different subsets of the data have previously been examined in articles such as Graham et al. (2017), Wood et al. (2018), and Lehdonvirta et al. (2019).

To ensure that we are comparing apples with apples, in this chapter we focus our quantitative analyses on projects categorized as writing work. We chose writing because it was what many of our interview informants were doing, it is relatively commodified in that the variation in rates is limited, it requires no formal qualifications, it is supplied by contractors from countries around the world, and it exists in large numbers in the records (34,352 projects in total). Also, since stereotypes of foreign countries vary across the world, we focused on U.S. and Canadian buyers. We chose these two countries because their combined market share is very high in global outsourcing in general and the platform economy in particular.

The structure of this marketplace and of online contracting in general calls for a multi-level study design: our smallest unit of analysis is an individual project; each project belongs to a contractor, and each contractor comes from a country. We are interested in whether the rates paid for a project vary depending on the contractor's country, and what country characteristics might account for this variance. These levels and the main variables of interest are depicted in Figure 5.1. A detailed description of the data and methodology is included at the end of the chapter.

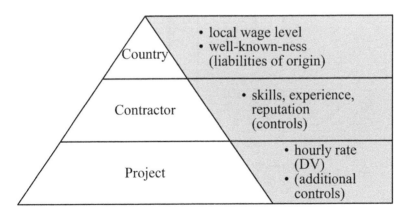

Figure 5.1   Three-level design, levels, and variables

1   GLOBAL EARNINGS DISPARITIES IN ONLINE WORK

Let us start our analysis of the transaction records by examining whether there are any obvious differences between how much workers from different countries are earning on the platform. Figure 5.2 shows how much workers from different countries earned per one hour of writing work on the platform. The figure reveals some familiar patterns. First, it suggests that there are significant earnings disparities between countries. For instance, with a rate of $4.26 per hour, the mean Kenyan earned only a third of what a mean U.S.-based worker was earning. Second, it shows that the earnings disparities are structured along a familiar high-income vs. lower-income country continuum. The four top-earning countries on the platform are all classified as high-income countries according to the World Bank, while the bottom five are classified as lower middle-income countries. The middle ground in platform earnings is occupied by a mix of middle-income countries (we will also use the terms emerging economy and lower-income country to refer to countries that are not classified as high-income countries).

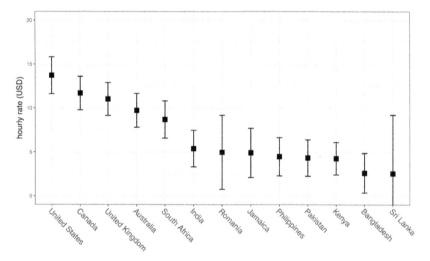

Figure 5.2   Predicted pay rate by country in USD (residual standard errors in bars

The values in Figure 5.2 are geometric means rather than the more familiar arithmetic means ("averages"). Geometric means are less affected by outliers, so they give a more reasonable idea of what a "typical" worker might be earning. They are lower than average pay rates: for instance, U.S.-based writers on average earned \$18.61 per hour, but their geometric mean earnings were just \$13.71 per hour. This is because a handful of superstars pushed the average up, with one writer earning as much as \$175 per hour in one project. At the same time, a long tail of U.S.-based novice online writers was charging next to nothing to try to break into the market. The geometric means in our case are very close to median pay rates, so they can be thought of roughly as what a "middle of the road" worker is earning. For brevity, we will refer to them simply as means.

We can also compute a "within-country correlation coefficient" for the model underlying Figure 5.2. This statistic tells us how much of the observed variation in workers' earnings rates on the platform is attributable to unexplained variation between countries rather than to variation between individuals or projects. This figure is approximately 35 percent – that is, 35 percent of the workers' pay rates seems to be determined by their countries of origin.

2   IMPACT OF CONTRACTOR QUALITY

To what extent are the stark rate differences that we found between countries explained by differences in human capital, that is the skills or quality of the labour supplied to the market? The United States has a better education system and various other institutional advantages over Bangladesh, so U.S.-based contractors might be expected to be more competent on average than workers based in Bangladesh. Though we don't have data on the workers' educational and other qualifications, we do have some quite straightforward measures of contractor competence. We know how many skill tests each contractor has successfully completed on the platform. These are voluntary computer-administered tests that assess the contractor's abilities in areas such as language skills, important software packages, and general business and communication skills. We also know how many projects they have previously completed on the platform. To the extent that experience translates into competence, this is another partial indicator of the contractor's competence. Finally, we know the average feedback rating that the contractor has received from previous clients. Taken together, these three imperfect measures can be used to provide a reasonable picture of contractor competence. Interview participants certainly felt that these measures were important determinants of pay on the platform:

> Once you're able to take a test for that skill you've acquired, you're telling your potential clients that I'm capable of doing this stuff: "Hey you can go see my profile; I'm capable of doing that." [Male, 23, Abuja]
> I ask for more money now than I asked for five years ago. I have more experience, and [...] many good feedbacks and clients can trust me on projects. [Male, 31, Ho Chi Minh City]

Table 5.1 presents the country means of the three contractor competence characteristics: experience, reputation, and skills. The countries are presented in the order of the sum of these three characteristics, which can be thought of as a simple human capital index for the online contractors from that country. Contrary to expectation, Bangladesh ranks slightly above the United States in this index. In fact, most of the lower-income countries in the list rank higher than the high-income countries with better education systems and other institutional factors. This counter-intuitive finding can be explained by the fact that highly competent workers in high-income areas are likely to have many opportunities in their local labour markets, with little need to turn to online labour markets for work. In contrast, highly competent workers in lower-income areas may find better opportunities online than in their local markets (Braesemann et al., 2020). Contractors from lower-income countries may also be investing more time into the skill tests if the opportunity cost of their time is lower.

Table 5.1   Contractor quality characteristics, averages by country

	Experience	Reputation	Skills	Sum
South Africa	4.06	4.63	8.55	17.25
Romania	3.43	4.90	6.89	15.21
India	3.51	4.54	5.13	13.18
Philippines	3.52	4.57	4.79	12.88
Pakistan	3.57	4.68	4.48	12.73
Bangladesh	3.37	4.53	4.70	12.60
United States	3.34	4.63	4.02	11.99
Canada	3.32	4.52	4.12	11.97
Kenya	3.55	4.39	3.80	11.75
United Kingdom	3.29	4.63	3.30	11.22
Sri Lanka	3.58	4.70	2.43	10.71
Australia	2.94	4.63	2.94	10.51
Jamaica	2.80	4.56	2.00	9.36

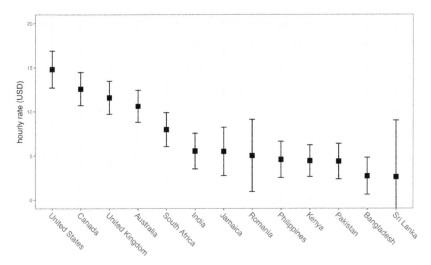

Figure 5.3   *Predicted pay rate by country in USD, controlling for worker experience, reputation, and skill tests (residual standard errors in bars)*

Although Table 5.1 already strongly suggests that differences in human capital are not going to explain why emerging economy workers earn less online, we can examine the link formally with a multi-level mixed-effects regression model. The variable being explained is the hourly rate (log-transformed), and the contractor quality characteristics are entered into the model as control variables. The resulting model allows us to predict how much workers in different countries would earn in a hypothetical world where all workers had exactly the same competence characteristics. The results are shown in Figure 5.3. Not much changes: the country mean earnings remain very close to those presented in Figure 5.2. Adding the time zone difference between the worker and the client to the model as an additional control variable likewise has no practically significant effect. The within-country correlation coefficient of the model increases slightly to 37 percent.

3   IMPACT OF LOCAL OPPORTUNITIES

Our analysis thus far shows that over a third of the variation in hourly rates is attributable to the workers' countries of origin, and that these country-level disparities don't seem to be explained by differences in human capital or time zones. The differences persist despite many lower-income countries supply-ing at least as good or more competent workers to the platform than many high-income countries, according to the available measures. Another possible explanation for the pay rate differences can be found in the combined effects of local wage levels and competition. Workers lacking well-paid opportunities available in the local labour market are presumably willing to accept online projects at lower rates. In contrast, workers whose local job market provides many well-paid opportunities will presumably find only higher-paying online projects worth accepting. Indeed, interview participants in many cases compared their online rates to what they could earn on the local labour market:

> I'm going to compare [the pay offer] with my daily – because that's what I can see myself working for the entire day, $30 [...] So that's my whole day's work, more or less the same salary [as] with my call center job. [Female, early 30s, Manila]

This intuition corresponds to the "reservation wage" model used in labour economics (Lippman & McCall, 1976). The salience of reservation wages is influenced by the level of competition in the market (Manning, 2011). If there is little competition between contractors, then contractors can charge whatever the client is willing to pay, and their local wage level doesn't enter into the picture. But if competition is intense and results in bidding wars, then the best alternative option in each contractors' local labour market determines the minimum rate at which it still makes sense for them to bid for a project online. We know that competition on platforms can be very intense, as they extend access to many workers around the world. Although demand-side entry barriers are also diminished (by for instance allowing work to be purchased in smaller chunks), the evidence suggests that there is currently more supply than demand on global platforms (Kuek et al., 2015; Graham et al., 2017), though this does vary by type of work (Kässi & Lehdonvirta, 2018). Differences in local wage levels together with intense competition could thus explain why contractors from lower-income countries such as the Philippines, Kenya, and Pakistan end up working at significantly lower rates than contractors from high-income countries such as the United States, the United Kingdom, and Canada.

We can examine this hypothesis by entering the local wage level as an additional control variable to our model predicting contractor pay. The results are depicted in Figure 5.4. This time the impact is significant. When the effect of the local wage levels is eliminated, the country differences in contractors' pay rates become less pronounced, and, more importantly, the order of the countries changes – the predicted top-earners are now contractors from India and Pakistan! The within-country correlation coefficient falls from 37 to 14 percent. In other words, a large share of the variation in the rates that contractors earn online seems to be attributable to differences in their local wage levels. Contractors from countries with lower wage levels are willing to take

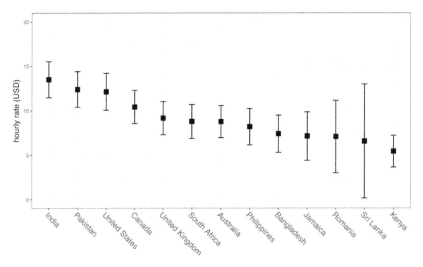

Figure 5.4   *Predicted pay rate by country in USD, controlling for worker experience, reputation, skill tests, time difference, and local wage level (residual standard errors in bars)*

up projects that pay lower rates. Contractors from high-income countries are more likely to only accept projects that pay a higher rate. Such projects occur perhaps because the client is in a hurry and cannot wait for lower bids, because they need a very particular skill set that the contractor happens to have, or because they simply wish to pay a higher rate for compliance or ethical reasons.

Nevertheless, even when the impact of the local wage level is controlled, most lower-income countries still rank below the high-income countries in terms of platform pay rates. Fourteen percent of the variation in pay rates is still attributable to unexplained country-level differences. Can this remaining impact of geography somehow be explained?

4   IMPACT OF CLIENT PERCEPTIONS

So far we have examined how factors stemming from the contractor's home country context influence pay rates and help to explain global pay disparities. As a final step, let us shift our attention to how the client country context may be generating or supporting global pay disparities. It is well established in the international marketing literature that clients' or customers' perceptions of foreign countries influence their perceptions of the quality of goods or services from those countries (Johansson et al., 1985; Verlegh & Steenkamp, 1999), and consequently their willingness to pay them (Laroche et al., 2005;

Koschate-Fischer et al., 2012). This is particularly the case when the good or service lacks a strong brand or reputation of its own (Maheswaran, 1994). It seems highly plausible that such perceptions might be influencing international clients' willingness to pay for platform-mediated labour as well. Many interview participants certainly felt that this was the case, as illustrated by this quote:

> This perception [of clients] that third world countries are not good. It hurts. It's very demoralizing. The perception, I really hate it because in this country we've come up with some of the most innovative ideas and if people in oDesk would just utilize such talents, they're here. [Male, 27, Nairobi]

In the international marketing literature, country images are typically conceptualized in terms of the associations attached to them (e.g. German cars), their valence (from positive to negative), and their strength (from strong to no image at all) (Shimp et al., 1993). These are typically measured with surveys. Since we do not have suitable survey data available, we adopt a more innovative approach: we measure the strength of a country's image, its "well-known-ness," with a proxy developed from Internet search volume data. Search volume data are increasingly used in social and economic research to measure aggregate human behaviors and attitudes (Choi & Varian, 2012; Preis et al., 2013), including racial attitudes (Stephens-Davidowitz, 2014). Using the Google Trends database, we captured the relative frequency of each of the countries among Google search queries performed in the United States. The resulting variable shows that Americans are most likely to type United States into their search boxes (relative frequency 480) and least likely to type Sri Lanka (4).

This approach has advantages and disadvantages. A country's relative popularity in searches is admittedly an imperfect proxy for how well-known the country is. But a significant advantage of this measure is that it is observational as opposed to self-reported, as honest survey responses on a person's knowledge and ignorance are difficult to elicit. The main drawback of this approach is that we are only measuring the strength of the country image, not its valence. Yet there are good reasons to expect that simply how well-known as opposed to obscure a country is – how familiar clients are with a country – is likely to affect clients' assessments of contractors from that country. Studies in both labour economics (Arrow, 1998) and social psychology (Fiske, 1998) suggest that familiarity diminishes the salience of (negative) stereotypes, and experiments in behavioral economics suggest that simply being able to recall a (country's) name from previous memory positively influences clients' assessments of it (Tversky & Kahneman, 1974). This intuition was articulated by an online worker, a woman from Lesotho, a small neighbor of South Africa. She explained:

> I am actually from Lesotho, not South Africa. I find it's easier to put South Africa on my profile than to put Lesotho, because not a lot of people know where it is and it's just easy for people to have a point of reference.

Entering our measure of worker home country well-known-ness into the model has a dramatic effect (Figure 5.5). When country differences in well-known-ness are eliminated, the remaining country differences in platform pay rates are slashed, and the order of the countries is completely revamped. The predicted earnings rates range from $10.08 (Kenya) to $15.41 (Pakistan), and United States is third from the bottom, with a predicted mean rate of $10.91. The within-country correlation coefficient falls to just 5 percent, which means that our model is now able to account for almost all of the causes of country-level disparities in platform pay rates – the most important of which turned out to be differences in local wage levels and differences in client perceptions of the contractor home country. The R^2 of the model is 43 percent, compared to 30 percent for the previous model without country well-known-ness.

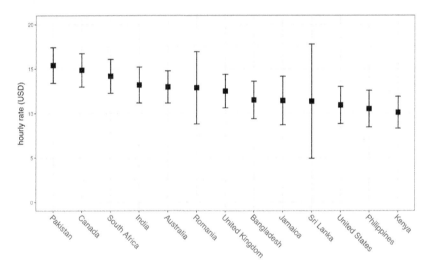

Figure 5.5   *Predicted pay rate by country in USD, controlling for worker experience, reputation, skill tests, time difference, local wage level, and country well-known-ness (residual standard errors in bars)*

DISCUSSION

In this chapter we examined how workers' geographic origin shapes their experience and pay rates in the platform economy. The question is brought to the fore by new technologies that expand the scope of labour markets from local to transnational. To frame the question, we adopted the concept of "liabilities of origin" (Ramachandran & Pant, 2010) from international business scholarship. As expected, our quantitative findings showed that there were large country-level differences in the rates that contractors earned online. Following the liabilities of origin approach, we examined how both the home country context and the client country context resulted in liabilities that disadvantage workers from emerging economy countries compared to their peers from high-income countries. We will discuss the implications and limitations of each of our findings in turn below.

Institutions and Human Capital

One of the ways in which the home country context is seen to disadvantage actors from emerging economy countries is that its institutions are weak or underdeveloped (Pant & Ramachandran, 2012). Some institutions act as enablers that determine whether contractors can access the online market in the first place; others influence how much human capital they bring to the market (Kuek et al., 2015). Our findings concern those individuals who do have access to the market. Somewhat contrary to expectations, our findings suggested that contractors from lower-income countries brought more human capital to the market than contractors from high-income countries, measured in terms of online contracting experience, reputation score, and number of skill tests completed (Table 5.1). This finding can be explained by a lack of opportunities in the local market in lower-income countries. High skill test counts in lower-income countries could also reflect an increased need to signal quality to counter buyer-side biases (Lehdonvirta et al., 2019). In any case, observed country differences in rates were clearly not driven by contractors from lower-income countries having less demonstrable experience, possessing fewer proven skills, or delivering lower-rated work; almost the opposite was the case.

This finding may have important implications to development policy. The UNDP's 2015 *Human Development Report*, with its focus on "rethinking work," centrally notes that "there has never been a worse time to be a worker with only ordinary skills and abilities" and that "this new world of work puts a high premium on workers with skills and qualifications in science and technology" (UNDP, 2015: 10). While that is undoubtedly true, our findings make it clear that it is only part of the story. Differences in human capital did not explain country differences in rates observed in the online labour market; this suggests that investments in evening out human capital differences may not succeed in evening out earnings gaps. Admittedly there are likely to be aspects of human capital or worker quality that our variables failed to capture, but the finding nevertheless strongly indicates that we should consider other explanations as well.

Local Markets vs. Global Opportunities

A much stronger way of explaining country disparities in platform pay rates turned out to be the impact of local wage levels. Workers in areas with high local wages performed online projects that paid more, while workers whose local wage levels were low accepted lower-paying online projects on the mean. This is easy to understand through the reservation wage model (Lippman & McCall, 1976): if the worker has a better-paying option on the local market, why accept a lower-paying task online? This means that workers from emerging economies don't necessarily do fewer high-paid projects, but that their mean earnings are pushed down by the fact that they *also* accept lower-paying tasks.

Another possible interpretation is that workers from high-income countries have some special skills, not captured by our contractor quality variables, for which reason they are more likely to be hired into more demanding projects. We tried to limit this possibility by focusing our analysis on projects categorized as writing work, as these are more homogeneous than for instance software development projects, which vary hugely in terms of the skills required. In Lehdonvirta et al. (2019) we performed similar analyses on projects categorized as graphic design work and with additional contractor competence control variables, with similar results. This supports our conclusion that workers with higher local wage levels simply self-select out of the lower-paying tasks. A positive implication from this for economic development is that if/when local wage levels in the world's marginalized regions grow, online contractors in these countries can be expected to shift toward higher-paying tasks as well. In the meanwhile, the reservation wage model suggests that any interventions that reduce the intensity of competition in online work – such as collective organizing (Wood et al., 2018) – should increase lower-income contractors' rates.

Client Perceptions and Digital Media

Turning to the client's side, we found that a measure of how well-known the contractor's home country was in the client's country was able to explain most of the remaining country-level disparities in platform earnings rates. A possible mechanism is that better-known countries are less susceptible to stereotyping (Fiske, 1998), or that familiar things are preferred over unfamiliar ones (Tversky & Kahneman, 1974). As a consequence, contractors from less well-known countries are disadvantaged on the global market.

However, this interpretation should be treated only as tentative. Cross-country analyses associating one variable with another are inherently low-N, and many social and economic development indicators are mutually correlated due to being bound up in webs of causal relationships. Many other variables besides well-known-ness might have yielded similar effects, and we did not use experimental or econometric techniques to attempt to identify the causal factor. Having said that, three factors lend credibility to our interpretation of the result. First, the finding stands on two empirical legs: some of our qualitative interview data as well as quantitative analysis of transaction records suggested that buyers attributed more value to online contractors from well-known countries. Second, our quantitative measure of country well-known-ness has significant conceptual and empirical distance from the usual suite of mutually correlated development indicators (GDP, HDI, Internet penetration, etc.). For example, though India scores lower than the U.K. (55 vs. 60), it scores much higher than the more economically developed South Africa (9) and even Australia (34). That such a measure can help explain variation in an unrelated economic variable (hourly rate) is not obvious at face value. Third, the finding has simple and reasonable theoretical interpretations, as discussed above. Still, most social science phenomena are massively overdetermined; many causes contribute to an outcome. This effect, to the extent that we believe in it, should be seen as an example of what is probably a wider family of client-side geographic biases shaping the everyday experiences of online contractors.

A biased reception based on one's country of origin is of course a common phenomenon in conventional labour markets as well. Studies in many national labour markets show a wage gap between migrants and locals, only part of which can be explained by differences in skills and other worker characteristics (ILO, 2015). Studies attribute the unexplained variation to factors such as discrimination arising from prejudice or distrust (Solé & Parella, 2003), perceived lower consumption needs and lack of representation in labour unions (ILO, 2015), and the difficulty of assessing foreign educational credentials (Barrett et al., 2012). Not all of these explanations may be applicable to remote platform work. Collective bargaining work appears next to non-existent so far (Wood et al., 2018), and the function of conventional educational credentials (which are practically unverifiable in the online context) is intended to be fulfilled by the platforms' own (verifiable) skill tests (Kässi & Lehdonvirta, 2018), in which we saw that lower-income workers actually appear to be better qualified.

Moreover, a significant difference between migrant labour and online contracting (or "virtual migration"; Horton, 2010) is that in the latter case the relationship is mediated by digital platforms, which influence what information is presented about the worker and how. We can draw on research in computer-mediated communication to understand some potential consequences of this to liabilities of origin. Levels of anonymity afforded by computer-mediated communication are known to contribute to depersonalization, that is a tendency of the participants to perceive each other as representatives of salient social categories rather than as individuals with idiosyncratic behaviors and needs (Lee, 2006; Postmes et al., 1998; Spears & Postmes, 2015). By leaving out many other cues about a contractor's identity while prominently displaying their country of origin, platforms may inadvertently be inviting clients to relate to contractors through country stereotypes more strongly than they would otherwise do. It is noteworthy that in contrast to conventional outsourcing firms, the online contractor is a "micro-provider" who has no organizational affiliation that would act as the most salient social category instead of their country (Lehdonvirta et al., 2019). The liability of origin in online contracting thus differs subtly in mechanisms and perhaps also in magnitude from both firm-based liability of origin and the migrant wage penalty. An interesting implication from this conclusion is that platforms may be able to influence buyer-side biases by manipulating the range of information displayed about contractors. For example, displaying a greater variety of identity cues could make the country less salient and reduce the depersonalization effect. But for now, this remains speculation.

CONCLUSION

In place of visions of revolutionary change brought about by ICTs that remove all barriers, we inevitably find a more nuanced reality, where technology opens up new options but also perpetuates some old patterns and biases. Platforms clearly provide new opportunities in marginalized regions of the world where local opportunities are constrained. These opportunities benefit especially people with valuable skills that are hard to put to use in the local labour market. Online contractors from marginalized countries are not necessarily inferior at all in quality to online contractors from high-income countries, at least in occupations such as writing that do not depend on highly specialized training available only in higher-income countries. At the same time, they do suffer some liabilities of origin relative to their peers from high-income countries. These liabilities are in many ways similar to the disadvantages faced by emerging-economy firms seeking to break into international markets, or immigrant workers entering a new labour market, except for one notable difference

– the role of the platform as the mediator of the exchanges and thus the shaper of the decision environment.

DETAILED METHODOLOGY

Overall Approach and Interview Data

Our overall empirical approach is an exploratory statistical analysis of data derived from records of transactions carried out on an online labour platform from March 1 to August 31, 2013. The transaction records were provided to us by a leading online labour platform company in an anonymized, privacy-protected form. The company did not wish to be identified by name. The platform facilitates the entire contracting relationship, from search and negotiation to supervision, delivery, billing, and post-project evaluation. It is an excellent context to study global online contract work, because it hosts clients and contractors from any country, and is among the largest such platforms.

The quantitative analyses are supplemented with quotes from face-to-face interviews with workers carried out in six countries between September 2014 and December 2015. In total, 107 workers were interviewed across Southeast Asia (in the Philippines, Vietnam, and Malaysia) and sub-Saharan Africa (in South Africa, Kenya, and Nigeria). The process of collecting the interviews is described in detail in the appendix of Lehdonvirta et al. (2019). For the purposes of this chapter, we selected quotes from these interviews that help to motivate and illustrate issues covered by the quantitative analyses. For more systematic analyses of this interview data, see e.g. Wood et al. (2018) and Wood et al. (2019).

Multi-level Random Intercept Model

The structure of the online labour market calls for a multi-level, nested study design, where projects belong to contractors, and contractors belong to countries (Figure 5.1). We are interested in whether the rates paid for a project vary depending on the contractor's country and, in particular, whether certain country characteristics (well-known-ness and local wage level) account for this variance. Besides the country-level variables of interest, we naturally also expect individual contractor characteristics such as skills and experience (that is, human capital or worker competence) to have a strong influence on the rates paid. Since these endowments may vary between countries, they must be included as control variables. The characteristics of different projects must likewise be controlled as far as possible. The resulting design can be expressed as the following three-level random intercept model (using the triple indexing notation of Snijders and Bosker, 1999):

$$Y_{ijk} = \gamma_{000} + \sum_n \gamma_n x^n_{..k} + \sum_n \beta_n x^n_{.jk} + \sum_n \alpha_n x^n_{ijk} + V_{00k} + U_{0jk} + R_{ijk},$$

where Y_{ijk} is the hourly rate paid in project i to contractor j belonging to country k. The term γ_{000} is the main intercept. The term $\sum_n \gamma_n x^n_{..k}$ refers to the country characteristics and their coefficients, and $\sum_n \beta_n x^n_{.jk}$ and $\sum_n \alpha_n x^n_{ijk}$ refer respectively to contractor and project-level characteristics and their coefficients. The last three terms are the country-, contractor-, and project-level random effects terms; residual variation in the dependent variable is decomposed into these different levels to address the question of how much contractors' countries influence the rates earned. Explanatory variables are not decomposed, as between-group effects are not assumed to differ from within-group effects.

Data and Variables

The full transaction records cover all 362,220 projects carried out on the platform from March 1 to August 31, 2013. Out of all the diverse types of projects contracted via the platform, we focused on one type of work: writing work, defined as projects categorized under "Blog & Article Writing," "Creative Writing," "Copywriting," or "Technical Writing" in the platform's ontology. Hourly rates can vary by orders of magnitude between different types of work (from a mean of $2.99 in "Data Entry" to $38.10 in the "Legal" category) and addressing this statistically in our multi-level design would result in a complex and opaque model. Limiting ourselves to one type of work allows us to compare apples with apples when it comes to country differences. We chose writing because it was what many of our interview informants were doing, it is relatively commodified in that the variation in rates is limited, it requires no formal qualifications, it is supplied by contractors from countries around the world, and it exists in sufficient numbers in the records to facilitate multi-level analysis (34,352 projects in total).

To eliminate sources of variation that would be difficult or impossible to control otherwise, we applied two further selection criteria. First, only projects billed on an hourly basis were included (9,243 projects). The platform also supports fixed-payment projects but controlling project size becomes a problem in these. Second, only projects where the client is from the United States or Canada were included, to eliminate variation in buyer-side biases across different buyer countries (5,390 projects). We focus on U.S. and Canadian buyers because their combined market share is very high in global outsourcing in general and on this platform in particular. Finally, projects with an undefined or zero hourly rate and projects where no money was charged were pruned as artifacts (5,256 projects remaining). Countries whose contractors performed fewer than 20 projects in total were pruned to satisfy model assumptions (4,817 projects remaining, belonging to 3,078 contractors from 13 countries).

Table 5.2   Levels, variables, and descriptive statistics

		Mean (s.d.), raw	Mean (s.d.), transformed
Project	Rate (DV)	11.01 (10.93)	1.99 (0.98)
(*n*=4,817)	Time difference	6.20 (4.86)	
Contractor	Experience	62.08 (82.76)	3.42 (1.32)
(*n*=3,078)	Reputation	4.58 (0.84)	-1.95 (1.55)
	Skills	4.40 (5.81)	
Country	Local wage level	7.59 (8.21)	1.08 (1.69)
(*n*=13)	Well-known-ness	59.62 (127.89)	3.06 (1.33)

Table 5.2 shows the variables used in the analysis and their descriptive statistics both in their raw form and after transformations were applied. *Rate* is the hourly rate paid to the project's contractor in U.S. dollars; as is common in studies of wages and earnings, it is right-skewed and entered into the model log-transformed. *Time difference* is measured as the absolute difference between the client's country's time zone and the contractor's country's time zone in hours; for countries spanning multiple time zones, an estimate of the country's center of population is used. *Experience* is measured as the number of projects the contractor has completed on the platform since joining the marketplace; it is right-skewed and entered into the model log-transformed. *Reputation* is measured as the contractor's mean feedback score from clients, on a scale from 0 to 5. As it is left-skewed (many providers have close to 5-star ratings), it is reflected and log-transformed. *Skills* is measured as the number of computer-administered skill tests the worker has successfully taken on the platform and published on their profile. These tests are voluntary and measure such skills as typing, language proficiency, and office software use.

The *local wage level* variable represents the country's average hourly wage across all sectors. The variable is expressed in U.S. dollars, converted using exchange rates rather than PPP to correspond with the method a contractor would use to convert their local labour market wage to their online asking rate. For eight out of the 13 countries represented in the data set, it was possible to calculate this variable using the Occupation Wages around the World (OWW) database (Oostendorp, 2012). For Kenya, Pakistan, South Africa, Sri Lanka, and Jamaica, it was necessary to rely on separate ILO and national reports, resulting in potentially inconsistent methodologies. The most recent year for which wage data could be obtained across the countries was 2008, so the variable is somewhat out of date compared with the rest of our data set. Despite these limitations, the variable fulfills its function of capturing the main contours of the stark differences in wage levels across the countries in our data set, from Sri Lanka's $0.43 to the United Kingdom's $19.64 per hour.

The *well-known-ness* of a country was measured with a proxy developed from Internet search volume data. Using the Google Trends database, we captured the relative frequency of each of the 13 countries among Google search queries performed in the U.S. on June 1, 2013. The resulting variable shows that Americans are most likely to type United States into their search boxes (relative frequency 480) and least likely to type Sri Lanka (4). This approach has advantages and disadvantages compared with the survey methods used in most studies of country-of-origin effects (e.g. Bracamonte & Okada, 2015). Search volume data cover the majority of the U.S. Internet user population instead of a small but possibly more targeted sample; in some studies this would be a problem, but in a study of online contracting, Internet users are a relevant population. The main drawback is that the resulting measure (country's relative popularity in searches) is an imperfect proxy for the construct of interest (how well-known a country is), which limits its validity. But a significant advantage is that the measure is observational as opposed to self-reported, which is likely to enhance its reliability, as honest survey responses on a person's knowledge and ignorance are difficult to elicit. All in all, we believe that this novel measure of country reputation is appropriate for this study and likely to have applications beyond the study as well.

We estimate model parameters using the restricted maximum likelihood method and assess mode fit using Nakagawa and Schielzeth's (2013) marginal (fixed effects only) and conditional (fixed and random) R^2. The key statistic in this study is the intraclass correlation coefficient (ICC), which we use to examine how much of the variation in the dependent variable is due to variation between countries. Model parameters for all the models are presented in Table 5.3. Since our data covers all the writing work transacted over the platform during the study period rather than a probabilistic sample of it, inferential statistics such as p-values are not shown. All the results are statistically significant; we are instead concerned with assessing their practical significance. Generalizations beyond the data in the discussion section are inductive rather than statistical in nature. Our combination of qualitative and quantitative evidence from a key site in the field provides us with a good basis for cautious inductive generalization.

Table 5.3   *Estimates for three-level random intercept models with log(rate) as the dependent variable*

	Null model		Model 1		Model 2		Model 3		Model 4
Fixed effects	*Coef.*	*S.E.*	*Coef.*	*S.E.*	*Coef.*	*S.E.*	*Coef.*	*S.E.*	*Coef.*
Intercept γ_{000}	1.777	(0.160)	1.284	(0.165)	1.273	(0.194)	0.151	(0.327)	0.241
Experience			0.123	(0.011)	0.123	(0.011)	0.123	(0.011)	0.123
Reputation			-0.032	(0.008)	-0.032	(0.008)	-0.032	(0.008)	-0.032
Skills			0.011	(0.003)	0.011	(0.003)	0.011	(0.003)	0.011
Time difference					0.001	(0.013)	0.005	(0.013)	0.015
Well-known-ness							0.354	(0.085)	0.222
Local wage level									0.223
Random effects	*Var.*	*S.E.*	*Var.*	*S.E.*	*Var.*	*S.E.*	*Var.*	*S.E.*	*Var.*
Country-level V_{00k}	0.32	(0.57)	0.33	(0.57)	0.33	(0.58)	0.13	(0.36)	0.03
Contractor-level U_{0jk}	0.49	(0.70)	0.45	(0.67)	0.45	(0.67)	0.45	(0.67)	0.45
Project-level R_{ijk}	0.11	(0.34)	0.12	(0.34)	0.12	(0.34)	0.12	(0.34)	0.12
Variance explained	*Prop.*		*Prop.*		*Prop.*		*Prop.*		*Prop.*
ICC	0.35		0.37		0.37		0.19		0.05
Marginal R^2	0.00		0.05		0.05		0.34		0.43
Conditional R^2	0.88		0.88		0.88		0.89		0.89

NOTE

1. This research was supported by grants from the International Development Research Centre (107384-001) and the European Research Council (639652).

REFERENCES

Arrow, K.J. 1998. What has economics to say about racial discrimination? *Journal of Economic Perspectives*, 12, 91–100.

Barrett, A., McGuinness, S., & O'Brien, M. 2012. The immigrant earnings disadvantage across the earnings and skills distributions: The case of immigrants from the EU's new member states. *British Journal of Industrial Relations*, 50(3), 457–481.

Bracamonte, V., & Okada, H. 2015. Is consumer perception of foreign online stores affected by the image of the country? An experimental study among Japanese consumers. *Proceedings of ASE BD&SI 2015*, October 7–9, Kaohsiung, Taiwan. https://dl.acm.org/doi/pdf/10.1145/2818869.2818923

Braesemann, F., Lehdonvirta, V., & Kässi, O. 2020. ICTs and the urban-rural divide: Can online labour platforms bridge the gap? *Information, Communication & Society*.

Choi, H., & Varian, H. 2012. Predicting the present with Google Trends. *The Economic Record*, 88, 2–9.

Ciravegna, L., Lopez, L., & Kundu, S. 2014. Country of origin and network effects on internationalization: A comparative study of SMEs from an emerging and developed economy. *Journal of Business Research*, 67, 916–923.

Fiske, S.T. 1998. Stereotyping, prejudice and discrimination. In Gilbert, D.T. & Fiske, S.T. (Eds.) *The Handbook of Social Psychology*, Fourth Edition. Oxford: Oxford University Press.

Ghani, E., Kerr, W.R., & Stanton, C. 2014. Diasporas and outsourcing: Evidence from oDesk and India. *Management Science*, 60(7), 1677–1697.

Graham, M., Hjorth, I., & Lehdonvirta, V. 2017. Digital labour and development: Impacts of global digital labour platforms and the gig economy on worker livelihoods. *Transfer: European Review of Labour and Research*, 23, 135–162.

Horton, J. 2010. Online labor markets. In *Internet and Network Economics: 6th International Workshop, Proceedings*. Berlin: Springer, pp. 515–522. http://john-joseph-horton.com/papers/online_labor_markets.pdf

ILO. 2015. *Global Wage Report 2014/15: Wages and income inequality*. Geneva: International Labour Office.

Johansson, J.K., Douglas, S.P., & Nonaka, I. 1985. Assessing the impact of country of origin on product evaluations: A new methodological perspective. *Journal of Marketing Research*, 22(4), 388–396.

Kässi, O., & Lehdonvirta, V. 2018. Online Labour Index: Measuring the online gig economy for policy and research. *Technological Forecasting and Social Change*, 137, 241–248.

Koschate-Fischer, N., Diamantopoulos, A., & Oldenkotte, K. 2012. Are consumers really willing to pay more for a favorable country image? A study of country-of-origin effects on willingness to pay. *Journal of International Marketing*, 20(1), 19–41.

Kuek, S.C., Paradi-Guilford, C., Fayomi, T., Imaizumi, S., Ipeirotis, P., Pina, P., & Singh, M. 2015. *The Global Opportunity in Online Outsourcing*. Washington, DC: World Bank.

Laroche, M., Papadopoulos, N., Heslop, L.A., & Mourali, M. 2005. The influence of country image structure on consumer evaluations of foreign products. *International Marketing Review*, 22(1), 96–115.

Lee, E.J. 2006. When and how does depersonalization increase conformity to group norms in computer-mediated communication? *Communication Research*, 33(6), 423–447.

Lehdonvirta, V. 2018. Flexibility in the gig economy: Managing time on three online piecework platforms. *New Technology, Work & Employment*, 33(1), 13–29.

Lehdonvirta, V., Kässi, O., Hjorth, I., Barnard, H., & Graham, M. 2019. The global platform economy: A new offshoring institution enabling emerging-economy micro-providers. *Journal of Management*, 45(2), 567–599.

Lippman, S.A., & McCall, J.J. 1976. The economics of job search: A survey. *Economic Inquiry*, 14(2), 155–189.

Maheswaran, D. 1994. Country of origin as a stereotype: Effects of consumer expertise and attribute strength on product evaluations. *Journal of Consumer Research*, 21, 354–365.

Manning, A. 2011. Imperfect competition in the labor market. In *Handbook of Labor Economics*, Vol. 4. Elsevier, pp. 973–1041.

Musteen, M., Datta, D.K., & Butts, M.M. 2014. Do international networks and foreign market knowledge facilitate SME internationalization? Evidence from the Czech Republic. *Entrepreneurship Theory and Practice*, 38, 749–774.

Nakagawa, S., & Schielzeth, H. 2013. A general and simple method for obtaining R^2 from generalized linear mixed-effects models. *Methods in Ecology and Evolution*, 4(2), 133–142.

Oostendorp, R.H. 2012. The Occupational Wages around the World (OWW) database: Update for 1983–2008. *World Development Report 2013 Background Paper*. Washington, DC: World Bank.

Pant, A., & Ramachandran, J. 2012. Legitimacy beyond borders: Indian software services firms in the United States, 1984 to 2004. *Global Strategy Journal*, 2(3), 224–243.

Postmes, T., Spears, R., & Lea, M. 1998. Breaching or building social boundaries? SIDE-effects of computer-mediated communication. *Communication Research*, 25(6), 689–715.

Preis, T., Moat, H.S., & Stanley, H.E. 2013. Quantifying trading behavior in financial markets using Google Trends. *Scientific Reports*, 3, 1684.

Ramachandran, J., & Pant, A. 2010. The liabilities of origin: An emerging economy perspective on the costs of doing business abroad. In Devinney, T.M., Pedersen, T., & Tihanyi, L. (Eds.) *Advances in International Management*, Vol. 23. Bingley, UK: Emerald, pp. 231–256.

Shimp, T.A., Samiee, S., & Madden, T.J. (1993). Countries and their products, a cognitive structure perspective. *Journal of the Academy of Marketing Science*, 21(4), 323–330.

Snijders, T., & Bosker, R. 1999. *Multilevel Analysis*. London: Sage.

Solé, C., & Parella, S. 2003. The labor market and racial discrimination in Spain. *Journal of Ethnic and Migration Studies*, 29(1), 121–140.

Spears, R., & Postmes, T. 2015. Group identity, social influence, and collective action online. In Sundar, S.S. (ed.) *The Handbook of the Psychology of Communication Technology*. Chichester, UK: John Wiley & Sons, pp. 23–46.

Stephens-Davidowitz, S. 2014. The cost of racial animus on a black candidate: Evidence using Google search data. *Journal of Public Economics*, 118, 26–40.

Tversky, A., & Kahneman, D. 1974. Judgment under uncertainty: Heuristics and biases. *Science*, 185(4157), 1124–1131.

UNDP (United Nations Development Programme) (2015). *Human Development Report 2015: Work for Human Development*. New York: United Nations.

Verlegh, P.W.J., & Steenkamp, J.-B.E.M. 1999. A review and meta-analysis of country-of-origin research. *Journal of Economic Psychology*, 20(5), 521–546.

Wood, A.J., Lehdonvirta, V., & Graham, M. 2018. Workers of the Internet unite? Online freelancer organisation in six Asian and African countries. *New Technology, Work and Employment*, 33(2), 95–112.

Wood, A.J., Graham, M., Lehdonvirta, V., & Hjorth, I. 2019. Good gig, bad gig: Autonomy and algorithmic control in the global gig economy. *Work, Employment and Society*, 33(1), 56–75.

6. Freelancing globally: Upworkers in China and India, neo-liberalisation and the new international putting-out system of labour (NIPL)

Wing-Fai Leung, Premilla D'Cruz and Ernesto Noronha

INTRODUCTION

Digitalisation has taken place at a global level, exporting business models across continents and increasing the possibility of casual work, while preventing unions and governments from scrutinising employment malpractice (Holtgrewe 2014; Moore 2018). The new digital workplace has profound effects on workers and their professional identities. The global expansion of digital 'platforms', whether entailing online (e.g., Amazon Mechanical Turk/ AMT) or offline (e.g., Uber) work also exports the Western entrepreneurial ideal as a universally valorised symbol of good work and an opportunity for democratic participation in the information society (Cohen 2015). The contemporary online 'gig economy' represents a new means of livelihood, taking forward its earlier manifestation as home-based medical transcription which was offshored to developing countries such as India (Noronha & D'Cruz 2008). Sitting at the cusp of neo-liberalism[1] and technology (D'Cruz 2017), online labour markets are seen as critical drivers in the further expansion of the service outsourcing/offshoring sector (Beerepoot & Lambregts 2015), thereby reconfiguring the international division of labour while extending global value chains (Huws 2013), to form a planetary labour market (Graham & Anwar 2019).

Crowdsourcing through digital platforms such as Upwork and Freelancer changes the nature of freelancing as the platforms allow the combination of 'crowd' and 'outsourcing' (Howe 2006), bridging a global market with individual workers, making it possible for workers to be hired for projects or tasks on short-term contracts. At the same time, crowdsourcing reflects the increasing casualisation of white-collar employment and the informalisation of work in the digital age (D'Cruz & Noronha 2019; de Stefano 2016a). However, existing studies mostly consider the experiences of workers in the West (Bergvall-Kåreborn & Howcroft 2014; Cushing 2013; Irani 2015), even though platforms are populated by large numbers of workers from across the world (Graham et al. 2017).

Platforms such as AMT and Upwork connect requesters and freelancers and extract revenue through fees. Freelancers can offer skills, bid for work, receive payment digitally and have flexibility and access to a wide range of potential employers. Firms or individual requesters can access workers at a low cost and avoid the legal costs (contracts, benefits, etc.) associated with conventional subcontracting (Bergvall-Kåreborn & Howcroft 2014; Ettlinger 2016). Clients have no responsibility towards freelancers beyond the scope of the projects/ jobs (D'Cruz & Noronha 2016). Moreover, platforms usually exist beyond any form of democratic oversight, whether regulatory, state linked or worker led (Pongratz 2018; Urry 2014), contributing to the deregulation of work, especially in Western neo-liberal economies.

If, on the one hand, digital platforms provide greater opportunity for participation in a virtual sphere, on the other hand, they also increment the options for exploitation of labour for capital accumulation in the service sector, offering increased autonomy to contract workers in exchange for low-paid and precarious work (Milkman & Ott 2014; Wood et al. 2018). The global workforce comprises workers from different countries competing with each other. In order to retain competitiveness, workers have to accept the demands of capital or production may simply be moved to other geographical locations where workers are more amenable, engendering new forms of labour exploitation (Bieler & Lee 2017a, p. 182; Fuchs 2013; Standing 1999). Global labour is supposed to manage their life as individual 'entrepreneurs' whereby 'the individual [flexible] subject […] progressively resembles the *homo economicus* imagined by neoliberal economists' (Ouellet 2010, p. 180).

We can consider digital platforms as a new form of the international division of labour (NIDL); the NIDL referred to industrial restructuring and the shift of manufacturing work from the developed world to the developing world, especially China and India. The rise of the term in the 1970s (Frobel et al. 1978) implied the zero-sum game between jobs in the West and the developing countries, with academic interest being predominantly about the effects the NIDL had on the Global North, especially on traditional manufacturing industries and the levels of unemployment. The effect in developing countries was characterised by 'proletarianization and impoverishment of ever-growing numbers of people' (Frobel et al. 1978, p. 124). Nash (1983) notes the weak bargaining power of workers from developing countries due to international capital investments. For instance, in the Indian context, Noronha (1996) argues that NIDL resulted in the demand for labour flexibility, an increase in non-standard jobs and the weakening of trade unions. Today, the production of information and information technology is part of an NIDL that shapes modes of production, distribution and consumption (Fuchs 2016). We contend that the platform economy continues and updates the practice of the NIDL whereby the workforce in developing countries, including China and India, participate in employer-labour interactions (control and bargaining) through platforms such as Upwork, with its invisible management logic and its individualist, entrepreneurial slant (Caraway 2010; D'Cruz & Noronha 2019). In addition, we argue that platforms and requesters can enjoy the benefits of the putting-out system such as inadequate employment law coverage and labour arbitrage emanating from global competition between freelancers, limiting worker solidarity and avoiding sunk costs (de Stefano 2016b). In fact, Kenney and Zysman (2016) argue that platform work has more than a passing resemblance to the putting-out economy that was prominent in the pre-Industrial Revolution era when companies would ship materials to people to assemble items such as shoes, clothing or firearms in their homes. In the current manifestation of the putting-out system, the platform, while still claiming to be only an intermediary, has unprecedented control over the compensation for and organisation of work. Platforms such as AMT, Upwork and InnoCentive have created similar global virtual labour exchanges which enable companies to crowdsource the performance of specific tasks that require human judgement; they are a modern form of the putting-out system (Kenney & Zysman 2016). Therefore, we hold that the platform economy combines the characteristics of the NIDL and the putting-out system which we term and develop as the *new international putting-out system of labour* (NIPL). We conceptualise NIPL to mean that, unlike the first wave of outsourcing which involved activity between different firms and organisations under NIDL, *digital work platforms can put out work from big firms, small businesses and individual clients directly to individual workers and small enterprises who telework from anywhere in the world.* This has been induced by neo-liberal policies which have reversed the movement of work from home-based artisanal workshops to factories, as evident in the industrial era, back to individuals in the current globalisation period (Noronha & D'Cruz 2019). Nonetheless, like the pre-industrial system, the NIPL eliminates or reduces employers' costs of real estate, equipment, supervision, management and labour while also providing product market flexibility and stalling workers' collective action (Finkin 2016; Noronha & D'Cruz 2008).

This chapter is a comparative study of Upwork freelancers from China and India, two BRICS countries, which represent rising economies but with contrasting political, social and cultural conditions. The GDP per capita of the two countries shows the different standards of living: US$8770 for China, US$2015 for India.[2] Globally, India is ranked second after the USA among freelancer nations, with about 15 million freelancers (Lal 2015) who take up 40 per cent of the freelancer jobs offered around the world (Elena 2017). The Oxford Internet Institute (OII) shows that within online platforms, while writing and translation are the top categories in the USA, in India, software development and technology dominate (55 per cent of market share), followed by creative work and multimedia. According to the OII, China was not in the top 20 countries where online labour workers were located. Developed countries dominate as the origin of online employers while 'the majority of work is carried out in low-income countries' (Graham et al. 2017, p. 142). Across the globe, the Chinese online workers were in the 90–100 percentile (US\$20.1–100) in terms of the median hourly pay requested, while their Indian counterparts were in the 10–25 percentile (US\$5.1–9.9) (Graham et al. 2017, p. 144). The two cases will, therefore, provide a valuable contribution to the debates around digital platform work.

In completing this comparison between Chinese and Indian Upworkers, our main concerns are to examine (a) the extent to which online freelance work in developing economies represents 'decent work',[3] and (b) how freelancers' participation in the global digital platform economy can be understood through the lenses of neo-liberalism and NIPL. After describing the Upwork platform and the methodology of each country's study, the chapter presents the findings in terms of labour conditions, referencing neo-liberalism, and freelancers' experiences of platform work. The chapter concludes with an analysis discussing online freelance work in terms of decent work and the NIPL.

1   FREELANCING ON UPWORK

Upwork is a skilled digital workplace (Kittur et al. 2013) formed in May 2015 as the result of a merger of Elance and oDesk. Upwork has 12 million registered freelancers and 5 million registered clients, with 3 billion jobs posted annually and more than US\$1 billion worth of work done annually (Graham & Anwar 2019). The platform allows members of the labour force to compete directly as independent freelancers with their international counterparts, offering their services to requesters around the world (Green et al. 2013; Huws 2013). Digital platforms such as Upwork carry no liabilities for clients and freelancers (Caraway 2010) but retain a percentage of the payment between these two parties as their fee (Aloisi 2015). Upwork hosts remunerative jobs of varying temporality and complexity (Green et al. 2013), with most clients coming from developed countries and most freelancers coming from developing economies and often being poorly rewarded (Graham et al. 2017).

The platform provides employment opportunities but acquiring requisite skills and training are left to individual freelancers. Workers are also responsible for the facilities and resources they need to carry out the work, including workspace, power, computer/mobile devices, software requirements and so on (Caraway 2010). Upworkers set up their own profile, bid for jobs, gain experience and endeavour to receive good reviews and build a reputation. Contracts and management of the requester-crowdsourced worker relationship are conducted through a series of online mechanisms such as reviews, escrow and arbitration. Work is risky both in terms of whether Upworkers can secure projects and whether their rights are respected. Freelancers are not covered by unions or government regulation. There is no legal protection since crowdsourcing is 'borderless' (Bergvall-Kåreborn & Howcroft 2014; Caraway 2010).

In spite of these shortcomings, Upwork has in place some mechanisms which protect the interests of freelancers (D'Cruz & Noronha 2019). First, the platform conducts identity checks of all those signing up, which lowers the risk of freelancers being misled. Second, the platform specifies a minimum remuneration for both hourly and fixed price projects. Third, the platform monitors freelancer and client behaviour to ensure that rules pertaining to gaining/posting jobs and interacting with freelancers and clients during the course of work are followed. Fourth, redress mechanisms available on the platform address freelancer and client grievances, covering task-related, payment-related and interpersonal issues which occur on the site (D'Cruz & Noronha 2016).

2   METHODOLOGY

Leung conducted research in 2016 on freelancers in Greater China (mainly China with a minority of participants based in Asia) who use the online platforms, Elance-oDesk and later Upwork. She carried out the study through a detailed questionnaire: a 40-question survey of 20 Upworkers who were Chinese-English/English-Chinese translators. She 'hired' the freelancers on Upwork to complete the survey as their task and each was paid for the work. In some of the cases, the researcher asked follow-up questions or clarification via email and the messaging service within Upwork. The job role of a translator was chosen as this group was more likely to interact with global clients. Leung also noted participants' profiles, which were publicly available, and detailed their work history, skills, jobs and ratings, where they were located and their qualifications. A grounded approach was used to organise and analyse the data.

D'Cruz and Noronha adopted a qualitative strategy to study Indian freelancers' subjective experiences of work on the online platform Elance-oDesk and later Upwork. In 2015, freelancers were contacted via a research call on various social networking sites as well as Internet searches. Twenty-four Elance-oDesk freelancers (15 full-timers and 9 part-timers) from across India, whose jobs on the platform included data entry, research assistance, content writing, marketing and public relations, business analytics and numerous information technology applications, completed the interview process. Participants' locations necessitated data collection via telephonic interviews. Unstructured conversational interviews were conducted and subjected to thematic analysis.

The comparative research does not match data sets, but rather analyses the themes emerging from the respective studies in China and India, which allows the researchers to focus on key issues: the experiences and quality of online work juxtaposed vis-à-vis decent work, and the role the platform economy serves in the global flows of digital labour, adopting the frames of neo-liberalism and NIPL.

3   LABOUR CONDITIONS IN CHINA AND INDIA AND NEO-LIBERALISATION

Since the Open Door policy of the late 1970s, there has been a gradual break-up of state-owned enterprises in China. The sharp decline of employment in the state sector, particularly from the late 1990s, was achieved mainly through downsizing, plant closures and privatisation of state-owned enterprises as part of state-driven reform. Consequently, the urban workforce employed in the state sector had been reduced from more than 78 per cent to around 19 per cent by 2012 (Cooke 2016). Since then, China has emerged as the assembly platform of global capital. In line with this assembly role, China's contribution is often limited to providing cheap labour to maintain international competitiveness (Hart-Landsberg 2015). Thus, despite moving rapidly into export of manufactured goods as part of the NIDL, China's production is mainly based on cheap labour, low value-added activities, dominated by foreign TNCs and highly dependent on access to markets elsewhere (Bieler & Lee 2017b). The shift from the protection of secure formal employment within state-owned enterprises to the rise of private businesses subject to fluctuating market demands accompanied the rise of the number of workers who do not have a formal contract or who perform casual work in an informal economy (Liang et al. 2016). According to the ILO (2018, p. 88), the percentage of workers in informal employment was 54.5 per cent. Most of the rise in informal employment has taken the form of casual workers who receive lower levels of remuneration and report lower subjective well-being than formal employees (Liang et al. 2016).

Unemployment rates in China have remained low at 4.4 per cent in 2019.[4] However, urban youth (16–24 years) unemployment is estimated to be 9.04 per cent (Schucher 2017, p. 79). While mass manufacturing has prompted the rapid development of the economy, high-skilled jobs are in fact in short supply, reflected in the postgraduate unemployment rates in urban China (10.4 per cent) and rural China (45.3 per cent) (ibid. p. 84). This is evidence that though education standards have risen over time, graduate jobs have recently become scarcer and therefore more competitive. In 2017, 8 million young people graduated from university, ten times more than ten years ago.[5] Desirable stable and highly skilled professional jobs are hard to come by. Nearly 12 per cent of graduates opted for flexible employment, such as freelancing, setting up one's own business or informal work (ibid. p. 85). For those who have access, freelancers on international work platforms can partake of job opportunities previously unavailable to the local labour market. However, the online platform economy, because of the regulatory challenges it faces, thrives on turning informal workers into platform labourers in China by appropriating labour and increasing vulnerability (Chen 2018).

Though India is counted among the emerging economies of the world, employment conditions remain dismal (India Labour and Employment Report/ ILER 2014). The poor availability of jobs, nature of the employment contract and problems associated with working conditions (Rustagi 2015) are more pronounced among particular social categories and in smaller cities and towns and rural areas, precipitating under-employment and unemployment (ILER 2014) and violating workers' rights (Kapoor 2014). Non-standard employment, with limited or no regulation, social protection and social dialogue (Williams 2017), accounts for over 92 per cent of the Indian workforce (ILER 2014). The latest census data of 2011 highlights the especially high unemployment numbers for youth between 15 and 29 years. Many unemployed are educated and looking for jobs commensurate with their abilities (ILER 2014). Good quality employment is 'rare', with access to it 'extremely unequal' (ILER 2014, p. 25). India's espousal of neo-liberalism in 1991, accompanied by the deregulation of employment and attempts at labour law reform, has led to a conscious policy to shift labour from formal to informal contracts (Noronha & Beale 2011; Noronha & D'Cruz 2018), accentuating the aforementioned scenario. In these circumstances, the IT industry has become an icon of development (Noronha & D'Cruz 2016). This is because IT employees benefit through higher salaries, better working conditions and mobility in terms of status in society. However, as part of the NIDL, they have to be satisfied with work which is at the lower end of the value chain (Noronha & D'Cruz 2016; Noronha et al. 2018). Similarly, crowdsourced employment, despite falling within the informal sector (de Stefano 2016a) with its entrepreneurial slant (Holtgrewe 2014) and its emphasis on merit, is an attractive alternative (D'Cruz & Noronha 2016).

The labour conditions in China and India, therefore, encourage the informal economy and freelancing, especially among younger, educated, Internet-savvy job seekers who are utilising the platforms to gain work that is not limited to the national job market. The major difference is that the proficiency level of English in India makes its educated population a more competitive workforce in the online marketplace. Undoubtedly, because of the necessity of computing equipment and skills and Internet access, usually coupled with proficiency in English (Pongratz 2018), it should not be surprising that online gig work is largely limited to particular classes and locations in the Indian subcontinent. Given the nature of work (Chinese-English/English-Chinese translation) of our Chinese participants, they also have to have a good degree in English in order to compete for work. Out of the 20 Chinese participants, 15 have a bachelor's degree and three are master's graduates; 9 out of the 24 Indian interviewees have a bachelor's degree, 13 are master's graduates and two are students. Even so, the expectation of a high level of English on a platform like Upwork generally puts many Chinese freelancers at a disadvantage vis-à-vis other nationalities, such as Indian workers, who have native or near-native proficiency in the language.

The Chinese Upworkers were attracted to the work because of its flexibility and the self-organisation of time and workload (nine), the opportunity for extra income (11), gaining customers globally (five), and learning new skills and working on more diverse projects (six). One of the Chinese workers stated, 'These platforms are like a door to the world for me, which enriches my professional life and always gives me new and creative ideas'. For the 15 Indian participants who worked full-time on the platform, the reasons for their choice were childcare (two), spouse's job/marriage which made location-specific jobs in the local labour market difficult (four), better earning opportunities and career growth (four) and living in small Indian cities and towns with poor labour market conditions which made crowdsourced employment a far more attractive option (five).

In both the Indian and Chinese studies, therefore, online work is a means to improve one's standard of living that can provide opportunities independent of the national labour condition, allowing access to international clients and skills development opportunities. The fact that the informal sector predominates in both countries and hence is not perceived as unusual or especially threatening (ILER 2014) accounts for Chinese and Indian participants' positive views of online platforms such as Upwork. Crowdsourced employment, with its entrepreneurial slant that encourages self-promotion and self-protection, is an attractive alternative for both Indian and Chinese freelancers. Entrepreneurialism has acquired romantic connotations of initiative, energy, boldness, independence, self-reliance and risk-taking (Keat 1991) and is seen as a remedy for broader societal problems, especially among the technical and educated elite in developed and developing Asian countries (see Leung 2018; Leung & Cossu 2019). Entrepreneurialism emphasises self-sufficiency and personal responsibility for success, being linked to the rise of neo-liberalism and aligned with the retreating welfare state, unfettered markets and lean corporations (Cohen 2015). Having to be entrepreneurial, while entailing self-control, self-commercialisation and self-rationalisation (Pongratz & Voss 2003), despite its accompanying uncertainty, variable income and limited statutory entitlements (Vosko 2009), was not seen negatively. Instead, both Indian and Chinese participants considered such commodification and marketisation of themselves to be the basis of their success, a neo-liberal turn that suggests they are co-opted into the American ideological apparatus (Leung & Cossu 2019).

4   AGENCY, FLEXIBILITY AND SKILLS DEVELOPMENT

A striking feature of online platform labour among the Indian and Chinese workforce is the involvement of the middle class and of educated graduates which brings this group, conventionally associated with standard employment, into the unorganised labour market (D'Cruz 2017). Since the economic reforms, Chinese workers are no longer guaranteed jobs for life in state-run work units, and the access to an international market through digital platforms has given the highly qualified Upworkers an individualised outlet. Similarly, India, being at the top of the league in matters of informal employment (Williams 2017), witnesses in its workforce greater individualism and competition for scarce opportunities and resources (Sinha, 2015). The platform economy provides an important means of livelihood, with its entrepreneurialism and merit bases perceived as proxies for agency and mastery (D'Cruz & Noronha 2016).

Seventeen of the Chinese participants earned less than 60 per cent of their household income from online jobs and only four of them worked over 30 hours per week online. The three participants who earned over 60 per cent of their household income from the platforms reported an annual income of over US$10,000.00. The highest annual income (US$20,000.00–29,000.00) represented 80–100 per cent of a participant's household income. Seven earned less than US$2500.00, and eight earned between US$2,500.00 and US$9,999.00. Thirteen Chinese participants worked part time, combining online work with other jobs; five of them were already freelance translators when joining Upwork. Due to the risks involved in online platform work, the majority of the Chinese participants were part-time and most did not rely on it as their sole source of income. Fifteen Indian participants were full-timers who had online freelance work as their only employment and source of income. Nine were part-timers (two of whom received more than half of their average monthly income from the platform and two were students). Compared to the Chinese Upworkers, the Indian freelancers appeared to rely on the digital platform more in terms of hours of work and income.

The majority of the Chinese participants were single workers (13), relatively free of childcare and the need to support other dependents. Among the five married participants, for example, only two had children, and in each case, a single child. Given the One Child Policy, this was unsurprising.[6] Among the Indian interviewees were women with children (two) as well as women whose husbands' jobs involved periodic relocations to other cities or who had family responsibilities (four). They chose platform work as a means of managing both work and family roles as they did not wish to forgo their links with the world of work. In that sense, Indian participants tended to be influenced by childcare and/or family responsibilities as a reason to use online work platforms. Care responsibilities are not the only reason for choosing online employment, though; 19 out of 20 Chinese participants agreed that online work fits in with their other responsibilities and tasks. Being able to combine personal and family demands, enjoying a satisfactory work trajectory and finding a suitable means of livelihood despite locational constraints were described as positive aspects of working on the platform by the Indian interviewees and as the reasons they opted for full-time crowdsourced employment. In addition, all Indian full-timers appreciated operating from home and avoiding difficult commutes as well as escaping from the micropolitics, supervisory controls and interpersonal issues that accompanied organisational life.

The Chinese sample gave an average of 6.5 out of 10 for being able to utilise their skills in the online jobs, and an average of 7.4 out of 10 for satisfaction with their online work. Correspondingly, they felt only 5.9 out of 10 for satisfaction with their current standard of living. However, many factors, aside from the use of online platforms, might have an impact on this. Being able to organise one's own work life is a sign of emerging individualism – an important aspect of contemporary life in China, and our participants showed a relative high degree of satisfaction with this dimension of work on the crowdsourcing platforms.

The opportunity to utilise one's skills and further one's abilities was considered advantageous by all Indian participants. However, developing new skills was undertaken by participants at their own initiative and cost. All participants appreciated their exposure to foreign clients and freelancers. They could interact with people across the globe, learning about the latter's work and culture. The work ethic of the West in terms of punctuality, precision and quality was praised. Chinese Upworkers reported similar satisfaction with being able to access international clients and with using their translation skills. This is broadly in line with what Graham and his colleagues call 'skill and capability development' (2017, pp. 151–152), though their argument that workers are kept at arm's length by platforms' invisible management, which then limits skill upgrading, contrasts with how the Indian and Chinese freelancers felt about their skill development.

5   PAY, MALPRACTICE AND DISCRIMINATION

Crowdwork platforms like Upwork have facilitated the digital outsourcing of work, mostly to countries where labour costs are lower. However, the experiences of the global Upworkers are rather different from the low-waged manufacturing working class that the original NIDL refers to. The workers we studied demonstrated a good level of satisfaction with the platform except for the high fees. Moreover, they observed that the structure of the platform offered some protection against cheating customers, though they reported some negative experiences. The new digital workers enter into their own time arrangement in terms of scheduling, but they are also often inadequately paid for their labour. For instance, 12 of the Chinese participants spent one or two hours a day performing non-paid functions including maintaining their profiles, checking messages, providing good service to gain positive feedback and bidding for work. These tasks were necessary to maintain a good online freelance profile but involved unpaid work. The majority of workers also worked outside of nine-to-five office hours and weekends, a necessity when interacting with international clients due to the time difference that put those located in China behind North America and in front of Europe. Of the Chinese workers, three charged under US$10.00/hour, with one charging only US$3.00/hour (the lowest). Seven requested an hourly fee between US$10.00 and US$20.00. Five charged US$25.00/hour or US$30.00/hour. Those who requested over US$10.00/hour tended to be more qualified and had had more success on the platform. Overall, 18 out of 20 freelancers in the Chinese sample improved their income through the online platforms. The Indian freelancers' rates varied from US$4.00 to US$20.00 per hour for part-timers and US$3.50 to US$50.00 per hour for full-timers, with the nature of task on offer, level of skill, duration of work experience, length of platform membership and specificities of platform profile impacting the rate being quoted. Indian IT freelancers sometimes asked for rates between US$35.00 and US$85.00 per hour for projects and these expectations were met with success. Indian full-timers considered their remuneration from the platform to be better than what the local job market could provide, while Indian part-timers were pleased with the additional income which supplemented the stable returns from their regular jobs.

Nonetheless, workers' pay is usually subject to pre-existing conditions within a global digital economy. Cost-savings for Western companies is a key feature of NIPL, and the platform economy reflects this; workers also have to negotiate fees individually, without recourse to collective bargaining. Average fees per hour vary but usually correspond with the work experience and the number of projects a freelancer has already undertaken. In order to compete with other freelancers, a platform like Upwork can downgrade the rate of pay, causing a 'race to the bottom' (Graham et al. 2017; Kneese et al. 2014). There are expectations that workers based in developing economies such as China and India will inevitably accept fees lower than their counterparts in Western countries for the same work, which was confirmed by a Chinese participant who said: 'People may think labour in China should be cheaper than in other regions, forgetting that this is the fastest developing market, with many expats and Chinese [who] have international experience and skills'. Echoing this, an Indian freelancer said:

> No doubt, we are paid less than the freelancers from US, UK, Australia, because we are from India. Even though we are skilled and we do good work, we get less. But because of the conversion rate, the money is good. I would get much less locally for the same work.

Similar to their Chinese counterparts, Indian workers spent time acquiring contracts, which involved checking job posts and preparing bids that showcased one's skills, experience, performance and appropriateness for the task. To this end, building a profile, maintaining a positive image, marketing oneself in general and for a job in particular, and being entrepreneurial were important facilitators. Since bids are generally posted during the Indian night (as they mostly originate in the West) and receive quick responses, participants who wish to have a steady supply of work and income have to extend their workdays by staying up to check posts and put together appropriate responses to them. The race to get work resulted in freelancers lowering rates based on the premise that clients' cost-savings agenda would favour less expensive bids in instances of comparable competences. Nonetheless, freelancers would maintain a particular minimum rate for themselves. That the platform also specifies minimum rates is seen as helpful to stall a complete downslide to the absolute bottom.

The Indian and Chinese Upworkers' experiences on the platform reflect the inequality within the NIPL. Thirteen Indians reported being cheated by clients who disappeared after project completion without making payments. Moving off the platform after initial discussions without a contract so as to save the platform fee for themselves and the client, initiating work in the pre-contract stage prior to clients funding the escrow account and opting for payments at the time of task completion in long-term fixed projects left freelancers vulnerable. Not only could clients disappear without paying them but redress via the platform would be limited to situations falling within the purview of stated conditions.

Similarly, twelve Chinese freelancers reported that they had encountered situations where they were not paid or were paid unfairly. Eight freelancers were not paid after completing the work. They reported experiences of clients using the timed project work mode rather than the escrow/fixed price structure, making it easier for clients to default after several milestones. Clients could also close the accounts before freelancers completed the work. Three participants reported that they had experienced clients who misrepresented the work involved, which usually meant that freelancers carried out additional work beyond what they were paid for. In these ways, the experiences of both Chinese and Indian workers were analogous. Being deprived of payments, clients' incorrect information about the work, having a greater workload than expected and not being paid overtime were common experiences for Chinese and Indian Upworkers. The platform provides a level of mitigation in the interaction between clients and workers, but workers have to remain vigilant.

The majority of Chinese participants (15) told us that they had not experienced discrimination, but only because it was difficult to know if it had occurred. Being discriminated against on such a platform usually resulted in the freelancers not getting jobs. Only four participants reported discrimination based on nationality, race and gender. The opportunities that were open to workers were constrained by their locations and by assumptions about global workers. For example, it was possible for employers to specify 'native English speakers' which often excluded workers by virtue of their nationality, locations or 'non-English' names. A Chinese participant from Singapore, one of the wealthiest and most developed Asian nations, considered herself a native English speaker as she was fully bilingual, and yet with an obvious Asian name she perceived that she was disadvantaged when the job listings specified 'native speakers'.

In the Indian study, racial discrimination from both clients and fellow freelancers was reported (for a detailed discussion on abuse on online platforms, see D'Cruz & Noronha 2018a, 2018b; Noronha & D'Cruz 2018). Similar to the Chinese case, such biases were usually covert and veiled, with obvious instances inviting reprimands from platform administrators. Clients' negative behaviour arose from doubts over freelancers' competence, sometimes with a view to reducing the latter's payments. Western freelancers' negative acts stemmed from competition linked to both skill and remuneration. Apart from seeing Indians as capable and hence threatening, other freelancers considered the lower rates solicited by the developing world as undercutting them and spoiling their earning opportunities.

Such discrimination and attitudes towards Chinese and Indian freelancers are another manifestation of neo-colonialism (Holtgrewe 2014), evidencing the hegemony of the Global North and adding aversive racism to the existing vulnerabilities of informal sector workers in developing countries. The dynamics of the platform economy indicate processes completely antithetical to the earlier claims of the democratisation of society through cyberspace (Ettlinger 2016). The organisation of crowdsourced work is orchestrated from the developed world, and though the crowd is global, supposedly leading to the dissolution of boundaries between the Global North and Global South and to the remunerative flattening of the global workforce (Ettlinger 2016), racial biases in selection, wages and interpersonal interactions persist (D'Cruz & Noronha 2016, 2018a).

CONCLUDING DISCUSSION

Outsourced Digital Labour as Decent Work

The platform economy has facilitated the absorption of global freelance workers into the world capitalist system and exports precarity associated with the virtual work business model. Despite the potential of exploitation that exists, Chinese and Indian Upworkers report largely positive experiences of using such platforms. Unfortunately, workers' rights and collective bargaining are not well developed in either country and, therefore, with online employment, Upworkers are as vulnerable as their offline counterparts. In China, the increase in crowdsourced work reflects the gradual adaptation of elements of a capitalist economy since the late 1980s, as a new generation of workers in China has grown up embracing the neo-liberal entrepreneurship ideal (Ong 2006, p. 173). The data discussed herein reveal that freelance workers are mostly young and highly educated and use the online platform to improve their income and work flexibility, enabled by their English language skills. They see freelance work on platforms such as Upwork as opportunities to garner skills and, more importantly, exercise control over their careers. Most of the Chinese participants are single, childless and unmarried. The underlying entrepreneurial ethos and individualism are new to China but represent ways of thinking which have been enthusiastically embraced, especially by younger graduates. While a similar trend can be seen in India, there are other pertinent issues as well. Indian workers who seek opportunities through the global crowdsourced platforms do so in response to poor labour markets and unfavourable working conditions nationally. Indeed, many of them are highly skilled and educated and belong to the middle class, and hence find the online platform a useful means to gaining challenging and satisfying work. Platform work privileges merit and competence, utilises and hones freelancers' skills, exposes workers to the global job market and allows flexible working hours, especially for those who need to combine work with household tasks, in particular childcare responsibilities. Despite the costs, risks and vulnerabilities, the platform strikes a chord with Indian freelancers on two important counts: (1) it represents a move away from the feudalistic ethos that pervades most Indian workplaces making them exploitative and sycophantic (D'Cruz & Noronha 2012); and (2) it coheres with the growing predominant notions of self-realisation and entrepreneurialism, especially among Indian youth, that are evident in the subcontinent thanks to neo-liberal and global influences (D'Cruz & Noronha 2016).

Though the Indian and Chinese freelancers' subjective experiences of online outsourced work encompassed feelings of well-being, a critical lens highlights several dimensions of disempowerment. This type of work embodies deficits across all four pillars of decent work, including the provision of full and productive employment, rights at work ensuring human dignity, social protection and social dialogue (ILO 1999). Looking at the criteria which include labour market security, employment security, job security, work security, skill reproduction security, income security and representation security (Kantor et al. 2006), freelancers have to put in concerted efforts to ensure labour market security (especially by bidding but undergirded by reputation), employment security (in spite of constraints, abuse and discrimination, etc., optimum performance and behaviour are required to maintain reputation, and platform and project continuity) and income security including long-term safety nets. Skill reproduction security including arranging for infrastructure is fully the freelancers' responsibility as is work security except for the platform's verification checks, behavioural guidelines and grievance redress. Many of the issues platform workers face are similar to those encountered by other precarious workers, making 'parallel and watertight dimension of the labour market with structurally separated feature and needs' (de Stefano 2016a, p. 2) superfluous.

Moreover, workplace mistreatment has been associated with precarious work, in particular poor labour market conditions, inter-worker competition, job insecurity, limited or no social protection and social dialogue, and partial or no regulation (Djurkovic 2018; Noronha & D'Cruz 2018). Contingent on their job contract and the availability of regulation, social protection and social dialogue, informal workers face varying degrees of liability (Kalleberg 2012; Standing 2011), which has implications for how they tackle situations of abuse and discrimination since mechanisms of redress within and outside workplaces can vary or be (un)available, depending on their particular employment situation (Noronha & D'Cruz 2018). Indian and Chinese participants share country-linked and capital-linked views of the importance of free market dynamics, glossing over how these harm their interests (D'Cruz & Noronha 2018b). In so doing, they are hemmed in by their cognition, and reinforce and perpetuate the context surrounding platform labour, furthering the hegemony of the platform and the sway of neo-liberal and cultural ideologies. Emancipatory discourse and social justice are subverted as macro-level thought processes colour individual sensemaking processes (Burbank & Martins 2010; D'Cruz & Noronha 2018b).

The New International Putting-Out System of Labour (NIPL)

The advantage of the putting-out system is that it enables the outsourcing of work so that employers' costs of real estate, equipment and supervision can be eliminated or reduced and collective action and legal regulation can be avoided, while increasing labour market flexibility emanating from the fluctuation in demand. Employers need not invest in a workplace for the work to be done, or provide the tools (Finkin 2016). In the case of Upwork, workers are also responsible for the workspace, power, computer/mobile devices and software requirements.

Nonetheless, we have developed a context-specific understanding of crowd-work in national conditions. By considering how Chinese and Indian freelancers make use of online opportunities to access international markets for their occupations and professions, we suggest that they are also acculturated to the assumed ethos in the platform economy – neo-liberalism, entrepreneurialism and individual responsibility towards one's career – and they inadvertently reduce the need for supervision. Chinese and Indian Upworkers in the digital economy must accept these notions – many of which are previously unfamiliar codes of work culture – that underpin the platform economy in order to participate in the global flows of virtual work. In the Asian context – shared by Indian and Chinese cultures – individualism is a relatively new ethic. Indian and Chinese workers have been incorporated into work processes that involve self-management, often without adequate compensation and safeguards of labour conditions. The relatively young and educated in both countries have been subsumed by the global discourse surrounding neo-liberalism, and they voluntarily enter into individually negotiated work arrangements with global clients. Besides this, employers can track their experience with workers electronically, thus overcoming the loss of supervisory capacity earlier putting-out systems entailed (Finkin 2016). Indian freelancers continue in these jobs, notwithstanding the challenges and problems, due to poor labour market conditions in their own country, which do not offer them equivalent employment alternatives. They cite the financial and material returns, career progression and upward mobility associated with the platform as important considerations in the trade-off. Race and class dynamics are not limited solely to the hegemony of the Global North, but class issues of the Global South, linked to people's aspirations, must also inform our understanding of the complexities of platform work as offshored means of informal yet unregulated and non-unionised employment.

While the NIDL manifested at the level of whole industry and international trade between corporations, digital platforms engender interactions between individual requesters and freelancers. The NIPL, therefore, advances the NIDL beyond specific manufacturing industries; rather, the outsourcing affects a series of occupations and professions (e.g., IT, translation) spread across different sectors, mostly focused on the service and knowledge economies. Therefore, for Chinese and Indian freelancers, while online platforms offer them opportunities to work with clients from developed countries, they have to negotiate the global job market as individuals, and many experience discrimination linked to their geographical locations and ethnicities. The experiences of these Upworkers represent the individual challenge of being part of the NIPL. The workers are neither drawn from the working classes nor engage in predominantly manufacturing industries. Nonetheless, the freelancers in our study also report difficulties negotiating transnational transactions and experiences of discrimination, with little possibility of addressing power differences due to their status as isolated contractors (Caraway 2010). Freelancers from developing economies such as China and India face discrimination by requesters from the developed world who, wishing to reduce labour costs, often assume low expectation of pay from workers from China and India. Freelancers from developed countries resent the fact that Indian workers may command lower fees and therefore are competing with them and lowering the overall standard of pay. The findings can be explained by labour conditions in China and India and by requesters' assumptions about workers according to their ethnicity and geographical location, exacerbated by the existing planetary power structure (Graham & Anwar 2019). While the NIDL originally theorises about global economic currents between industries, countries and economies, digital platforms allow us to consider individual implications, comparing the effects beyond the Western viewpoint. The discrimination that has been cited reminds us of offshoring operations and the concerns of imperialism by the Global North (Noronha & D'Cruz 2009), which only reinforces the position that digital labour operates within the hierarchies of the New Global Division of Labour (Huws 2012; Su 2009), which exist both offline and online (D'Cruz 2017). As the neo-liberal project progresses against a backdrop of unprecedented technological innovation and expansion (D'Cruz & Noronha 2016), and despite purported greater worldwide integration into global oneness (Castells 2010), the hegemony of the developed world persists (Posthuma & Nathan 2010), emphasising the 'societal embeddedness' of global production networks which militate against any reduction of pre-existing inequalities (Coe et al. 2008).

Unlike the previous waves of manufacturing outsourcing, digital platforms participate in facilitating the NIPL through exporting the weightless knowledge industry and the labour conditions associated with precarious, insecure employment. It is difficult for Chinese and Indian freelancers to address these labour conditions given that the idea of the putting-out system is meant to avoid legal regulations. In the context of platforms, this is achieved by constructing an arms-length relationship with self-employed independent contractors (Finkin 2016). In pitching workers from the developing world against workers from the developed world, global platforms such as Upwork impact individual workers in matters of wages and job security. Importantly, workers from the originating economies of the Global North come into direct competition with their counterparts from the Global South. This means that workers' potential for collective action against their putative employers is substantially reduced. Further, as in the putting-out system, freelancers experience a lack of contact with other workers, a constant need for new work and a wide array of potential purchasers of their services which stymie the growth of collective action (Finkin 2016). Although subsumed under the capitalist logic of global crowdsourcing platforms, Upworkers in China and India are not the impoverished blue-collar workers that the NIDL originally theorises about. What is relevant here is the NIPL, which incorporates individual workers, including freelance professionals, and exports not only 'jobs' but also ideas associated with neo-liberal economies including entrepreneurialism and individualism. Overall, Chinese and Indian freelancers on online platforms are happy with the opportunities to realise both participation in the world economy and self-sufficiency within the increasingly valued ethos of individualism. This is an emerging trend to note, given that both India and China are considered to be collectivist societies (Hofstede 1980); the increase in engaging with platform work, therefore, speaks to changes in the national ethos arising due to global influences in thought processes as well as economic imperatives, particularly in the era after the global economic crisis of the late 2000s (D'Cruz & Noronha 2016; Hansen & Svarverud 2010; Schmalz & Ebenau 2012). Clearly, cultural differences, far from being fixed and static, are in fact dynamic, fluid and situationally constructed (Noronha & Magala 2017). Freelancers' participation in global capital is conditioned by their compliance with the mechanisms and stipulations centralised through the platform (resembling the panopticon; Ouellet 2010). Platforms such as Upwork engender the individualisation of labour, perceived as empowering workers, while absorbing freelancers into a new capitalist logic within national and international conditions.

NOTES

1. David Harvey defines neo-liberalism as 'a theory of political economic practices that proposes that human well-being can best be advanced by liberating individual entrepreneurial freedoms and skills within an institutional framework characterized by strong private property rights, free markets, and free trade' (2005, p. 2).
2. https://data.worldbank.org/indicator/NY.GDP.PCAP.CD (accessed 14 December 2019).
3. Promulgated by the ILO since 1999 as a means of worldwide labour regulation to address the emerging global business context, decent work comprises four pillars: full and productive employment, rights at work ensuring human dignity, social

protection, and social dialogue (ILO 1999), encompassing the ILO's core labour standards and demonstrating its new commitment to workers previously excluded from these provisions (Ghai 2003; Vosko 2002). It focuses on eight core conventions (against child labour and forced labour and for free collective bargaining and non-discrimination on grounds of religion, gender, race, etc.) within a broad non-binding framework whose conditions are not fixed by the ILO but engender international consensus about fairness at work, with specific details being worked out locally (Ghai 2003; Moore et al. 2015).

4.   https://data.worldbank.org/indicator/SL.UEM.TOTL.ZS (accessed 14 December 2019).

5.   China National Bureau of Statistics. https://www.weforum.org/agenda/2017/04/higher-education-in-china-has-boomed-in-the-last-decade (accessed 14 December 2019).

6.   The policy was changed in 2015, but the effects of this would not have been apparent in the sample in 2016.

REFERENCES

Aloisi, A. (2015), 'The Rising of On-demand Work: A Case Study Research on a Set of Online Platforms and Apps', The 4th ILO Conference on Regulating for Decent Work, ILO, Geneva, 8–10 July.

Beerepoot, N. & Lambregts, B. (2015), 'Competition in Online Job Marketplaces: Towards a Global Labour Market for Outsourcing Services?', *Global Networks*, **15**(2), 236–255.

Bergvall-Kåreborn, B. & Howcroft, D. (2014), 'Amazon Mechanical Turk and the Commodification of Labour', *New Technology, Work and Employment*, **29**(3), 213–223.

Bieler, A. & Lee, C. (2017a), 'Chinese Labour in the Global Economy: An Introduction', *Globalizations*, **14**(2), 179–188.

Bieler, A. & Lee, C. (2017b), 'Exploitation and Resistance: A Comparative Analysis of the Chinese Cheap Labour Electronics and High-Value Added IT Sectors', *Globalizations*, **14**(2), 202–215.

Burbank, P.M. and Martins, D.C. (2010), 'Symbolic Interactionism and Critical Perspective: Divergent or Synergistic?', *Nursing Philosophy*, **11**(1), 25–41.

Caraway, B. (2010), 'Online Labour Markets: An Inquiry into oDesk Providers', *Organisation, Labour and Globalisation*, **4**(2), 111–125.

Castells, M. (2010), *The Power of Identity: The Information Age: Economy, Society, and Culture*. Chichester: Blackwell.

Chen, J.Y. (2018), 'Thrown Under the Bus and Outrunning It! The Logic of Didi and Taxi Drivers' Labour and Activism in the On-demand Economy', *New Media & Society*, **20**(8), 2691–2711.

Coe, N.M., Dicken, P. & Hess, M. (2008), 'Global Production Networks: Realizing the Potential', *Journal of Economic Geography*, **8**(3), 271–295.

Cohen, N. (2015), 'Entrepreneurial Journalism and the Precarious State of Media Work', *South Atlantic Quarterly*, **114**(3), 513–533.

Cooke, F.L. (2016), 'Employment Relations in China'. In G.J. Bamber, R.D. Lansbury, N. Wailes & C.F. Wright (eds), *International and Comparative Employment Relations: National Regulation, Global Changes*. Sage Publications Ltd, pp. 291–315.

Cushing, E. (2013), Amazon Mechanical Turk: The Digital Sweatshop. *UTNE Reader*. https://www.utne.com/science-and-technology/amazon-mechanical-turk-zm0z13jfzlin (accessed 10 September 2018).

D'Cruz, P. (2017), 'Partially Empowering but Not Decent? The Contradictions of Online Labour Markets'. In E. Noronha & P. D'Cruz (eds), *Critical Perspectives on Work and Employment in Contemporary India*. New Delhi: Springer, pp. 173–198.

D'Cruz, P. & Noronha, E. (2012), 'High Commitment Management Practices Re-examined: The Case of Indian Call Centres', *Economic and Industrial Democracy*, **33**(2), 185–205.

D'Cruz, P. & Noronha, E. (2016), 'Positives Outweighing Negatives: The Experiences of Indian Crowdsourced Workers', *Work Organization, Labour and Globalization*, **10**(1), 44–63.

D'Cruz, P. & Noronha, E. (2018a), 'Target Experiences of Workplace Bullying on Online Labour Markets: Uncovering the Nuances of Resilience', *Employee Relations*, **40**(1), 139–154.

D'Cruz, P. & Noronha, E. (2018b), 'Abuse on Online Labour Markets: Targets' Coping, Power and Control', *Qualitative Research in Organizations and Management*, **13**(1), 53–78.

D'Cruz, P. & Noronha, E. (2019), 'Indian Freelancers in the Platform Economy: Prospects and Problems'. In K.R. Shyamsundar (ed.), *Globalization, Labour Market Institutions, Policies and Processes in India*. New Delhi: Palgrave, pp. 257–276.

De Stefano, V.M. (2016a), *The Rise of the 'Just-in-Time' Workforce*. Geneva: ILO. https://www.ilo.org/wcmsp5/groups/public/---ed_protect/---protrav/---travail/documents/publication/wcms_443267.pdf (accessed 13 December 2019).

De Stefano, V.M. (2016b), 'Introduction: Crowdsourcing, the Gig-economy and the Law', *Comparative Labor Law & Policy Journal*, **37**(3), 1–10.

Djurkovic, N. (2018), 'Workplace Bullying in Precarious Employment'. In P. D'Cruz et al. (eds), *Handbooks of Workplace Bullying, Emotional Abuse and Harassment: Special Topics and Particular Occupations, Professions and Sectors*. Singapore: Springer, pp. 1–28.

Elena, S. (2017), The Secrets of the World's Second Largest Freelance Economy – India. YKA. https://www.youthkiawaaz.com/2017/10/the-rise-of-indias-freelance-economy/ (accessed 10 September 2018).

Ettlinger, N. (2016), 'The Governance of Crowdsourcing: Rationalities of the New Exploitation', *Environment and Planning A: Economy and Space*, **48**(11), 2162–2180.

Finkin, M. (2016), 'Beclouded Work in Historical Perspective', *Comparative Labor Law & Policy Journal*, **37**(3), 16–12.

Frobel, V., Heinrichs, J. & Kreye, O. (1978), 'The New International Division of Labour', *Social Science Information*, **17**(1), 123–142.

Fuchs, C. (2013), 'Class and Exploitation on the Internet'. In T. Scholz (ed.), *Digital Labor. The Internet as Playground and Factory*. Abingdon: Routledge, pp. 211–224.

Fuchs, C. (2016), 'Digital Labor and Imperialism', *Monthly Review*, **67**(8), 14.

Ghai, D. (2003), 'Decent Work: Concept and Indicators', *International Labour Review*, **142**(2), 113–145.

Graham, M. & Anwar, M.A. (2019), 'The Global Gig Economy: Towards a Planetary Labour Market?', *First Monday*, **24**(4) n.p. https://firstmonday.org/ojs/index.php/fm/rt/printerFriendly/9913/7748

Graham, M., Hjorth, I. & Lehdonvirta, V. (2017), 'Digital Labour and Development: Impacts of Global Digital Labour Platforms and the Gig Economy on Worker Livelihoods', *Transfer: European Review of Labour and Research*, **23**(2), 135–162.

Green, A., De Hoyos, M., Barnes, S., Baldauf, B., Behle, H. & Stewart, J. (2013), *Exploratory Research on Internet-enabled Work Exchanges and Employability*. Seville, Spain: Publications Office of the European Union.

Hansen, M.H. & Svarverud, R. (2010), *iChina: The Rise of the Individual in Modern Chinese Society*. Copenhagen: NIAS Press.

Hart-Landsberg, M. (2015), 'From the Claw to the Lion: A Critical Look at Capitalist Globalization', *Critical Asian Studies*, **47**(1), 1–23.

Harvey, D. (2005), *A Brief History of Neoliberalism*. Oxford & New York: Oxford University Press.

Hofstede, G. (1980), *Culture's Consequences: International Differences in Work-related Values*. Beverly Hills, CA: Sage.

Holtgrewe, U. (2014), 'New New Technologies: The Future and the Present of Work in Information and Communication Technology', *New Technology, Work and Employment*, **29**(1), 9–24.

Howe, J. (2006), 'The Rise of Crowdsourcing', Wired. https://www.wired.com/2006/06/crowds/ (accessed 10 September 2018).

Huws, U. (2012), 'The Reproduction of Difference: Gender and the Global Division of Labour', *Work Organisation, Labour & Globalisation*, **6**(1), 1–10.

Huws, U. (2013), 'Working Online, Living Offline: Labour in the Internet Age', *Work Organization, Labour and Globalization*, **7**(1), 1–11.

ILER (2014), *Workers in the Era of Globalization*. New Delhi: IHD and Academic Foundation.

ILO (1999), Decent work: Report of the Director-General to the International Labour Conference. http://www.ilo.org/public/english/standards/relm/ilc/ilc87/rep-i .htm(accessed 20 February 2015).

ILO (2018), *Women and Men in the Informal Economy: A Statistical Picture*. Third edition. Geneva: ILO.

Irani, L.C. (2015). 'Difference and Dependence among Digital Workers: The Case of Amazon Mechanical Turk', *South Atlantic Quarterly*, **114**(1), 225–234.

Kalleberg, A.L. (2012), 'Job Quality and Precarious Work: Clarifications, Controversies, and Challenges', *Work and Occupations*, **39**(4), 427–448.

Kantor, P., Rani, U. & Unni, J. (2006), 'Decent Work Deficits in Informal Economy: Case of Surat', *Economic and Political Weekly*, **41**(21), 2089–2097.

Kapoor, R. (2014), 'Creating "Good Jobs"', *Economic and Political Weekly*, **59**(46), 16–18.

Keat, R. (1991), 'Introduction: Starship Britain or Universal Enterprise'. In R. Keat & N. Abercrombie (eds), *Enterprise Culture*. London: Routledge, pp. 1–17.

Kenney, M. & Zysman, J. (2016), 'The Rise of the Platform Economy', *Issues in Science and Technology*, **32**(3), 61–69.

Kittur, A., Nickerson, J.V., Bernstein, M.S., Gerber, E.M., Shaw, A., Zimmerman, J., Lease, M. & Horton, J.J. (2013), 'The Future of Crowd Work', Conference on Computer Supported Cooperative Work, San Antonio, Texas, 13 February.

Kneese, T., Rosenblat, A. & Boyd, D. (2014), 'Understanding Fair Labor Practices in a Networked Age', Open Society Foundations. https://www.datasociety.net/pubs/fow/FairLabor.pdf (accessed 10 September 2018).

Lal, S. (2015), 'Thanks to Internet, India has Most Freelance Professionals after US', *Hindustan Times*. https://www.hindustantimes.com/tech/tech-internet-combine-to

-create-unconventional-career-options/story-1kHKXGcYpUiEMgyTYT9nNO.html (accessed 10 September 2018).

Leung, W.F. (2018), *Digital Entrepreneurship, Gender and Intersectionality: An East Asian Perspective*. London: Palgrave Macmillan.

Leung, W.F. & Cossu, A. (2019), 'Digital Entrepreneurship in Taiwan and Thailand: Embracing Precarity as a Personal Response to Political and Economic Change', *International Journal of Cultural Studies*, **22**(2), 264–280.

Liang, Z., Appleton, S. & Song, L. (2016), *Informal Employment in China: Trends, Patterns and Determinants of Entry*. Bonn: Institute for the Study of Labor (IZA).

Milkman, R. & Ott, E. (2014), *New Labor in New York*. Ithaca, NY: Cornell University Press.

Moore, P. (2018), *The Threat of Physical and Psychosocial Violence and Harassment in Digitalized Work*. Geneva: ILO.

Moore, P., Dannreuther, C. & Möllmann, C. (2015), 'Guest Editors' Introduction: The Future and Praxis of Decent Work', *Global Labour Journal*, **6**(2), 127–137.

Nash, J. (1983), 'Introduction'. In J. Nash & M.P. Fernandez-Kelly (eds), *Women, Men and the International Division of Labour*. Albany: State University of New York.

Noronha, E. (1996), 'Liberalisation and Industrial Relations', *Economic and Political Weekly*, **31**(8), L14–L20.

Noronha, E. & Beale, D. (2011), 'India, Neo-liberalism and Union Responses: Unfinished Business and Protracted Struggles'. In G. Gregor, A. Wilkinson & R. Hurd (eds), *The International Handbook of Labour Unions: Responses to Neo-liberalism*. Cheltenham, UK and Northampton, MA, USA: Edward Elgar, pp. 167–186.

Noronha, E. & D'Cruz, P. (2008), 'The Dynamics of Teleworking: Case Studies of Women Medical Transcriptionists from Bangalore, India', *Gender, Technology and Development*, **12**(2), 157–183.

Noronha, E. & D'Cruz, P. (2009), *Employee Identity in Indian Call Centres: The Notion of Professionalism*. New Delhi: Sage.

Noronha, E. & D'Cruz, P. (2016), 'Still a Distance to Go: Social Upgrading in the Indian ITO-BPO-KPO Sector'. In D. Nathan, M. Tewari & S. Sarkar (eds), *Labour in Global Value Chains in Asia*. Cambridge: Cambridge University Press, pp. 423–449.

Noronha, E. & D'Cruz, P. (2018), 'Indian Freelancers' Experiences of Bullying on Online Labour Markets: Insights into Digital Workplaces in the Informal Economy'. In P. D'Cruz et al. (eds), *Indian Perspectives on Workplace Bullying: A Decade of Insights*. Singapore: Springer, pp. 147–172.

Noronha, E. & D'Cruz, P. (2019), 'Organization Advantage: Experience of Telework in India'. In J. C. Messenger (ed.), *Telework in the 21st Century*. Cheltenham, UK and Northampton, MA, USA: Edward Elgar Publishing, pp. 255–285.

Noronha, E. & Magala, S. (2017), 'Going Dutch, Remaining Indian: The Work Experiences of IT Expatriates'. In E. Noronha & P. D'Cruz (eds), *Critical Perspectives on Work and Employment in Globalizing India.* Singapore: Springer, pp. 283–303.

Noronha, E., D'Cruz, P. & Banday, M.U.L. (2018), 'Navigating Embeddedness: Experiences of Indian IT Suppliers and Employees in the Netherlands', *Journal of Business Ethics*. DOI: 10.1007/s10551-018-4071-3.

Ong, A. (2006), *Neoliberalism as Exception: Mutations in Citizenship and Sovereignty*. Durham, NC: Duke University Press.

Ouellct, M. (2010), 'Cybernetic Capitalism and the Global Information Society: From the Global Panopticon to a "Brand" New World'. In M. Paterson & J. Best (eds), *Cultural Political Economy*. London: Routledge, pp. 177–196.

Pongratz, H.J. (2018), 'Of Crowds and Talents: Discursive Constructions of Global Online Labour', *New Technology, Work and Employment*, **33**(1), 58–73.

Pongratz, H.J. & Voss, G.G. (2003), 'From Employee to "Entreployee": Towards a "Self-entrepreneurial" Work Force?', *Concepts and Transformation*, **8**(3), 239–254.

Posthuma, A. & Nathan, D. (2010), *Labour in Global Production Networks in India*. New Dehli: Oxford University Press.

Rustagi, P. (2015), 'Informal Employment Statistics: Some Issues', *Economic and Political Weekly*, **50**(6), 67–72.

Schmalz, S. & Ebenau, M. (2012), 'After Neoliberalism? Brazil, India, and China in the Global Economic Crisis', *Globalizations*, **9**(4), 487–501.

Schucher, G. (2017), 'The Fear of Failure: Youth Employment Problems in China', *International Labour Review*, **156**(1), 73–98.

Sinha, J.B.P. (2015), *Psychosocial Analysis of the Indian Mindset*. New Delhi: Springer.

Standing, G. (1999), *Global Labour Flexibility*. New York: St. Martin's Press.

Standing, G. (2011), *The Precariat: The New Dangerous Class*. New York: Bloomsbury.

Su, Z. (2009), 'Place of China in the New International Division of Labour', Proceedings of Global Management Conference, Río de Janeiro.

Urry, J. (2014), *Offshoring*. Cambridge: Polity.

Vosko, L.F. (2002), 'Decent Work: The Shifting Role of the ILO and the Struggle for Global Social Justice', *Global Social Policy*, **2**(1), 19–46.

Vosko, L.F. (2009), *Managing the Margins: Gender, Citizenship, and the International Regulation of Precarious Employment*. Oxford: Oxford University Press.

Williams, C.C. (2017), 'Re-classifying Economies by the Degree and Intensity of Informalization: The Implications for India'. In E. Noronha & P. D'Cruz (eds), *Critical Perspectives on Work and Employment in Contemporary India*. New Delhi: Springer, pp. 113–132.

Wood, A.J., Graham, M., Lehdonvirta, V. & Hjorth, I. (2018), 'Good Gig, Bad Gig: Autonomy and Algorithmic Control in the Global Gig Economy', *Work, Employment and Society*, **33**(1), 56–75.

PART III

Labour process and labour relations in platform capitalism

7. Digitalised management, control and resistance in platform work: a labour process analysis

Simon Joyce and Mark Stuart

INTRODUCTION

The era of platform work has presented employment researchers with a number of challenges.[1] In this chapter, we focus on conceptual and theoretical issues; specifically, the problem of how best to understand platform worker contestation and resistance. To do this, we develop an application of labour process theory (Braverman 1974; Edwards 1989, 1990; Hyman 1987; Littler 1982; Thompson 1990). While the control–resistance duality of labour process approaches is fairly familiar in platform work research, to date there has been a significant – indeed, problematic – overemphasis of control, while platform worker resistance has been correspondingly downplayed (for instance, Gandini 2019; Howcroft and Bergvall-Kåreborn 2019; Rosenblat and Stark 2016; Shapiro 2018; Sharma 2020; Veen et al. 2020; Wood et al. 2018). The overemphasis of control in previous research – while in some ways understandable, given the novelty of algorithmic technology – has skewed accounts of platform work's nature and dynamics. In particular, platform worker resistance has been under-researched and under-theorised. This chapter aims to redress the balance.

Despite the widespread focus on control, evidence of platform worker resistance continues to accumulate. Most obviously, there is regular coverage in news media of platform worker strikes, protests, and legal challenges (see below). Some academic and activist researchers have explicitly examined – indeed, championed – such resistance (Cant 2020; Tassinari and Maccarrone 2020; Woodcock 2018). Other evidence of platform worker resistance appears in research focussed on control, where it is often assumed to be of little consequence, or easily disarmed by platform control mechanisms (Griesbach et al. 2019; Rosenblat and Stark 2016; Shapiro 2018; Sharma 2020; van Doorn and Badger 2020). Such accounts often reproduce problematic notions of control familiar from previous eras; in particular, mirroring heavily criticised 'electronic panopticon' accounts of 1990s ICT systems (for an explicit revival of this analysis, see Woodcock 2020; for a critical review of earlier debates, see Bain and Taylor 2000; Moore and Joyce 2020). Consequently, despite the obvious empirical persistence of platform worker resistance, it appears as something of an anomaly in the absence of any adequate theorisation.

Our argument in this chapter is that labour process theory can provide an explanation for both the nature and dynamics of platform worker resistance, as well as its persistence. To date there has been little systematic effort to apply labour process theory to platform work. Gandini (2019) argues that a labour process approach might be fruitful in this area (see also Moore and Joyce 2020), and Tassinari and Maccarrone (2020) show how labour process analysis can be applied to a detailed case study of food delivery platform workers. We build on these foundations to develop a broader account. In particular, we show how aspects of platform work usually associated with the control of labour are also key sites of platform worker resistance.

The starting point for our analysis is the understanding that platform work establishes a labour–capital relationship between workers and the company running the app (Gandini 2019; Joyce 2020). For labour process theory, capitalist labour processes are characterised by a dual tendency towards both control over the labour process by managers, as well as resistance to that control by workers. As a result, the labour process is a site of inherent conflict and contestation. The digitalised management methods of platform work, we argue, represent an evolution in the systems utilised by managers to control workers at the point of production, but this solution is no more able to resolve the intractability of worker resistance than was any management system that came before it. In consequence, platform management methods do not represent a complete solution to the problems capital faces in managing labour. Rather, and despite their undoubted novelty, platforms represent another example of what Hyman (1987, p. 30) has aptly characterised as 'different routes to partial failure'.

We begin with a discussion of the conceptual framework of labour process theory. Next we set out an understanding of platform work as a set of management methods for organising work and managing a workforce. Subsequently, we apply our labour process analysis to empirical evidence on platform work and platform worker resistance, drawn from own and others' research.

1   CONTROL AND RESISTANCE IN LABOUR PROCESS THEORY

Labour process theory (LPT) permits the analysis of work organisation on two levels. First, LPT identifies the underlying dynamics common to all forms of paid work under capitalist relations of production: specifically, a dual dynamic of control and resistance. Second, LPT examines specific management methods for organising work and extending control over the labour process; methods which vary historically and across different industries and workplaces, which can be more or less effective from management's point of view, but which can never do away entirely with the underlying dynamics of control and resistance. As we show below, the dual level analysis of LPT is particularly useful for clarifying issues in platform work.

For its understanding of the employment relationship, LPT draws heavily on Marx's account of the exploitation of labour at the point of production – *viz.*, that capital seeks to extract surplus labour by ensuring (or attempting to ensure) that workers produce a greater quantity of value than is returned to them in the form of wages. For LPT, as for Marx, this underlying dynamic is present regardless of whether any given capitalist in fact makes any profit. An equivalent dynamic is also present in parts of the economy – such as the public sector – where profits as such are never made (Fine and Saad Filho 2010). Although aspects of the labour process were already studied in fields such as industrial relations and the sociology of work, LPT took off as a more or less coherent research project following the publication of Braverman's (1974) account of the labour process under 'monopoly capital' conditions. Despite Braverman's avowedly Marxist approach, however, during the 1980s LPT explicitly moved away from any commitment to Marxism as a wider theory of society and history, despite retaining a number of its key conceptual insights. Thompson (1990, pp. 99–101) codified the 'core theory' of LPT, based on four main components:

- the labour process is a site of the exploitation of labour
- the logic of accumulation 'forces capital constantly to revolutionise ... production'
- the logic of accumulation leads to a 'control imperative ... [to] regulate the labour process'
- 'the social relation between capital and labour is an antagonistic one' which gives rise to 'a variety of forms of conflict and resistance'.

Thompson claims, though, that this account 'is not in my view Marxist', because it detaches Marx's wider theory of society and history; specifically, the notion of social change through class struggle (ibid., p. 102). Likewise, Edwards (1986) distances his broadly comparable account from Marx on similar grounds, while nevertheless retaining a nearly-Marxist notion of 'structured antagonism' in labour–capital relations based on exploitation, which may or may not be expressed in overt struggle or resistance.

The key link in LPT analysis is that the drive to extract surplus labour means that capital must achieve some level of control over the labour process, over aspects such as the speed and intensity of labour, quality standards of production, what equipment, tools and raw materials are used, and how. The dynamic to establish control is rooted in a fundamental uncertainty within the capitalist labour process, commonly termed the *indeterminacy of labour* (Thompson and Smith 2010). Again, this analysis is drawn from Marx: the commodity that workers sell to capitalists (in exchange for a wage) is not labour but the *capacity to labour* (Edwards 1986), termed 'labour power' by Marx (1976). Workers' capacity to labour is bought by a capitalist, usually for a specified number of hours each day, but it is then up to the capitalist – or, more usually, managers acting on behalf of capital – to ensure that each worker's capacity to labour is transformed into actual concrete labour, of a specific type, standard and intensity (Thompson 1990). That is, for LPT, control means *control of the labour process*. It is not necessary, from this perspective, for managers to control the hearts and minds, or subjectivity, of workers – even though some managers seem to want that.

Despite – or, perhaps, because of – the centrality of control within the LPT tradition, the concept has been a focus of considerable controversy. Famously, Braverman (1974) saw deskilling[2] as management's main weapon in a long historical process whereby capital increasingly took control of the labour process from the hands of skilled workers, through a progressive application of Taylorist 'scientific management', including: separating the conception and execution of labour; breaking down complex work into simple routinised tasks; and replacing skilled labour with machinery and semi- or unskilled workers. Despite its huge (and continuing) impact, however, Braverman's account was almost immediately criticised as deterministic and one-dimensional. Critics pointed out that, historically, there was no clear correspondence of deskilling and control. For the 19th century, Samuel (1977) showed that many groups of skilled workers showed little sign of rebellion against capital, and Lazonick (1979) demonstrated that the introduction of machinery by managers was usually driven not by the need to control skilled labour, but by moves to improve and standardise products for rapidly expanding markets. Moreover, there is plenty of evidence from the 20th century that semi- and unskilled (i.e. deskilled) workers could prove extremely resistant to managerial control (for instance, Beynon 1984). Critics of Braverman pointed out that managers in fact use a variety of methods for achieving control over the labour process. Friedman (1977) distinguishes two strategies: 'direct control' and 'responsible autonomy'; while Edwards (1979) identifies three methods: 'simple', 'technical' and 'bureaucratic' control. While Edwards viewed his three methods in terms of a historical evolution, Freidman linked his two strategies to core and peripheral labour markets.

Although Edwards and Friedman recognise variation in forms of management control, they also retain a problematic structural determinism apparent in Braverman's account (Edwards 1989, 1990, 1992; Hyman 1987; Storey 1985). The theoretical problem, summed up by Storey (1985, p. 194) is that many accounts 'rest on functionalist premises that capital must and can devise coherent systems of control to ensure the structurally necessary extraction of surplus value', resulting in a 'single-track search for definitive and comprehensive modes of work control which are assumed to exist'. The problem with such approaches is that, both historically and theoretically, management methods, systems and practices are fractured, partial and contradictory. Control is rarely – if ever – the central strategic concern of management (Hyman 1987). Even the purchase of new machinery is seldom primarily concerned with the control of labour. Other pressing issues for managers include production schedules, purchasing, marketing, finance, sales, and so on. As Hyman (1987, p. 35, original emphasis) puts it: 'The contradictory role of management as both co-ordinator of a complex and often baffling productive operation, and simultaneously a vehicle of discipline and disruption, is almost inevitably reflected in consequential contradictions both *between* and *within* the various managerial specialisms'.

This is not to say that managers are not concerned with labour control; rather, it is to emphasise that management cannot be treated as the undifferentiated 'self-conscious agent of capitalist compulsion to subordinate labour' (Hyman 1987, p. 34). Contradictory tendencies within the management function form the irreducible setting for management strategies for control of the labour process. As a result of these contending pressures, managerial strategies rarely mesh together neatly. These structural constraints undermine management strategies – including strategies for control – reducing them, as Hyman (ibid., p. 30) puts it, to 'different routes to partial failure'.

The second level of analysis in LPT examines particular, concrete management methods for controlling the labour process. One of the great strengths of LPT research is the large quantity of empirical research accumulated over some four decades, mostly in the form of detailed case studies. Problems arise, though, if the two levels of analysis are conflated; in particular, by the assumption that management methods intended to control the labour process are straightforwardly able to do so. Theoretically, such an assumption abolishes the underlying dynamics within the labour process, as well as contradictions within management. The theoretical challenge, then, is to maintain an understanding of both the underlying dynamic of control and resistance, as well as the variety and specificity of management practice, including methods of control. To this end, Edwards (1990, p. 145) distinguishes between *general control*, at the level of 'the overall effectiveness of the production system', and *detailed control*, at the level of the immediate labour process. Similarly, Storey

(1985, p. 198, original emphasis) poses the problem in terms of '"levels" and "circuits" of control' in which there exits 'a *variety* of means of control'. While it is not possible fully to explore these rich debates within the confines of this chapter, the key point is that adequate analysis of the labour process must examine the specificity of management methods, while retaining an understanding of the contradictions of management, the variety of management methods and the necessarily partial nature of systems of managerial control.

Often, however, evolving forms of management methods are heralded as entirely new and revolutionary, as if they have resolved previous difficulties once and for all (Edwards 2007). Littler (1982, p. 5) terms this the 'panacea fallacy', which repeatedly claims to have identified 'the magic strategy that successfully stabilised capital–labour relations'. It is not surprising that corporate and managerialist narratives promote such claims. It is important, though, that platform work research avoids the temptations of the panacea fallacy; for instance, by assuming that claims made about the technical capacities of platform technology actually describe the labour processes of platform work and the experience of platform workers. As discussed below, many aspects of platform work are not new at all; furthermore, others are significantly less monolithic than is often assumed.

For LPT, control – however partial and contradictory – is not the end of the story. The drive to control brings with it a corollary: the drive to resist. That is, LPT identifies a *dual dynamic* within the capitalist labour process, which entails both *control and resistance*. As a result, all management strategies for control face not only the challenge of contradictions within the management function, but also the intractability of worker resistance (Ackroyd and Thompson 1999). Importantly, LPT sees the drive to resist as an underlying dynamic which may or may not result in actual resistance. Moreover, where resistance does emerge, its nature and outcome are not predetermined. Resistance may be collective or individual, large or small, organised or unorganised, effective or ineffective. But it is seldom absent.

Despite the centrality of resistance to the labour process framework, theoretical discussion of this key concept is undeveloped by comparison to control. For some accounts, resistance may be largely symbolic (see Ackroyd and Thompson 1999), or may even end up reinforcing control mechanisms; although this latter approach has been hotly disputed (Thompson and Smith 2010). Often, especially in the debates following Braverman, resistance was treated more or less as a constant, assumed presence, which management control methods are designed to overcome. In these accounts, 'workers come to the factory gates as the bearers of a universal recalcitrance to capitalist authority' (Littler 1982, p. 27). What is missing from such accounts is an understanding of the specific ways that the experience of paid work is itself central to generating worker resistance. Hyman (1975) provides a general reminder that the labour–capital relationship – including management methods, is a *generator* of disruption and conflict. Labour process theory provides theoretical means to go beyond this (essential) insight, to analyse specific forms of worker resistance as responses to evolving methods of managerial control. Edwards (1989, p. 188) identifies an 'informal' level of worker resistance, drawing on the work of Mars (1982) and Ditton (1977) examining work 'fiddles'; that is, common practices of rule-breaking by workers, ranging from petty short-cuts to outright criminal activity, intended to shift the balance of effort and reward (see also Ackroyd and Thompson 1999). Edwards highlights the role of informal work groups in devising and perpetuating such practices, some of which may be known about and even encouraged by managers seeking to smooth production. Edwards (1989) also recognises more formal collective resistance such as strikes and other unionised activity (see also Edwards 1992, 2007). Applying a similar approach, Moore and Joyce (2020) distinguish 'grassroots' and 'trade union led' resistance among platform workers. Despite these discussions, frameworks for grasping resistance remain underdeveloped.

In a celebrated intervention, Burawoy (1979) argued that a simple dichotomous framework of control *versus* resistance is inadequate, and added the notion of *consent* to capture the non-conflictual effort of workers in a Chicago engineering factory. This contribution has been much debated. Clawson and Fantasia (1983, p. 671) argue that Burawoy downplays the reality of worker contestation and resistance by presenting an undialectical analysis in which 'all social processes benefit the capitalist class'. Furthermore, Edwards (2007) points to the fundamental problem of excessive generalisation from one case study. Despite these problems, Burawoy's influence has been considerable.

Burawoy is important in the context of platform work because studies that focus on its algorithms often overstate the extent to which platform technology ensures compliance with, or even internalisation of, platform company priorities and rationalities (for instance, Ajunwa and Greene 2019; Griesbach et al. 2019; Wu et al. 2019). Aside from theoretical difficulties, the empirical problem with the over-enthusiastic use of control and consent in platform work research is the sheer scale of non-consent and non-control evident in a growing number of studies, as well as in news media reporting. In reality platform work is the location of globally significant levels of worker organisation, protest and resistance, often of a very militant type (Joyce et al. 2020). While Burawoy's 'consent' may be useful in some contexts, it is far from clear that it is universally applicable, especially in platform work.

Consequently, we retain the classic control–resistance approach developed in accounts such as Thompson (1990; also Thompson and Smith 2010) and Edwards (1986, 1990). Most importantly, we wish to emphasise the *dual nature* of the underlying dynamic within the capitalist labour process, comprising both control and resistance. Accounts that see only one side of this duality are, at best, limited. As we show below, platform management methods offer managers opportunities for enhanced control of the labour process, while at the same time providing sites for platform worker resistance and contestation.

2 PLATFORM WORK AS MANAGEMENT METHOD

Platforms and platform work have been defined in various ways. For some, platforms are a technical arrangement of computer hardware, software and processing power (Kenney and Zysman 2016). For others, platforms represent novel economic formations, based on processing data as a raw material (Srnicek 2016), or new ways of engaging a workforce (Vallas and Schor 2020). Some focus on the role of platforms as intermediaries for economic transactions (Agrawal et al. 2013; Ajunwa and Greene 2019; Bergvall-Kåreborn and Howcroft 2014; Hall et al. 2019; Hall and Krueger 2018; Horton and Zeckhauser 2016; Schmidt 2017), sometimes distinguishing between 'capital platforms' mediating the sale or rent of goods and services, and 'labour platforms' mediating paid work (Farrell and Greig 2016). Others, though, point to the highly active role of platforms in shaping markets, including labour markets, as evidence that a passive 'mediator' definition is problematic (Forde et al. 2017). Further definitions highlight what are seen as the novel social relations of platforms, in the 'triangular' relationship of worker–platform–customer (Calo and Rosenblat 2017; Harris and Krueger 2015; Lehdonvirta et al. 2019; Schörpf et al. 2017). When it comes to platform work, perhaps a common shared definition might be, 'paid work mediated by and online platform' (Forde et al. 2017).

These definitions all capture certain aspects of platform work. For present purposes, however, we would emphasise its character as a *management system*. Regardless of definition, the companies that run platforms are rapidly innovating and refining a new fusion of methods for organising work and managing workers. Some elements of this fusion are recent developments; most obviously, the digital technology of apps and algorithms. Other elements are much older: for instance, work carried out as-and-when required; payment by piecework; worker-provided equipment; 'triangular relationship between the producer, the end-user and the intermediary' (Stanford 2017, p. 384) – the latter being strongly similar to putting-out systems found in the earliest period of industrialisation (see Leung et al., this volume). Moreover, the fusion of management methods developing within platform work are already disseminating far more widely. For instance, in the application of algorithmic distribution and monitoring of work, in settings where the standard model of employment is still firmly in place (Moore and Joyce 2020).

In this sense, platform work represents an evolution of management methods, in the same way that previous systems emerged, such as Taylorism, human resource management or lean production. In adopting this approach, we understand platform work as a portfolio of methods that managers can use for organising and managing a workforce. Here, we follow Moore and Joyce (2020), who see *platform management methods* as a composite of technological and organisational forms that managers can deploy, in various combinations, in order to organise work and manage workers, and to exercise a degree of control over the labour process. Moore and Joyce (ibid., p. 5) identify a number of management methods within the platform model, including:

- algorithmic allocation of work
- digital tracking and monitoring of workers
- integration of customer ratings into performance management systems
- setting of prices for services provided and rates of pay for work conducted
- extraction of commission on every transaction
- engagement of workers on self-employed or independent contractor status
- legal and regulatory arbitrage[3] concerning worker status and service provision.

Platforms that mediate paid work tend to use most of these methods, but it is not necessary that they use them all. Platform companies adopt different business models, with variation in how labour is managed. For instance, platforms such as Amazon Mechanical Turk and Upwork allow users to set prices, whereas platforms such as Uber set all the terms of each transaction. Similarly, some platforms – for instance, Upwork – allow customers to monitor workers, while others monitor workers directly via GPS tracking, etc. It is not even the case that platform workers are always engaged on a self-employed basis; for instance, prior to its withdrawal from the market, Foodora riders in Germany were legally employees, as the company took advantage of 'mini-job' regulations (Ivanova et al. 2018). Elsewhere, court rulings and changing legal frameworks are leading to shifts in the employment status of platform workers away from self-employment (see below). One advantage of a multi-strand approach to conceptualising platform work is that it can encompass change and variation as platform work evolves. Conceptualising platform work in this way also avoids the problem of 'monism' identified by Storey (1985, p. 207) – that is, 'the tendency for commentators to seek definitive singular types of control'. For the approach proposed here, platform work is one option available for capitalist firms: alternatives include Taylorism, lean production and HRM, as well as partial adoption of these models, hybrids and other firm-level variations.

Conceptualising platform work as a system for managing labour also informs the development of labour process analysis, and in doing so highlights the dynamic relations between methods of control and patterns of worker resistance. The platform menu of platform management methods listed above fall into three main groups: algorithmic management (allocation of work, digital tracking and monitoring, integration of customer ratings); pay (setting of prices and rates of pay, extraction of commission); and wider forms of regulation (self-employed or independent contractor, legal and regulatory arbitrage). Each of these methods carries specific implications for control of the labour process. In the next section, we set out evidence to show that these broad dimensions of platform management control also generate and shape emergent platform worker resistance.

3   CONTROL AND RESISTANCE IN PLATFORM WORK

In this section, we apply the labour process framework outlined above to show how platform management methods shape emerging patterns of platform worker resistance. Theoretically, the important point is that methods of control and patterns of resistance are linked via the dual control–resistance dynamic within capitalist labour processes. In other words, platform methods do not simply impose control; they are also key drivers of platform worker resistance. Our argument returns to Hyman's insistence that capitalist management, because of its exploitative nature, is a principal source of conflict and contestation. In addition to this first level of analysis in terms of underlying dynamics, we are also able to add second level analysis of specific forms and categories of platform worker resistance, linked to specific aspects of platform management methods. The section therefore follows the three broad categories of platform management methods outlined above – algorithmic management, pay, broader regulatory issues – and, for each, outlines aspects of management control and empirical evidence of platform worker resistance.

3.1   Algorithmic Management

The obvious place to start any discussion of control and resistance in platform work is with algorithms and their surrounding technology. Algorithm-related issues around the allocation of work, digital tracking and monitoring of workers, and ratings systems have featured heavily in platform work research. This research effort has identified important aspects of the functioning of the platforms of platform work. However, these features have been seen almost exclusively in terms of control. As a result, the extent to which platform algorithms are malleable and open to challenge and modification has been downplayed, leading to a one-sided understanding of the extent to which platforms have succeeded in resolving the inherent indeterminacy of labour.

Several important aspects of algorithms are directly related to management efforts to control the labour process. Most obviously, algorithms are central to the allocation of work and, often, to monitoring its completion. Early research on platform work identified the integration of customer ratings into algorithmic performance management systems as an often harsh and non-transparent mechanism for allocating work (Berg 2016; Bergvall-Kåreborn and Howcroft 2014; Chen et al. 2015; De Stefano 2015; Irani 2015; Rosenblat and Stark 2016). If ratings slipped below a certain level, workers would lose access to the best-paying jobs, or would even be barred from the platform altogether: 'deactivation', as it became known (De Stefano 2015). Consequently, pressure to maintain high ratings becomes a constant but unpredictable disciplining force standing over many platform workers. Research has shown that this pressure can and does result in workers putting up with abusive or discriminatory language from customers, threatening or violent behaviour, criminal activity and even sexual assault, for fear that speaking out or self-defence may result in lower ratings and consequent loss of earnings (Huws et al. 2017; Moore 2018; Raval and Dourish 2016). The fact that ratings cannot be transferred between platforms means that workers become tied to the site where they have built up a good reputation (Kokkodis and Ipeirotis 2016).

Algorithms can also be set to adjust rates of pay according to fluctuating demand for labour, in the infamous 'surge-pricing' systems of Uber and other transportation companies. As anyone who has talked to experienced app-based drivers or riders will testify, different platforms manage 'surge' conditions by different methods, and many of these change with bewildering speed, often un-announced, leading to unexpected fluctuations in earnings – more importantly, usually only in a downward direction (Berg and Johnston 2019; Sharma 2020). On many platforms, algorithms not only direct jobs to particular workers, and monitor their completion, but also keep track of any work refused, which can also lead to deactivation (Raval and Dourish 2016; Ravenelle 2017; Rosenblat and Stark 2016). Some apps track worker locations, as they drive or ride around a city. While some have termed these algorithmic prompts 'gamification' (Woodcock and Johnson 2018), in reality, changing rates of pay to get more effort from workers, or threatening them with loss of work and earnings, are well-established employment practices, which represent the direct continuation of very old-school methods for labour management and control. On these platforms, work is not becoming more like a game; it is becoming more like a job.

What is striking, but seldom discussed, about even these most algorithmic of management methods, is evidence that platforms have neither been able to overcome the underlying dynamic of worker resistance nor eliminate worker contestation in practice. At an individual level, Attwood-Charles (2019) has shown that couriers can avoid platform rules with little consequence. (Wood et al. 2018) have shown that digital freelancers are able to avoid surveillance of their work by the platform. Taxi-app drivers use online forums to exchange information about changes to platform algorithms, as well as tips on how to avoid getting caught breaking platform rules (Rosenblat and Stark 2016). Online clickworkers use forums to exchange information about the platform, and to warn each other about customers who pay poorly or not at all (Irani and Silberman 2013). Food delivery riders gather in town squares or outside restaurants and exchange information about algorithmic changes and ways of maximising income, and how best to deal with problems with the platform (Cant 2020). Although these types of everyday resistance[4] have begun to feature more often in research, it seems clear that much remains to be discovered and investigated.

A further feature of platform work is that algorithms change in response to external pressures, including driver/rider shortages, increased orders, or bad weather. Over time, workers learn how to take advantage of this. Research shows that platform workers, for instance grocery delivery drivers on Instacart in the US, have learned that rejecting low-paying jobs will train the algorithm to channel higher-paying jobs. One worker commented: 'I feel like I trained the computer what I'll do. Eventually that computer knows I'm not going to take all kinds of $10 orders. So they stop sending them to me and they send me more decent stuff' (Griesbach et al. 2019, p. 6).

What is more, these workers had collectivised these tactics for training the algorithm via online social media groups. Another reported that if workers refused to accept low-paying orders: 'the system starts to learn that that's not going to work because then that makes the orders late and we have unhappy customers' (ibid., p. 6).

Effectively, these workers have reinvented the age-old practice of output restriction, a well-known tactic for increasing pay rates under piecework systems, recognised by Taylor as 'soldiering' (Braverman 1974). Instead of bargaining with a foreman, however, these workers were training an algorithm, in an elementary form of pay bargaining. In a similar approach, we have interviewed clickworkers who combined collectively to manipulate algorithmic preference settings in order to secure increased rates of pay. It is also well-established that experienced clickworkers use software patches and browser extensions to increase access to better-paying tasks, and that these are effectively collectivised through online forums (Irani and Silberman 2013; Salehi et al. 2015). Taking a more straightforwardly technical approach, Chen (2018) reports Didi drivers in China using additional code with the algorithm, so that they could reject low-paying jobs without the app realising. In our own research, we have encountered two groups of delivery riders who were attempting to reverse-engineer apps in order to gain a clearer understanding of their operation. Veen et al. (2020, p. 400) found food delivery workers engaged in 'manipulation of geo-spatial data, theft of food ... and evasion of shift work'. Other research reports delivery riders: using software to interfere with the app to hide GPS tracking data; using coordinated data-requests under Europe's GDPR data protection regulations to interfere with the platform company's use of data, and to restrict deactivations; and combining multiple data-requests in legal challenges to platforms' use of data (van Doorn and Badger 2020, pp. 11–13).

The point of these examples is not to claim that workers have overcome, or are on the verge of overcoming, the technical capacities of platform algorithms. These examples are important for two reasons. First, they demonstrate the continuing relevance of the 'panacea fallacy' (Littler 1982, p. 5). There are many previous examples of new systems of work technology being introduced, with accompanying predictions that worker organisation and resistance would be eliminated as a result. The best-known example is the introduction of the moving production line in auto factories in the first decades of the 20th century, which was widely expected to provide the panacea for management efforts to control union organisation (Edwards 1979). Such expectations now look faintly ridiculous, given the history of worker militancy in auto plants. The process of workers figuring out the new technology, learning where the pressure-points are, what tactics work and what don't, what forms of organisation are most appropriate, these processes take time; commonly, around 25 years (Moody 2018). We would therefore expect worker resistance to algorithmic management to develop over a period of years and the emergent evidence represents the early development of such a process. While the problems of extrapolating a trend into the future are well known, this expectation seems less unlikely than the repeatedly mistaken claim that a panacea has this time been discovered. Indeed, if anything, platform workers are ahead of the curve.

The second reason why these examples are important is that they have emerged from research that is, generally, not looking for worker resistance, not expecting to find any, and often dismissive of its significance. We would argue that this reticence on the part of platform work research often reflects an incautious approach to dealing with claims made on behalf of algorithmic technology. It is in accounts of its digital technology that platform work research comes closest to expressing a version of the 'panacea fallacy'. Certainly, platform companies and Silicon Valley publicists have made such claims very loudly over recent years; so much so that even the *Financial Times* headlined its review of Uber's valuation as 'mythbusting' (Kaminska 2016). Algorithmically focused research commonly discusses 'control' in platform work, but resistance is addressed much more rarely. A key benefit of the labour process approach is that it sensitises research to the dual dynamic of control and resistance, and places worker resistance much higher up in the list of research questions.

3.2   Pay

Pay is a central aspect of platform management methods, and one that has been much commented on but little researched. This is surprising, given that pay has long been recognised a fundamentally important aspect of control in management of the labour process (for an exception, see Wu et al. 2019). Very commonly, platform work involves some version of piecework. The range of piecework systems in platform work is great. At one end of the scale, 'click-workers' on platforms such as Amazon Mechanical Turk or Microworker can earn as little as two cents per microtask, and overall earnings – such as they are – are made up from many such small and brief tasks (Berg 2016; Berg and Rani 2018). Elsewhere, drivers on ride-hailing apps are paid per trip, in much the same way that taxi-drivers have been paid for many decades previously. Similarly, freelance-type platform work is still paid by the project, in fairly recognisable continuity with non- or pre-platform freelance work (Florisson and Mandl 2018). Other work, such as cooked meal delivery, was established prior to the advent of platforms, but is now far more widespread, and, again, payment is per delivery.

Much of the literature on platform work views piecework as a pernicious and distinctive feature of platform work, especially in accounts that empha-sise its 'gig' aspect. Certainly, piecework has often, though not always, been associated with the 'sweated trades' and the bottom end of the labour market (Webb and Webb 1902). For Marx (1976, pp. 692–700), piecework was the payment system most aligned to capitalist relations of production. Historically, however, piecework has a more varied record, and has been used almost interchangeably with time-based payment systems, according to the changing requirements of employers. The reason for this is that piecework and time-based systems are not as different as is often assumed. As noted by Schloss (1898, p. 13) more than 120 years ago:

> in the practice of industry, whether a man [sic.] be employed on a time-wage or on a piece-wage, both the time occupied and the work done are, as a rule, taken into account. To put it roughly, time-wage very often has a piece-basis, and piece-wage has in practically all cases a time-basis.

The irreducible link between worker output and time in all payment systems applies no less in the case of platform work: microtasks, which take moments to complete, are paid in cents; taxi-app trips take longer and cost a little less than non-app taxi rides (and journeys that take longer are paid more); freelance projects that last for several days are priced considerably higher. In these cases and others, platform piecework rates clearly entail some calculation as to the time each takes to complete. The low rates of pay for many types of platform work, compared with their non-platform equivalents, is less to do with the piecework system as such – which also applies in non-platform settings – and more to do with the greatly increased competition between workers that platforms have enabled, and evasion of regulations controlling service charges and/or pay (see below).

For managers, the obvious appeal of piecework is that it encourages effort. While some see piecework as encouraging workers to 'internalise' the priorities of the platform (Woodcock 2020), in fact the opposite is the case: with piecework, it doesn't matter at all how much a worker identifies with the platform (or any other company) because the same economic compulsion applies to all workers (cf. Marx 1976, p. 899, *et passim*). As a study of dockworkers in 1970s London put it, in a description of piecework that could apply equally to Deliveroo riders cycling the streets of any city, 'payment systems that rewarded physical effort could be applied, because the pace of work was operator-controlled and not dependent on machines' (Hill 1976, p. 118). Research on platform work shows the same mechanism in operation time and time again. Platform workers continually calculate how many deliveries they need to make in an hour, or how many passenger trips, to achieve a certain level of earnings, or how many hours they need to work per shift to hit their daily earnings target (Aslam and Woodcock 2020; Wu et al. 2019). On food delivery platforms, or taxi-apps, workers often complain about changes to the app, or about non-transparent decisions by the platform algorithms. But what is striking in even the most algorithmically focused research, is that worker complaints over changes to the algorithm very often centre around the impact on pay (Rosenblat and Stark 2016). Workers complain that the app changed and now they are earning less.

As a result, piecework not only contributes towards control: it is also a significant trigger of worker resistance. As the study of London dockers cited above put it, 'piecework also creates numerous occasions for conflict' (Hill 1976, p. 110). Indeed, where workers are sufficiently well organised, managers have abandoned piecework altogether, in order to regain control over the labour process (Brown 1962). Research also suggests that payment-by-results systems in general have a tendency to undermine worker commitment, to breach the 'psychological contract', and to undermine the link between effort and reward, precisely because of widespread perceptions of unfair decision-making. Examples of platform workers complaining of unfair changes to pay are common. One of the most well-known involves the US grocery-delivery app Instacart, where management reset algorithms to include tips in the total pay calculation for each delivery, thereby effectively keeping the tip and deducting it from payment instead of the worker receiving it in addition to payment. In this case, when workers noticed the change, they took screenshots of pay details, posted them to social media websites, and notified sympathetic journalists and labour advocates (Captain 2019; for similar events at other delivery platforms, see Ghaffary 2019; Griesbach et al. 2019). As a result of using these tactics over a campaign lasting several weeks, the platform company adjusted its payments upwards. Although the workers did not win all they had hoped for, real changes were forced on the platform, under pressure of public shaming, in what might be the world's first case of collective bargaining by social media. Indeed, the use by workers of screenshots in their challenges to platforms – whether collective public campaigns or individual queries over missing pay – seems to be relatively commonplace. We have interviewed food delivery workers who say they 'screenshot everything' in case payments are less than expected or there are other instances of perceived unfair treatment. This tactic of worker protest reflects a peculiar aspect of algorithmic control in platform work: everything is written down. Or, at least, a great deal is written down. This stands in sharp contrast to many jobs at the lower end of the labour market, where proving what a manager said or did is a fundamental problem for many worker grievances – where, consequently, we might say that informational imbalances are in some respects even greater than in platform work (Cruz et al. 2017).

As these examples illustrate, and contrary to much commentary on platform work monitoring and 'quantification', the fundamental problem for piecework systems is not how to quantify output. The real difficulty is how output is linked to earnings. This calculation – usually made by managers – is always subjective, and always potentially open to contestation (Burchill 1976). A central and recurring site of worker contestation and resistance within piecework systems, therefore, arises every time pay rates are recalculated. As research has shown, on some platforms this happens very often, and usually with no explanation. It is not surprising, then, that worker complaints over rates and levels of pay figure highly in a great deal of platform work research. Often, researchers focus on the algorithm as the source of the grievance. We would suggest that pay is more likely to be the main issue.

Problems relating to pay are becoming increasingly apparent in platform worker resistance. In some cases, worker grievances over perceived imbalances between effort and reward lead to worker resistance of the 'fiddles' variety (discussed above). To date, practices of this type barely register in academic research. Yet, examples uncovered by online news media investigation include survey findings that around one-third of food delivery workers report eating some of the food they were delivering (Gilbert 2019), and the practice of platform delivery workers offering their platform job for hire to other workers on a short-term basis, coordinated via social media sites (McCulloch 2019). Examples from our own research include logging on using a friend's account while suspended, and registering with a food delivery app as a bicycle rider but using a car while working. In the case of job renting, some degree of informal collective organisation is clearly present.

Other research suggests that pay is by some distance the leading cause of conflict and resistance by platform workers. Working from databases of global online news reporting, the Leeds Index of Platform Labour Protest has documented a global total of 527 worker protest events involving workers on food delivery platforms, across 18 platforms and 36 countries, between January 2017 and May 2020. The evidence suggests that grievances over pay were an issue in almost two-thirds (63.4 per cent) of these protests across all continents, and accounted for over half of all platform-worker strikes and log-offs (Joyce et al. 2020). Clearly, protests of these types are more organised and public in nature than the fiddles noted above. Nevertheless, the Leeds Index research has found varying degrees of formalisation. Some protests involve union organisation – sometimes traditional unions, sometimes more radical grassroots organisations – while others are based on completely informal work groups (cf. Edwards 1989). Case study evidence from various types of platform work also supports the view of pay as a significant cause of platform worker grievances (Cant and Woodcock 2020; Chen 2018). To date, however, research in this area, as in other aspects of platform worker resistance, remains undeveloped.

3.3 Wider Regulatory Issues

Finally, legal and regulatory aspects of platform management methods – in particular, self-employed or independent contractor status workforce, and legal and regulatory arbitrage more generally – form aspects of platform business models that offer direct cost-savings to platform companies, as well as enhanced opportunities for control over the labour process. The classification of platforms workers as self-employed brings immediate financial benefits in the form of direct cost savings. For instance, in the European Union, companies engaging a workforce on self-employed terms save the equivalent of around 25 per cent of their wages bill, by avoiding social security payments and other labour taxes, including paid vacations and entitlements for maternity leave. Moreover, in most jurisdictions, minimum wage regulations do not apply to self-employed workers. This well-established platform strategy, of placing themselves outside normal business regulations, has been termed 'legal and regulatory arbitrage', and in the case of Uber has even been described as the ride-hailing platform's main business advantage over competitor transport companies (Calo and Rosenblat 2017; Fleischer 2010; Kaminska 2016). For Uber, this strategy has centred on efforts to have itself regulated as a technology company, rather than as a transportation provider (Borkholder et al. 2018).

In terms of labour process theory, the avoidance of standard business regulation provides platforms with several advantages. Most obviously, in many countries the lack of legal employee status means that platform workers are deprived of important employment and social protections, leaving them more reliant on the platform that provides their income, while removing rights to organise, to bargain and even to be heard (Cherry and Aloisi 2016; Forde et al. 2017; Johnston and Land-Kazlauskas 2018). As a result, worker capacities to resist control over the labour process are reduced. In addition, avoidance of taxi regulations has allowed taxi-app companies to avoid licencing requirements in some locations, to greatly increase driver numbers, and to leverage the resulting oversupply of labour to undermine worker opposition to labour practices, changes to the app, increased commission charges, and so on.

Nevertheless, the legal and regulatory aspects of platform management control methods have also been the sites of considerable worker resistance. In particular, challenges to the classification of platform workers as self-employed have become commonplace in many jurisdictions. Evidence from the Leeds Index (Joyce et al. 2020) suggests that such challenges tend to be concentrated in parts of the globe where the standard model of employment is more common; that is, largely but not exclusively in the global North. The reasons for this are obvious. There is both the legal means to challenge platform companies over worker classification, and the benefits of doing so are greater in countries with more developed employment and social protections. Legal challenges have been brought by individual workers, by established trade unions, by radical grassroots unions and even by platform customers (Cherry 2016; Joyce et al. 2020). As a result, platform companies have been required to treat workers as employees (or are under legal pressure to do so), or else workers have won some sort of 'intermediate' legal status between employment and self-employment, which nevertheless results in greater security or employment and/or increased access to social protections such as paid leave of minimum wage regulations (Forde et al. 2017). Perhaps most notably, efforts by California courts and legislature to reclassify platform workers as employees has led to a lengthy struggle in which platform worker unions have been active participants. The passage of Assembly Bill 5 and the campaign by platform companies, first, to resist its provisions and then – in a $200 million campaign – to overturn it completely, has yet to reach a final conclusion (Conger 2020; Park 2021). Moreover, it seems unlikely that California's initiative will be the last such episode.

Elsewhere, authorities have moved to re-regulate taxi-app platforms as transport companies. The European Court of Justice has ruled that Uber must be regulated as a transportation company not a tech firm (Khan and Ram 2017). In London – one of Uber's few profitable markets – Uber temporarily lost its licence to operate following a series of scandals involving failure to report criminal activities or to properly vet drivers (Bradshaw 2019). New York has implemented a cap on licence numbers and moved to extend minimum hourly wage regulation to include taxi-app drivers – linked to occupancy rates – in an attempt to reduce congestion as well as to improve driver incomes both for taxi-app drivers and for yellow cab drivers, after a tragic series of driver suicides (Berg and Johnston 2019). As a result of this re-regulation, driver earnings have increased, drivers are more secure and platform management prerogatives are restricted (Parrott and Reich 2018). The New York Taxi Workers' Alliance now has some 21,000 members across yellow cabs, taxi-apps and other hire-car services, and keeps up a lively campaign of protests, direct action and legal challenges, directed towards taxi-app companies and regulators alike (NYTWA 2020). Unions elsewhere have similarly sought to organise and represent platform workers, especially those involved in driving, delivery and courier work, and have often used legal and regulatory means to do so.

This brief survey of evidence is by no means intended to claim that unions have in any sense overcome the challenge posed by platforms and platform management methods. However, as the *Financial Times* pointed out in 2016, the market advantage of companies such as Uber largely rested on the avoidance of standard business regulation; that is, the strategy of 'legal and regulatory arbitrage' (Kaminska 2016). However, as the *FT* warned at the time, these advantages would run out to the extent that drivers became organised and authorities began to re-regulate taxi-apps as transport. In many parts of the world, this has begun to happen in relatively significant ways. For the present argument, then, these developments represent another aspect of platform management methods where control and resistance are jointly present.

DISCUSSION AND CONCLUSIONS

The contribution of this chapter is to demonstrate that patterns of platform worker resistance are linked to platform management methods of control. Theoretically, we have argued that the dual control–resistance dynamic within the labour process means that specific management control measures are likely to generate corresponding patterns of worker resistance. Empirically, despite limitations of space and rather incomplete evidence, we have shown that platform worker resistance has tended to cluster around the three main components of platform management – algorithmic management, pay, and wider regulatory issues – in what might be termed *channels of resistance*. In addition to channels of resistance (where resistance arises), we can identify three broad *forms of resistance* (by which it is expressed). First, there are micro-level fiddles and individual resistances, such as eating food during delivery or training algorithms to offer higher pay. This form is also partially collectivised as workers pass around information, whether face to face or, as is often the case, via social media and online forums. Second, we can identify informal collective actions – including strikes/log-offs or demonstrations – carried out by groups of platform workers, but without the involvement of unions or other representative organisations. The third form of resistance involves actions organised by unions or other worker representation and advocacy groups, on a more formal basis. These may be collective actions such as strikes/log-offs and demonstrations, but may also include legal action against platforms and campaigns for regulatory reform, which may comprise a mix of individual and collective action. We would view distinctions between different channels and forms of resistance as variations on a continuum rather than as sharply defined typologies. For instance, training the algorithm to offer higher pay could potentially be bracketed with algorithmic management or pay; and distinguishing in practice between types of informal collective and semi-collective action can be tricky. Nevertheless, the two dimensions – channels of resistance and forms of resistance – offer a basic conceptual framework for further research and analysis.

In highlighting the importance of resistance for an adequate understanding of platform work, it is not our intention to suggest that platform control methods are insignificant, or that worker resistance can easily overcome them, the technologies they embed, and the companies that run them. Rather, our argument is that accounts which view platform work narrowly, as a form of control only, are partial and therefore problematic. Platform management is not overthrown but neither does it run without frictions caused by workers' deliberate actions. While evidence remains scarce, what there is suggests that for workers, as Vallas and Schor (2020) put it, platform work is not a cage; at least, no more than many other forms of wage labour at the bottom end of the labour market. As with other methods of labour process control, platform management faces non-trivial levels of worker resistance. As time goes by, workers learn about platform management methods. Workers devise fiddles, figure out which jobs pay best and how to get them, and learn the basics of what rights they have or might claim. As a result, some management imperatives are frustrated, some control measures blunted. Managers adjust their approach, introduce new methods, or modify existing ones, and sometimes make concessions to worker grievances in order to reinforce longer-term objectives. Here, Edwards' (1990) distinction between general control and detailed control is useful: platforms may make concessions on the latter to sustain the former. Accounts of platform work that focus excessively on control miss this wider reality: the dialectic of control and resistance, expressed in patterns of reciprocal (if uneven) influence, each shaping the development of the other (if unevenly), as moments of the dual dynamic of the labour process.

The approach outlined here is compatible with accounts such as Edwards (1989, 1990), Storey (1985) and Hyman (1987), which understand managerial methods as comprising different forms, levels or circuits of control, which exist alongside – and sometimes in contradiction with – other managerial strategies and priorities. We have characterised platform work as, *inter alia*, a system for organising work and managing a workforce, identifying a number of distinct elements (cf. Moore and Joyce 2020). This differentiated account of platform management methods avoids the problematic 'functionalist premises that capital must and can devise coherent systems of control', and any associated 'single-track search for definitive and comprehensive modes of work control' (Storey 1985, p. 194). Contradictions within platform management (Hyman 1987; Storey 1985) are exemplified by the problems that many platforms have encountered in classifying workers as self-employed, while at the same time trying to maintain detailed control over the labour process. This contradiction has led to numerous legal challenges by workers over their employment status. One result has been that platforms have changed parts of their labour control regime in response. Of course, it remains to be seen how exactly these contradictions develop. Broader tensions can be identified between labour process control and other pressing matters that platform managers must deal with: not least, crucial issues of financial management, such as securing sufficient supplies of venture capital and, more fundamentally, actually making a profit. Not only is platform work not a panacea for control of the labour process, but it remains far from clear that platform work offers a viable business model outside a few niche areas.

The framework outlined here could be developed further. Most obviously, the shortage of systematic research on platform worker resistance presents significant obstacles to further theoretical development. Nevertheless, we can point to some potentially useful directions for future research. In particular, there is considerable scope for developing understandings of the different forms of resistance of platform workers, especially micro-level fiddles and resistances, and ways that these may be (partially) collectivised, as well as forms of informally organised collective action. There is also room to develop greater understanding of platform work channels of resistance, exploring, in particular, how these are related to specific methods of labour process control, and how these vary across different platforms and types of platform work. Finally, there is almost no research at all on tensions and contradictions between different aspects of platform work management methods, or between strategies for managing platform work and other aspects of managing a platform (such as financial management, or technology development functions). If we take as our starting point Hyman's (1987, p. 30) insight that different management strategies represent 'different routes to partial failure', the challenge remains to understand how, how far and how fast this process develops for platform work.

NOTES

1. We would like to thank the editors for helpful comments and suggestions, and for very great patience. As part of the Digital Futures at Work Research Centre (Digit), this work was supported by the UK Economic and Social Research Council (grant number ES/S012532/1), which is gratefully acknowledged.
2. Although Braverman never expressed it as such.
3. The term 'regulatory arbitrage' refers to the practice whereby companies reduce costs by structuring their business to avoid normal regulatory arrangements. Key examples in platform work include classifying workers as self-employed or independent contractors, thereby avoiding employment and social welfare contributions, and companies that provide transport services classifying themselves as technology firms, thereby avoiding costs associated with transport regulation. For discussion of regulatory arbitrage as a business practice see Fleischer (2010); for applications to platform work see Calo and Rosenblat (2017) and Kaminska (2016).
4. For an alternative list of such everyday resistance see Vallas and Schor (2020, p. 167).

REFERENCES

Ackroyd, S. and P. Thompson (1999), *Organisational Misbehaviour*, Sage, London.

Agrawal, A., J. Horton, N. Lacetera and E. Lyons (2013), *Digitization and the Contract Labor Market: A Research Agenda*, w19525, Cambridge, MA, National Bureau of Economic Research, October, accessed at https://doi.org/10.3386/w19525

Ajunwa, I. and D. Greene (2019), 'Chapter 3 Platforms at Work: Automated Hiring Platforms and Other New Intermediaries in the Organization of Work', in S. P. Vallas and A. Kovalainen (eds), *Research in the Sociology of Work*, Vol. 33, Emerald Publishing Limited, pp. 61–91.

Aslam, Y. and J. Woodcock (2020), 'A History of Uber Organizing in the UK', *South Atlantic Quarterly*, **119** (2), 412–21.

Attwood-Charles, W. (2019), 'Dimensions of Platform Labor Control and the Experience of Gig Couriers', paper presented at SASE Conference 2019, Fathomless Futures: Algorithmic and Imagined, New York, 27 June.

Bain, P. and P. Taylor (2000), 'Entrapped by the "electronic panopticon"? Worker resistance in the call centre', *New Technology, Work and Employment*, **15** (1), 2–18.

Berg, J. (2016), *Income Security in the On-Demand Economy: Findings and Policy Lessons from a Survey of Crowdworkers*, International Labour Office, p. 41.

Berg, J. and H. Johnston (2019), 'Too Good to Be True? A Comment on Hall and Krueger's Analysis of the Labor Market for Uber's Driver-Partners', *ILR Review*, **72** (1), 39–68.

Berg, J. and U. Rani (2018), *Digital Labour Platforms and the Future of Work*, Geneva, International Labour Office, p. 160.

Bergvall-Kåreborn, B. and D. Howcroft (2014), 'Amazon Mechanical Turk and the Commodification of Labour: Amazon Mechanical Turk', *New Technology, Work and Employment*, **29** (3), 213–23.

Beynon, H. (1984), *Working for Ford*, 2nd edn, Penguin, London.

Borkholder, J., M. Montgomery, M. S. Chen and R. Smith (2018), *How Transportation Network Companies Buy, Bully, and Bamboozle Their Way To Deregulation*, New

York, National Employment Law Project and the Partnership for Working Families, p. 39.

Bradshaw, T. (2019), 'Uber loses licence to operate in London', *Financial Times*, 25 November 2019, accessed at https://www.ft.com/content/78827b06–0f6a-11ea-a225 -db2f231cfeae?emailId=5ddbaa65eee916000436d737&segmentId=3d08be62–315f -7330–5bbd-af33dc531acb

Braverman, H. (1974), *Labor and Monopoly Capital: The Degradation of Work in the Twentieth Century*, Monthly Review Press, New York.

Brown, W. (1962), *Piecework Abandoned: The Effect of Wage Incentive Systems on Managerial Authority*, Heinemann, London.

Burawoy, M. (1979), *Manufacturing Consent: Changes in the Labor Process under Monopoly Capitalism*, The University of Chicago Press, Chicago.

Burchill, F. (1976), *Introduction to Payment Systems and Pay Structures with a Note on Productivity*, Open University Press, Buckingham.

Calo, R. and A. Rosenblat (2017), 'The Taking Economy: Uber, Information, and Power', *SSRN Electronic Journal*, accessed at https://doi.org/10.2139/ssrn.2929643

Cant, C. (2020), *Riding for Deliveroo: Resistance in the New Economy*, Polity, Cambridge.

Cant, C. and J. Woodcock (2020), 'Fast Food Shutdown: From Disorganisation to Action in the Service Sector', *Capital & Class*, 030981682090635.

Captain, S. (2019), 'Instacart is raising minimum pay again', *Fast Company*, 6 February 2019, accessed at https://www.fastcompany.com/90303309/instacart-is -raising-minimum-pay-again

Chen, J. Y. (2018), 'Thrown Under the Bus and Outrunning it! The Logic of Didi and Taxi Drivers' Labour and Activism in the On-demand Economy', *New Media & Society*, **20** (8), 2691–2711.

Chen, L., A. Mislove and C. Wilson (2015), 'Peeking Beneath the Hood of Uber', in Proceedings of the 2015 ACM Conference on Internet Measurement Conference – IMC '15, Tokyo, Japan, ACM Press, pp. 495–508.

Cherry, M. A. (2016), 'Beyond Misclassification: The Digital Transformation of Work', *Comparative Labor Law & Policy Journal*, **37** (3), 544–77.

Cherry, M. A. and A. Aloisi (2016), '"Dependent Contractors" in the Gig Economy: A Comparative Approach', *SSRN Electronic Journal*, accessed at https://doi.org/10 .2139/ssrn.2847869

Clawson, D. and R. Fantasia (1983), 'Beyond Burawoy: The Dialectics of Conflict and Consent on the Shop Floor', *Theory and Society*, **12** (5), 671–80.

Conger, K. (2020), 'Uber and Lyft Consider Franchise-Like Model in California', *New York Times*, 18 August 2020, accessed at https://www.nytimes.com/2020/08/18/ technology/uber-lyft-franchise-california.html

Cruz, K., K. Hardy and T. Sanders (2017), 'False Self-Employment, Autonomy and Regulating for Decent Work: Improving Working Conditions in the UK Stripping Industry', *British Journal of Industrial Relations*, **55** (2), 274–94.

De Stefano, V. (2015), 'The Rise of the "Just-in-Time Workforce": On-Demand Work, Crowd Work and Labour Protection in the "Gig-Economy"', *SSRN Electronic Journal*, accessed at https://doi.org/10.2139/ssrn.2682602

Ditton, J. (1977), *Part-time Crime: An Ethnography of Fiddling and Pilferage*, Springer, London.

Edwards, P. (1986), *Conflict At Work: A Materialist Analysis of Workplace Relations*, Basil Blackwell, Oxford.

Edwards, P. (1989), 'Patterns of Conflict and Accommodation', in D. Gallie (ed.), *Employment in Britain*, Blackwell, Oxford.

Edwards, P. (1990), 'Understanding Conflict in the Labour Process: The Logic and Autonomy of Struggle', in D. Knights and H. Willmott (eds), *Labour Process Theory*, Macmillan, Basingstoke, pp. 125–52.

Edwards, P. (1992), 'Industrial Conflict: Themes and Issues in Recent Research', *British Journal of Industrial Relations*, **30** (3), 361–404.

Edwards, P. (2007), 'The State of the Labour Process Debate after 25 Years: Some Reflections from Industrial Relations and Industrial Sociology', in *Notes for Remarks to Plenary Panel at the 25th International Labour Process Conference, Amsterdam*, April 2007, accessed at https://warwick.ac.uk/fac/soc/wbs/research/irru/publications/recentconf/pe_lpc07.pdf

Edwards, R. (1979), *Contested Terrain: The Transformation of the Workplace in the Twentieth Century*, Heinemann, London.

Farrell, D. and F. Greig (2016), *Paychecks, Paydays, and the Online Platform Economy*, JPMorgan Chase & Co. Institute, Washington DC.

Fine, B. and A. Saad Filho (2010), *Marx's Capital*, 4th edn, Pluto Press, London.

Fleischer, V. (2010), 'Regulatory Arbitrage', *Texas Law Review*, **89**, 227–75.

Florisson, R. and I. Mandl (2018), *Platform Work: Types and Implications for Work and Employment – Literature Review*, Eurofound, Dublin.

Forde, C., M. Stuart, S. Joyce, L. Oliver, D. Valizade, G. Alberti, K. Hardy, V. Trappmann, C. Umney and C. Carson (2017), *The Social Protection of Workers in the Platform Economy*, EMPL committee of the European parliament, D-G Internal Policies, European Commission, Brussels.

Friedman, A. L. (1977), *Industry and Labour: Class Struggle at Work and Monopoly Capitalism*, Vol. 82, Macmillan, London.

Gandini, A. (2019), 'Labour Process Theory and the Gig Economy', *Human Relations*, **72** (6), 1039–56.

Ghaffary, S. (2019), 'DoorDash is still pocketing workers' tips, almost a month after it promised to stop', *Vox Recode*, 20 August 2019, accessed at https://www.vox.com/recode/2019/8/20/20825937/doordash-tipping-policy-still-not-changed-food-delivery-app-gig-economy

Gilbert, B. (2019), 'Almost 30% of delivery drivers admit to taking food from an order, according to a new survey', *Business Insider*, 31 July 2019, accessed at https://www.businessinsider.com/uber-eats-delivery-drivers-eating-food-2019–7?r=US&IR=T

Griesbach, K., A. Reich, L. Elliott-Negri and R. Milkman (2019), 'Algorithmic Control in Platform Food Delivery Work', *Socius: Sociological Research for a Dynamic World*, **5**, 237802311987004.

Hall, J. V. and A. B. Krueger (2018), 'An Analysis of the Labor Market for Uber's Driver-Partners in the United States', *ILR Review*, **71** (3), 705–32.

Hall, J. V., J. J. Horton and D. T. Knoepfle (2019), 'Pricing Efficiently in Designed Markets: The Case of Ride-Sharing', *Semantic Scholar*, p. 76, accessed at https://www.semanticscholar.org/paper/Pricing-Efficiently-in-Designed-Markets%3A-The-Case-Hall-Horton/c96ad4e51587c3d7ed900f7a90da1d2dd86337bb

Harris, S. D. and A. B. Krueger (2015), *A Proposal for Modernizing Labor Laws for Twenty-First-Century Work: The "Independent Worker"*, Discussion Paper 2015–10, Brookings, Washington, DC.

Hill, S. (1976), *The Dockers: Class and Tradition in London*, Heinemann Educational Books, London.

Horton, J. J. and R. J. Zeckhauser (2016), *Owning, Using and Renting: Some Simple Economics of the "Sharing Economy"*, No. w22029, National Bureau of Economic Research, p. 42.

Howcroft, D. and B. Bergvall-Kåreborn (2019), 'A Typology of Crowdwork Platforms', *Work, Employment and Society*, **33** (1), 21–38.

Huws, U., N. H. Spencer, D. S. Syrdal and K. Holts (2017), *Work in the European Gig Economy: Research Results from the UK, Sweden, Germany, Austria, The Netherlands, Switzerland and Italy*, FEPS and Uni-Europa, Brussels.

Hyman, R. (1975), *Industrial Relations: A Marxist Introduction*, Macmillan, London.

Hyman, R. (1987), 'Strategy or Structure? Capital, Labour and Control', *Work, Employment & Society*, **1** (1), 25–55.

Irani, L. (2015), 'Difference and Dependence among Digital Workers: The Case of Amazon Mechanical Turk', *South Atlantic Quarterly*, **114** (1), 225–34.

Irani, L. C. and S. Silberman (2013), 'Turkopticon: Interrupting Worker Invisibility in Amazon Mechanical Turk', in *Proceedings of the SIGCHI Conference on Human Factors in Computing Systems – CHI '13*, Paris, France, ACM Press, p. 611.

Ivanova, M., J. Bronowicka, E. Kocher and A. Degner (2018), 'The App as a Boss? Control and Autonomy in Application-Based Management', *Arbeit | Grenze | Fluss – Work in Progress Interdisziplinärer Arbeitsforschung*, accessed at https://doi.org/10.11584/ARBEIT-GRENZE-FLUSS.2

Johnston, H. and C. Land-Kazlauskas (2018), *Organizing On-Demand: Representation, Voice, and Collective Bargaining in the Gig Economy*, 94, Geneva, International Labour Office, p. 54.

Joyce, S. (2020), 'Rediscovering the Cash Nexus, Again: Subsumption and the Labour–Capital Relation in Platform Work', *Capital & Class*, March 2020. doi:10.1177/0309816820906356

Joyce, S., D. Neumann, V. Trappmann et al. (2020), *A Global Struggle: Worker Protest in the Platform Economy*, ETUI Policy Brief, 2/2020, ETUI, Brussels.

Kaminska, I. (2016), 'Mythbusting Uber's valuation', FT Alphaville, *Financial Times*, 13 September 2016.

Kenney, M. and J. Zysman (2016), 'The Rise of the Platform Economy', *Issues in Science and Technology*, **32** (3), 61–9.

Khan, M. and A. Ram (2017), 'ECJ rules Uber can be regulated as taxi company', *Financial Times*, 20 December 2017.

Kokkodis, M. and P. G. Ipeirotis (2016), 'Reputation Transferability in Online Labor Markets', *Management Science*, **62** (6), 1687–1706.

Lazonick, W. (1979), 'Industrial Relations and Technical Change: The Case of the Self-acting Mule', *Cambridge Journal of Economics*, **3** (3), 231–62.

Lehdonvirta, V., O. Kässi, I. Hjorth, H. Barnard and M. Graham (2019), 'The Global Platform Economy: A New Offshoring Institution Enabling Emerging-Economy Microproviders', *Journal of Management*, **45** (2), 567–99.

Littler, C. R. (1982), *The Development of the Labour Process in Capitalist Societies: A Comparative Study of the Transformation of Work Organization in Britain, Japan, and the USA*, Heinemann Educational Publishers, London.

Mars, G. (1982), *Cheats at Work: An Anthropology of Workplace Crime*, George Allen and Unwin, London.

Marx, K. (1976), *Capital: A Critique of Political Economy*, Vol.1, Penguin, London.

McCulloch, A. (2019), 'Deliveroo and Uber Eats face questions over worker black market', *Personnel Today*, 7 January 2019, accessed at https://www.personneltoday.com/hr/deliveroo-and-uber-eats-face-black-market-worker-questions/

Moody, K. (2018), *On New Terrain*, Haymarket, Chicago.

Moore, D. P. V. (2018), *The Threat of Physical and Psychosocial Violence and Harassment in Digitalized Work*, International Labour Office, p. 54.

Moore, P. V. and S. Joyce (2020), 'Black Box or Hidden Abode? The Expansion and Exposure of Platform Work Managerialism', *Review of International Political Economy*, **27** (4), 1–23.

NYTWA (2020), New York Taxi Workers' Alliance, http://www.nytwa.org/

Parrott, J. and M. Reich (2018), 'An Earnings Standard for New York City's App-based Drivers: Economic Analysis and Policy Assessment', Report for the New York City Taxi and Limousine Commission, Center for New York City Affairs, New School, New York.

Park, J. (2021), 'Court rules California gig worker initiative is unconstitutional, a setback to Uber and Lyft', *Sacramento Bee*, 20 August 2021, accessed at https://www.sacbee.com/news/politics-government/capitol-alert/article253647838.html#storylink=cpy

Raval, N. and P. Dourish (2016), 'Standing Out from the Crowd: Emotional Labor, Body Labor, and Temporal Labor in Ridesharing', in *Proceedings of the 19th ACM Conference on Computer-Supported Cooperative Work & Social Computing – CSCW '16*, San Francisco, California, ACM Press, pp. 97–107.

Ravenelle, A. J. (2017), 'Sharing Economy Workers: Selling, not Sharing', *Cambridge Journal of Regions, Economy and Society*, **10** (2), 281–95.

Rosenblat, A. and L. Stark (2016), 'Algorithmic Labor and Information Asymmetries: A Case Study of Uber's Drivers', *International Journal of Communication*, **10**, 3758–84.

Salehi, N., L. C. Irani, M. S. Bernstein, A. Alkhatib, E. Ogbe, K. Milland and Clickhappier (2015), 'We Are Dynamo: Overcoming Stalling and Friction in Collective Action for Crowd Workers', in *Proceedings of the 33rd Annual ACM Conference on Human Factors in Computing Systems – CHI '15*, Seoul, Republic of Korea, ACM Press, pp. 1621–30.

Samuel, R. (1977), 'Workshop of the World: Steam Power and Hand Technoloy in Mid-Victorian Britain', *History Workshop Journal*, **3** (1), 6–72.

Schloss, D. F. (1898), *Methods of Industrial Remuneration*, Williams and Norgate, London.

Schmidt, F. A. (2017), *Digital Labour Markets in the Platform Economy*, Friedrich-Ebert-Stiftung, p. 32.

Schörpf, P., J. Flecker, A. Schönauer and H. Eichmann (2017), 'Triangular Love-Hate: Management and Control in Creative Crowdworking', *New Technology, Work and Employment*, **32** (1), 43–58.

Shapiro, A. (2018), 'Between Autonomy and Control: Strategies of Arbitrage in the "On-demand" Economy', *New Media & Society*, **20** (8), 2954–71.

Sharma, P. (2020), 'Digitalisation and Precarious Work Practices in Alternative Economies: Work Organisation and Work Relations in E-cab Services', *Economic and Industrial Democracy*, 0143831X2092446.

Srnicek, N. (2016), *Platform Capitalism*, Polity Press, Cambridge.

Stanford, J. (2017), 'The Resurgence of Gig Work: Historical and Theoretical Perspectives', *Economic and Labour Relations Review*, **28** (3), 382–401.

Storey, J. (1985), 'The Means of Management Control', *Sociology*, **19** (2), 193–211.

Tassinari, A. and V. Maccarrone (2020), 'Riders on the Storm: Workplace Solidarity among Gig Economy Couriers in Italy and the UK', *Work, Employment and Society*, **34**(1), 35–54.

Thompson, P. (1990), 'Crawling from the Wreckage: The Labour Process and the Politics of Production', in D. Knights and H. Willmott (eds), *Labour Process Theory*, Macmillan, Basingstoke, pp. 95–124.

Thompson, P. and C. Smith (2010), 'Debating Labour Process Theory and the Sociology of Work', in P. Thompson and C. Smith (eds), *Working Life: Renewing Labour Process Analysis*, Palgrave Macmillan, Basingstoke, pp. 11–28.

Vallas, S. and J. B. Schor (2020), 'What do Platforms Do? Understanding the Gig Economy', *Annual Review of Sociology*, **46**, 273–94.

van Doorn, N. and A. Badger (2020), 'Platform Capitalism's Hidden Abode: Producing Data Assets in the Gig Economy', *Antipode*, anti.12641.

Veen, A., T. Barratt and C. Goods (2020), 'Platform-Capital's "App-etite" for Control: A Labour Process Analysis of Food-Delivery Work in Australia', *Work, Employment & Society*, **34** (3), 388–406.

Webb, S. and B. Webb (1902), *Industrial Democracy*, Longman, London.

Wood, A. J., M. Graham, V. Lehdonvirta and I. Hjorth (2018), 'Good Gig, Bad Gig: Autonomy and Algorithmic Control in the Global Gig Economy', *Work, Employment and Society*, **33** (1), 56–75.

Woodcock, J. (2018), 'Digital Labour and Workers' Organisation', in M. Atzeni and I. Ness (eds), *Global Perspectives on Workers' and Labour Organizations*, Springer, Singapore.

Woodcock, J. (2020), 'The Algorithmic Panopticon at Deliveroo: Measurement, Precarity, and the Illusion of Control', *Ephemera*, 21.

Woodcock, J. and M. R. Johnson (2018), 'Gamification: What It Is, and How to Fight It', *The Sociological Review*, **66** (3), 542–58.

Wu, Q., H. Zhang, Z. Li and K. Liu (2019), 'Labor Control in the Gig Economy: Evidence from Uber in China', *Journal of Industrial Relations*, **61** (4), 574–96.

8. Collective organization in platform companies in Argentina: between trade union traditions and adaptive strategies

Cora Arias, Nicolás Diana Menéndez and Julieta Haidar

INTRODUCTION

This study is a contribution to the debate around the possibilities of workers' collective action and union organization in platform capitalism (Vandaele 2018; Collier et al. 2017; Tassinari and Maccarrone 2019). In brief, this debate engages with the organizational difficulties facing workers who find themselves in a paradigm of work in which companies promote the figure of the entrepreneur and self-employment, refusing to recognize the existence of an employment relationship, in practice as well as before the law.

Various studies (Jolly 2016; Rosenblat 2016; Vandaele 2018) assert that there is greater potential for workers' organization on the platforms known as *on demand*, through apps; meaning those for which work is done offline, taking a physical form, in a specific circumscribed territory (De Stefano 2016). In this perspective, these characteristics create better conditions for workers to form alliances, a situation which is rather more difficult on *crowdwork* platforms, which have hundreds of workers spread across the internet.

In this vein, the study produced by Collier et al. (2017) emphasizes that Uber workers find themselves in more advantageous conditions for coordinated action, due to four characteristics: a high level of control over working conditions, Uber itself being the single target of complaints shared by drivers, the existence of physical spaces where drivers can meet up during their working hours (such as airports), and the emergence of blogs and forums on which information circulates. However, these authors maintain that it has not been transport unions but rather 'substitute' actors (other unions, alternative labour organizations, lawyers) who have more often taken the lead in defending the drivers' interests and demands, generally in courts and legislatures.

In summary, the characteristics of labour organizations on the platforms pose serious challenges for workers' coordination and collective action, and even in more advantageous situations (on offline platforms), it is not clear that the unions can take on the task. Thus, the question of the effectiveness of the unions as the main organizational form for workers is a particularly pertinent one in the light of the new challenges engendered by platform capitalism. The question is whether an institution born more than a century ago to confront the exploitation of factory labour, after almost five decades of an offensive on the part of capital and the worsening of working conditions and rights, has the capacity to restore a relative balance between labour and capital in the face of algorithmic exploitation.

In our consideration this is a complex question, and in order to attempt to respond it is necessary to move beyond a decontextualized standpoint. We understand unions to be a socio-historical category which has gone through transformations along with changes to the society of which it is a partial expression. As Hyman points out, treating unions as though they were formal organizations plucked out of their social context is to disregard the impact of the institutional framework of power which the unions continuously interact with (Hyman 1975). In this regard, analysing union responses to platform capitalism requires that we consider a group of aspects with the aim of outlining the complexity of the phenomenon; among other aspects: global tendencies and pressures, business strategies, the characteristics of labour relations models, and types of unions.

In a prior study (Haidar et al. 2020), we analysed how the characteristics of algorithmic management, i.e. the supervisory practices, governance and control of the workers carried out by algorithms (Möhlmann and Zalmanson 2017), create conditions that obstruct or facilitate workers' organization, and how those organizations harness those resources of power in order to resist the platform capitalists' offensive and advance their demands. To put it another way, in that study we showed that in order to understand the characteristics of workers' organizational processes, it is necessary to take a view which transcends the organization itself and analyse how the platform companies organize the labour process.

On the basis of the progress made in our research, we understand that algorithmic management stakes out possibilities and limitations for the construction and use of resources of union power. In this chapter we aim to incorporate another dimension into our analysis which engages with the ways in which the unions respond to the challenges of platform work: the trade union traditions.

For the purposes of this study, we define trade union traditions as the ensemble of discursive and extra-discursive practices that influence the modalities of intervention, the styles of political-union construction, and the levels of institutional plasticity of a union organization. *Modalities of intervention* refers to the repertoires of collective action, the *styles of political-union construction* relate to types of leadership and the modes of decision-making, and *institutional plasticity* refers to the capacity to interpret and process the changes occurring in the composition of the workforce and the activities it engages in. Traditions are social constructions, and are therefore dynamic, and the object of transformations and disputes.

In this chapter we analyse the responses of two unions organizing platform delivery workers in Argentina: the Association of Platform Workers (APP), and the Association of Motorcyclists, Messengers and Services (ASIMM) that possess characteristics associated with two different union traditions. Expressed schematically: the first union is more associated with a rank and file type of organization, with horizontal and combative features, while the latter is closer to a hierarchical, vertical, bargaining-oriented organization.

This case is relevant because in Argentina the unions hold significant social and political power and continue to constitute the main form of workers' organization in spite of the processes which have weakened the workers' movement, from successive military coups throughout the 20th century to the neoliberal offensive which was initiated in the mid-1970s and intensified in the 1990s. The processes of organization and struggle undertaken by delivery workers are an expression of this strength. On the one hand, APP was founded in 2018 as the first platform workers' union in Latin America, when the structural conditions and the profile of the workers seemed to deter organization. On the other hand, ASIMM is an occupation-based union (couriers) that pre-existed the phenomenon of platforms and which faces a challenge from these new companies, as well as the new group of workers with different profiles and dynamics.

On the basis of qualitative research conducted in the city of Buenos Aires,[1] we analyse the positions and actions taken by each organization in the light of the algorithmic management of delivery platforms, according to the characteristics of traditional unions they adopt, not in terms of stereotypes or fixed models, but as extracted types which were constructed in the analysis (McKinney 1966). The practices of APP and ASIMM are not immutable, but rather undergo transformations in the process of interaction between both organizations, the workers, the companies and governments.

The Argentinian experience is of interest insofar as it highlights the fact that although the platform companies are indeed powerful, and organize the labour process in such a way that the existence of employment relations is obscured, which creates huge obstacles for workers' organization and struggle, there are several dimensions that can contribute to combating these difficulties: the degree of power held by unions in society, the characteristics of traditional unions, the levels of institutional plasticity of the unions, the winning of partial victories in a longer term struggle, and the political-ideological orientations of governments.

This chapter is arranged into four sections: first, we outline a brief characterization of the main union traditions in Argentina; second, we describe the development of delivery platforms in Argentina; and in the third and fourth sections we analyse the two organizational experiences of delivery workers, taking into consideration the dimensions of analysis of union traditions: styles of construction, modalities of political-union intervention, and institutional plasticity. Lastly, in the final conclusions we analyse the two experiences of organizing and highlight what the main contributions of this study are to the research field of unions and platform work.

1   THE UNION MODEL IN ARGENTINA

From their birth at the end of the 19th century, workers' organizations have been a key political actor in Argentina. Anarchist and communist ideas transmitted by immigrants arriving mainly from Italy and Spain over that period exerted a strong gravitational influence during the emergence of local labour unionism (Suriano 2001): they formed cooperatives, unions and associations that delivered social services to the workers and also organized protest action and struggles such as strikes and boycotts. With the assumption of Juan Perón's government (1943–1955), workers acquired new rights and unions multiplied in number while increasing their power, coming to constitute the 'backbone' of Peronism.

The vagaries of Argentinian political and economic history affected the unions, which enjoyed two periods in which they held greater power and others in which they were displaced from power. However, even in the most adverse conditions for workers, the unions continued to wield authority and their participation in the political arena was indisputable.

Union life in Argentina is governed by the Trade Union Law which establishes that workers have the right to freely form union organizations to defend their economic interests (according to official data from 2016, there are currently 3,376 unions). The law requires that organizations submit an application to the Ministry of Labour in order to obtain state recognition, requesting registration in a special union register. Once that application has been completed, unions acquire 'union registration' and along with it a series of rights. However, the Ministry only grants 'union recognition' to the most representative union in the sector (that with the greatest number of dues-paying members), which confers exclusivity or priority in relation to certain rights, fundamentally collective bargaining rights (according to the official data of the 3,376 registered unions only 1,667 have state recognition).

Despite state incentives for workers' organizational unity, in contemporary Argentina there are various cases of union diversity and coexistence in the same economic sector (Arias 2010). Furthermore, various rulings from the Supreme Court of Justice have ushered in the possibility of constructing rank and file organizations with the same rights as the unions granted state recognition.

Over the period of their existence, we can identify two major union traditions in Argentina which here we reconstruct and characterize with the aim of being able to interpret the experiences of ASIMM and APP more clearly. In a schematic way, we define the first tendency as being bargaining oriented, and the other as more confrontational.

The *bargaining tradition* in Argentina is characterized by a vertical style of political-union construction, featuring limited plurality, and decision-making capacity concentrated in the hands of the leadership. With regards to the *modalities of intervention*, political-institutional bargaining with governments and companies takes precedence, and the resource of collective action is scarcely utilized. Similarly, in terms of *institutional plasticity*, we can observe a high degree of permeability with regards to the context, and a tendency towards frequent appeals to the administrative authorities.

The *confrontational tradition* features a *style of political-union construction* that incorporates a larger degree of plurality and prioritizes rank and file decision-making in assemblies, with less static leaderships. Collective action plays a prominent role in its *modalities of intervention*, with political-institutional bargaining as a complementary resource. With regards to its *institutional plasticity*, this tradition is characterized by greater permeability when processing new identities and demands.

In the 1990s these traditions found expression in two main union confederations: the General Confederation of Labour (CGT), founded in 1930, represents the bargaining tradition,[2] and the Argentinian Workers' Confederation (CTA), established in 1992 as an opposition to market reforms, represents the confrontational tradition. The crystallization of both of these traditions into two separate confederations should not obscure the historical lineage of workers' organizations in Argentina, which Gilly (1986) described as the 'Argentinian anomaly'. This anomaly lies in the high levels of activism and politicization of the rank and file in the workplaces, which historically has put pressure on unions to make more substantial demands beyond the political-institutional alliances made by the union leadership.

The other aspect of this anomaly is institutional power. Indeed, a noteworthy feature of the Argentinian union traditions is the greater orientation of demands to the government rather than to capital, which Bunel (1992) points out as a fundamentally political hallmark of action, above all the level of the union leaderships (Diana Menéndez 2017).

In between these poles of bargaining and confrontation, attempts to reach agreements with governments and rank and file movements, the dynamic of organizing the delivery workers' struggle in Buenos Aires developed. The two experiences which we analyse in this chapter, APP and ASIMM, enable us to explore the diverse modes of confronting the challenges represented by the new modalities of management and exploitation. To further that aim, some of the questions which orient our research into the positions and actions taken by the unions are: How to organize a new group of workers who often do not recognize themselves as such? How are demands presented to companies that refuse to recognize the employment relationship? What are the regulatory proposals that could guarantee rights without relinquishing the benefits of autonomy?

2   DELIVERY PLATFORMS IN ARGENTINA

The delivery platforms operating in Argentina are Rappi, Glovo and PedidosYa.[3] These were established in almost ideal conditions: (1) a neoliberal government (under the presidency of Mauricio Macri from 2015–2019) which promoted entrepreneurship and the dismantling of institutions which protected labour rights; (2) a labour market characterized by rising unemployment (7.2 per cent in the fourth quarter of 2017, 9.1 per cent in the same period in 2018 according to official data), and the precarization of working conditions; (3) the arrival of various groups of immigrants, mostly Venezuelans, needing to quickly find work; and (4) the pre-existence of food delivery as a pattern of consumption.

Indeed, the appearance of these companies was facilitated by the government by a law passed in 2017 ('Support for Entrepreneurial Capital'), which expedited the creation of businesses with negligible capital, in only 24 hours. Likewise, the government promoted a labour reform which included a new legal figure in Argentinian legislation: the autonomous employee. According to the government, this figure would enable a new regulatory framework for new types of workers, such as riders, but the unions and labour lawyers opposed the initiative warning that the project would flexibilize and increase the precarization of employment, starting with riders but later extending to all workers.

Although the government promoted the operation of these new companies, the delivery service model is not a new one in Argentina; the difference being that while previously businesses employed their own delivery workers or subcontracted other companies to provide them with delivery workers, the new platforms use technology based on algorithmic management to connect supposedly independent workers with customers and providers. Therefore, riders are considered to be self-employed workers who can work when and how they wish, without there being any employment relationship from the perspective of the companies themselves, which is concealed by the discourse of entrepreneurship and algorithmic management. In fact, while the companies promise that riders can connect how and when they wish, in the concrete practices we can observe that the algorithms organize and control the labour process and the workers: they constantly monitor and assess the riders' behaviour, implement decisions automatically, and modify their working and payment practices and the rules of the game unilaterally and without prior warning (Haidar et al. 2020).

Currently the different delivery companies operating in Argentina conform to these characteristics. While PedidosYa had started to operate in Argentina in 2010 as a go-between for providers and customers, and later began to hire workers under a contractual arrangement, after the arrival of Rappi and Glovo onto the scene, it adapted to the new management model and started to use independent riders without any type of employment relationship. The fact that PedidosYa was the first platform company to use contracted employees meant that ASIMM, the pre-existing union, became the main organizer and representative of its workers. APP, in contrast, was founded by activists working for Glovo and Rappi, with the latter being the strictest in terms of controls, and with the worst track record of mistreatment and lack of protection for workers (Haidar et al. 2020). Over the following paragraphs we will analyse in detail the positions and actions taken by both unions in relation to the workers, the companies and the government.

3   APP: FROM RANK AND FILE ORGANIZATION TO POLITICAL OUTLET

Simón Rodriguez, the famous Venezuelan educator, coined a phrase that two centuries later would be put into practice by some of his compatriots: 'Either we invent or we fail'. In October 2018 a group of riders applied to the Secretary of Labour for the Nation for union registration for the Association of Platform Workers (APP), the first platform workers' union in Latin America. The union's constitution – still not recognized by the Ministry for Labour – was the expression of a preceding organizational process carried out by platform delivery workers in the city of Buenos Aires.

3.1   Styles of Political-Union Construction

The organization of work on delivery platforms opened the possibility for workers to meet in a new workplace: the streets. Delivery workers are highly visible (they ride bicycles or motorbikes with large eye-catching red, yellow or orange boxes) and they are a ubiquitous presence on bicycle lanes and the pavements outside restaurants while they wait for food packages to deliver. Rappi riders have the most free time for meetings as the company does not organize delivery shifts, while on Glovo and PedidosYa the distribution of shifts and the permanent assigning of deliveries means that spare time allowing communication between workers is reduced.

The possibility of face-to-face meetings and the discontent generated by the maltreatment workers experience from the companies (sudden unilateral changes to working conditions, lack of response to queries and proposals posed by the delivery workers, delays in payments, etc.) created the conditions in which Rappi riders have become the architects of collective organization. The delivery workers, predominantly Venezuelans and Colombians, began to share – first on a face-to-face basis, and then through WhatsApp groups – their concerns and complaints about abuses on the app, which was crucial to constructing a commonly held interest and an identity as workers. After virtual meetings they developed the process of organization and started to hold face-to-face meetings, taking the form of a kind of informal assembly which was held in the main neighbourhoods of Buenos Aires.

Gradually, without any external guidance to signpost the way, problems which a priori seemed of a personal nature began to be constructed as collective demands: working hours, rest periods, health insurance and health and safety, wages, and transparency of information. Driven by a sensation of injustice, the workers' organization began to grow from below. WhatsApp groups were set up, along with meeting points for each of the main neighbourhoods in the city, and in each one a representative or leader emerged who collected complaints and offered advice. The traditional Argentinian figure of the rank and file workplace delegate returned through this new experience. Workers we interviewed perceived this phenomenon as follows: 'She (an activist) is a lion … she is the struggle, a fighter. You (Argentinians) are world famous for your unions and mobilizations: that's her' (personal interview with Rappi worker).

'If he (an activist) said today we won't work, in Belgrano (a neighbourhood in Buenos Aires) nothing would move and that's a third of the platform' (personal interview with a lawyer for APP).

As mobilization theory (Tilly 1978; Kelly 1998; Darlington 2002) and historical experience suggests, the leaders constituted the main organizers of discontent; it was they who provoked the transition from complaints to direct action which we will analyse below: strikes, boycotts and mobilizations. It was of crucial importance to the process that a group of labour lawyers with strong links to the Confederation of Argentinian Workers (CTA) approached the assemblies and their leaders. The CTA, as mentioned above, is a confederation rooted in the rank and file union tradition and open to the organization of new groups of workers. These lawyers helped the riders, who were mostly migrants with no prior union experience, to develop an awareness of the need to organize their union, APP.

The formal constitution of the union, with members and delegates, represented more of a means than an end, in other words it was a path to obtaining recognition of the employment relationship (Haidar et al. 2020). The argument was as follows: there is an economic, organizational and legal relationship, there is also a union, therefore there is a relationship of employment.

As occurred in Argentina at other historical moments in which a new occupation with new workers and modes of working appeared (such as call centres in the first few years of the 21st century), the emergence of a new union was not the first option chosen by the workers. On the contrary, the riders initially contacted the pre-existing union ASIMM, but the relationship proved to be highly conflictive; the riders' leaders successfully organized struggles with a collective character, they wanted to make progress with their demands, and they found themselves in conflict with a union that wanted to control them. A worker explained it in this way:

> When we left (a meeting with company representatives after a strike) … as if by magic representatives from the motorbike couriers' union (ASIMM) appeared to tell us that they were going to help us, that they were going to negotiate with the company because this couldn't be allowed to happen, that they were going to join us, blah blah blah; they invited us to go to the union building the next day (…) What ASIMM did was they told us to calm down, not to talk to the media, that they had resolved everything, that they were going to hire employees. It turns out that the agreement was only to hire 22 workers per month, when there were 6,000 of us registered. (Personal interview with Rappi worker)

ASIMM's efforts to contain the activists included threats and physical attacks on APP representatives, practices which are well-established in a tradition for which the struggle for union control between different factions had long been expressed through violence, and practices which persist till today in a minority of male-dominated unions. After these experiences, the links between the riders' leaders and ASIMM were severed completely, and their paths bifurcated as the former set up their own union.

3.2   Modalities of Intervention

The dynamic guiding APP was marked by direct action as the main protest mechanism: boycotts, mobilization and strikes. On the one hand, the workers took advantage of their high degree of visibility in the city of Buenos Aires and the discussion of the phenomenon of platforms in the media to make their demands public. In a kind of cultural boycott, they used social networks and invitations to participate in television programmes in order to denounce their exploitative working conditions and in that way tarnish the reputation of the platform companies.

A *boycott* is a tactic used by old trade unions and is fundamental to the service sector. In this case the measure was successful, taking into consideration that the issue became widely discussed (in public opinion) and that the companies' spokespeople had to make public statements defending themselves.

On the other hand, the riders also organized mobilizations, a tool generally used by Argentinian unions, above all when the possibilities of calling a strike are limited (due to the union's uncertain capacity to win its members to the action, or the limited impact that the strike would make), or when the aim is to have a political influence on the government rather than the company. The mobilizations organized by the delivery workers corresponded with a combination of these factors. First, the riders demonstrated outside the companies' offices with the goal of being acknowledged and gaining admittance. Once the organizational process was well under way, the delivery workers also mobilized outside the Secretariat for Labour in order to demand employment regulations. On certain occasions they attracted the support of social organizations who joined the mobilizations, realizing the possibility of articulating the struggle with other precarious sectors.

In this case the action was unsuccessful, the national government and the local government of the city of Buenos Aires did not acquiesce to the workers' demands; on the contrary, they ideologically and practically supported the companies. However, thinking beyond the immediate outcome, the action taken shows that the delivery workers rapidly absorbed lessons from the traditional Argentinian unions and availed themselves of a traditional recourse in union history in Argentina: seeking protection and negotiation with the government, an aspect which we will explore in more detail below.

The third and most resonant tactic was the strike, a worker's right which is deeply enshrined in Argentinian law. The labour process was simultaneously a learning process for the workers, who with time learnt that if they refused to carry out deliveries, the business would grind to a complete halt and the platforms would be adversely affected.

With this idea at the forefront, Rappi riders took strike action using an original technique: one Sunday in July 2018 at a peak business hour they met in the commercially busiest neighbourhood squares, remained connected to the app, but made no deliveries for over an hour. In order to carry out this protest action they needed the participation of a large number of workers, coordinated geographically with the assistance of the WhatsApp groups.

The strike was effective, since as could be predicted the orders accumulated in local businesses, causing huge losses for the platforms. Multiple phenomena were expressed in this protest action: the worker's capacity for organization and leadership, but also the limits of rank and file action in platform capitalism. After the strike, the company invited the activists to participate in talks and responded positively to the demand for an increase in delivery rates. However, sometime later the activists were blocked from the app: effectively the company had sacked them. In this way Rappi was able to restrain the workers, generating fear and seriously weakening their collective action. This was partly a reflection of the limitations of the rank and file action taken by workers confronting companies which hold tremendous power at a global scale, with the backing of governments which allow them to operate without regulations, and the characteristics of algorithmic management which impose order, which control and which punish surreptitiously.

3.3   Institutional Plasticity

In spite of the lack of clarity or agreement about the possible modalities of employment (indefinite employment contracts, day labour or some form of self-employment), the demands of the workers organized through APP were focused on winning a raft of protection encompassing working hours, rates, health insurance, health and safety. This set of demands was mainly aimed at the state, as a union organizer explained:

> … we are asking the state to stop taking an indifferent stance because this should have been controlled from the outset. Who is it that regulates? The state (…) If the state doesn't regulate this then who will? (…) The law covers these problems and has ways to deal with them, what we need is for the state to take action against these companies that are waving around the false slogan of freelance and are creating precarity at a thousand kilometres an hour. (Personal interview, APP activist)

This union sought to achieve regulation for the work and the employment relation, and did not promote or support a strategy aimed at prohibiting this type of work altogether. This became evident in their disagreement with the ruling of a judge in the city of Buenos Aires who, dealing with the case of the platforms' infringement of urban health and safety measures, ordered their suspension (which was never carried out).

The prosecution of the activity of the platform companies had been advocated by ASIMM in a strategy which, as we shall examine in the following section, was intended to pressure the companies either to conform to the typical modality of employment or to close down. This prohibitionist stance could not repress the demands of workers who above all wanted to maintain their source of work and the relative freedoms that the platform system permits.

APP, by contrast, appealed to the courts to demand the reinstatement of leaders who had been blocked (fired) for their union activity, and in this way they aimed to demonstrate the existence of an employment relationship with the company. These court cases alternated between progress and repeated setbacks over the course of 2019 and still have no definitive outcome. The interesting aspect of this process is that the union, after having been weakened by the effective dismissal of its organizers and suffering a depleted workers' participation, began to move away from the practice of rank and file mobilization and towards a strategy sharing more in common with the political-institutional tradition.

In interviews we conducted in 2019 with new rank and file workers (it is an occupation with high levels of turnover), we observed that very few were aware of the existence of APP and its previous struggles, that they were broadly satisfied with the platforms, and that they had no interest in union organizing. The union activists we interviewed during the same period remarked that the workers were wary of unions due to the fear of being dismissed or losing their job as a result of a court ruling that could force the companies to suspend their activities.

Along with this characterization of the relation of forces in terms of the relative weakness of the union as compared with the platforms, the activists incorporated the most traditional mode of defining strategy particular to Argentinian unions: interpreting and adapting to the political conjuncture by taking into account who is currently in governing positions of power, and how they could benefit or harm them. This reflects a high degree of institutional plasticity, meaning a capacity to interpret and process transformations in occupations and the composition of the labour force, changing union strategies as a result.

Hence, activists who a year previously had organized assemblies and protest action, now placed their hopes in the idea that a change of government in Argentina would benefit them (in October 2019 Alberto Fernández of the more worker-friendly Peronist party was elected president). Their expectations regarding the new government were: that APP would be granted legal recognition through administrative channels (union registration) which the previous government had denied them; that through legislative channels it would pass legislation to regulate the occupation and enshrine labour rights; and that through legal channels a resolution would be enacted which would compel companies to reinstate sacked union leaders. With regards to the outcomes of these expectations, it is important to point out that halfway through 2021, there has been no advance towards the legal recognition of APP, nor towards a legal resolution regarding the dismissal cases; however, the new government is drafting a project to enact a 'statute' for platform workers,[4] which would be a regulatory tool that establishes rights and obligations for workers with highly flexible working hours (in Argentina there is an already existing statute for domestic, rural and construction workers among others).

The reconstruction and analysis of the development of delivery workers' organization in a new union reveals various elements that contribute to thinking about different union strategies towards large platform companies. First, the importance of the historical legacy of unionism in Argentina given that the (young, migrant) workers took an early decision to form a union instead of another more original type of organization as occurred in other countries where workers faced the same phenomenon. Second, the tradition of a rank and file, participative and direct action-oriented unionism has enabled workers to achieve certain progress with their demands but has also revealed its limitations in confrontation with the power of the platforms. Among these achievements, one which stands out is the construction of an identity for the riders as workers and as part of a workers' collective in opposition to an employer-other which the platform companies represent; raising platform work as an issue on the public and governmental agenda; and winning an immediate demand, an increase in rates paid, as a result of an innovative protest action, the virtual strike. At the same time, the experience highlights the fact that when confronting powerful companies without government support, direct action without institutional union recognition has serious limitations, as exemplified by the fact that after agreeing to increase delivery rates the companies continued to operate without recognizing the employment relationship, and then turned to a classic tactic of industrial conflict: following the strike, union activists were sacked (blocked), with a subsequent disciplinary process applied to the whole group of workers. Third, the institutional plasticity of the union proved to be key to recognizing the limitations of direct action and shifting to pursuing a political-institutional strategy, a practice which is familiar to the bargaining tradition of unions in Argentina. Fourth, a government with a political-ideological orientation which is more favourable to workers can indeed contribute to resolving conflicts via political channels; conflicts that, given an unfavourable correlation of forces, would be difficult to resolve through industrial action.

4   ASIMM: A MODEL TO DISMANTLE

ASIMM is a union with state recognition which adheres to the most rigid union model here called bargaining, although it has a relatively recent history. It was founded in 2001 to represent couriers who were employed by small and medium-sized businesses. The sector was disrupted by the emergence of platforms, the implementation of online administrative procedures, and the expansion of e-commerce, which overall had the effect of reducing the demand for courier services. Along with the decline of the sector ASIMM lost members; only a few years previously the union had around 5,000 members, and the number fell to less than half that in 2019.

The abrupt decline of membership and the radical transformations in the sector called in to question the validity of the established union model.

Likewise, the emergence of a new union (APP) reflects the inability of the established union to adequately deal with the working conditions, demands and expectations of a new group of workers. However, ASIMM went through a process of relative adaptation, shifting from very rigid positions towards greater flexibility.

4.1   Styles of Political-Union Construction

ASIMM is affiliated to the CGT, the oldest and most traditional of the Argentinian union confederations. The iconography associated with ASIMM, both on social network sites as well as at their offices and headquarters, is replete with symbols associated with Perón's leadership, with Catholicism and nationalism; all features of a conservative political-ideological orientation. Furthermore, courier services are carried out on motorbikes and its workers are strongly associated with a masculine 'biker' culture and heavy metal. In fact, there is no woman in the upper echelons of the union.

In contrast with that tradition, the appearance of platforms attracting a new group of young migrant workers on bicycles, and with many women (although still not constituting a majority), changed the characteristics of the rank and file. The new workers became objects of suspicion for the union, as an organizer expressed it:

> ... There is a shocking problem here that there are kids from Glovo who steal from each other, they eat the food orders ... 'I'll order some food myself, I'll eat it, and then I'll say that my customer didn't want the order but actually I ate it' ... It's all just anarchy ... There's a photo on Google of a guy that ordered a pizza and they ate half of it before he got it delivered ... . (Personal interview, ASIMM leader)

Thus, ASIMM was unreceptive to the demands that the new generation of workers were raising, among them the possibility of exercising the benefit of labour rights while also conserving their autonomy in relation to working hours. In this regard, the union defended a more traditional concept of employment which implied, among other aspects, fixed working hours:

> A kid from Rappi said 'I want to be registered', and we said 'but it would be good if you knew which days you are going to work ... Friday, Saturday and Sunday at least', and he answered 'no, on Fridays I play football and Tuesdays I can't work ...', so actually do you want to work at all? (Personal interview, ASIMM leader)

From the perspective of the traditional interpretive framework of the union, the new demands and interests that the workers proposed were alien to them, something which found expression in the thwarted dialogue with the workers who would eventually go on to set up APP. Over time, with the growth of the number of platform workers and the emergence of APP, ASIMM found itself obliged to modify its discourse and accept the existence of a new labour force: young women and men, a large section of whom rode bicycles (very little in common with biker culture), and a majority of whom were Venezuelan migrants.

4.2 Modalities of Intervention

ASIMM's first intervention into the conflict took place immediately following the strike organized by Rappi workers described above. One of the recommendations the union made was to not discuss the strike publicly in the media, which is an approach that stems from the union tradition prioritizing bargaining and conceives of conflict as a last resort. Thus, ASIMM approached Rappi to negotiate the hiring of a limited number of workers as contracted employees, a position that was rejected both by the company and by the rank and file leaders who saw this bargaining position as a betrayal of their collective demands. This, added to the violent intimidation of the rank and file activists, marked a parting of the ways between ASIMM and the workers who would later organize themselves through APP.

After the negotiations collapsed, ASIMM implemented new modalities of intervention and made a turn towards collective action, principally mobilizations outside public institutions and 'noise demonstrations' (a gathering of workers with implements that make noise to attract attention) outside company offices. A leader describes it:

> We organized marches to the Ministry, last November we held a mobilization at the obelisk [a famous monument in central Buenos Aires] with the Argentine Federation of Transport Workers to see if we could raise public awareness a bit … . (Personal interview, ASIMM leader)

The mobilization at the obelisk, supported by other transport unions, placed the debates and demands in a context with broader social resonance: provoking a public debate about the conditions of platform workers. Similarly, the conflict which was sparked off in PedidosYa towards the end of 2018, when the company dismissed 400 registered workers in order to shift to a new model of self-employed delivery workers, motivated the union to support the sacked workers. On that occasion the workers decided to occupy an administrative office belonging to the company.

This marked a turning point for ASIMM, which from then on began to collaborate with and support the delivery workers. While the dismissals directly impacted the main rank and file base of the union, as they were contracted workers, the action taken by ASIMM forged links with other workers who valued the close relationship with an already established union structure:

> ... it was more a question of acceptance, of lowering our guard with people from ASIMM ... We started to realize that there was a lot of prejudice against ASIMM, and we got to know them, they were there and it was the only political group that stepped in and dealt with the sackings and made it a much wider issue ... they opened up a lot of spaces for us in the union and a lot of places where we could also help the rest of the workforce ... . (Personal interview, PedidosYa activist)

The visibility of the conflicts and the threat of a rank and file organization in competition for the representation of platform workers encouraged ASIMM to modify their modalities of intervention and relax their resistance to incorporating new workers.

4.3   Institutional Plasticity

Initially, ASIMM clung firmly to the institutional logic which leaves no space for the representation of informal workers. Even the union itself had institutional barriers to incorporating new workers:

> the statute says that we can register employed workers, even though affiliation is voluntary, it's just a question of joining ... We can't enrol them in the system because there has to be an employer, we can't give them a membership number to be more specific ... . (Personal interview, ASIMM leader)

The union strategy seems to exclusively revolve around demanding from the administrative authorities that the platform companies formally employ their workers, recognizing the employment relationship and thus subscribing to the collective bargaining agreement. There does not seem to be a strategy of encompassing the diverse forms of work that would provide leadership to and empower the organization of rank and file workers. On the contrary, from the union's perspective, the state was the only actor that could, through political-institutional channels, resolve the problems that arose as a result of the new mode of working: 'Whenever we noticed that the company breached a regulation, we reported it, the problem is that if the state, which should be penalizing infractions, does nothing, we have our hands tied ...' (personal interview, ASIMM leader).

The demands aimed at pressuring the state and the companies included a strategy to ban the new form of work for breaching the existing regulations, but in a politically adverse context (the neoliberal government of Mauricio Macri between 2015 and 2019) that was ineffective, above all due to the unfavourable balance of forces with regards to the power of the companies. Given these limitations on the deployment of a traditional bargaining strategy aiming to subsume platform delivery work under existing institutional frameworks, ASIMM underwent an internal overhaul that involved a higher degree of institutional plasticity. As mentioned above, this was expressed in the willingness to support the workers' demands with protest action and attempts to devise a collective agreement that would specifically cover the new characteristics of platform work. In that regard, ASIMM, along with APP, hoped that a new government would be more receptive to the union's demands; an expectation that corresponds with the union tradition of relying on political channels to resolve industrial conflicts.

An analysis of the positions and actions taken by ASIMM at different moments enables us to account for some noteworthy features of traditional unionism facing the phenomenon of platform work. First, a distinctive feature of the Argentinian case compared with experiences in other countries is the pre-existence of a specific union for couriers and delivery workers, which is possible due to the union model of forming organizations along occupational lines, even when the particular economic sector is relatively small. In principle, the existence of a specific pre-existing union provided delivery workers with more advantageous conditions in which to organize. Second, this experience shows that the bargaining tradition has drawbacks when entering into conflict with multinational companies operating at an international level that refuse to recognize the existence of employment relations, and which evade regulations. Third, it demonstrates that the willingness of a union to adjust its original conservative positions and develop greater institutional plasticity is key to broadening its base and sphere of action, incorporating workers with new identities, demands and forms of taking action. Fourth, a union from the bargaining tradition is better placed to intervene and win demands when there is a government with a more worker-friendly political-ideological position, one that is willing to use political channels to attempt to partially balance out the power inequalities that exist in the industrial sphere. In view of the new government's project to draft a statute for platform workers, the focus of political unionism that directs its demands towards the state seems to have regained effectiveness in the context of the reality imposed by the platform companies.

CONCLUSIONS

The unprecedented speed at which these transformations to labour processes have recently taken place has had an impact on academic and political debates. The end of work, the disappearance or weakening of the unions, the crisis of the established labour relations model are now questions discussed globally. In this chapter we have been concerned with analysing the potential that the unions have to organize platform workers and to confront companies that

appropriate the discourse of entrepreneurialism and algorithmic management in order to conceal the existence of employment relations and evade
regulations.

Drawing on our analysis of the process of organization and struggle undertaken by delivery workers in two unions in Argentina, we are able to outline
some conclusions that can contribute to examining union strategies facing
global platform companies. An initial conclusion we can draw from this experience is that the historical legacy of unionism has an impact on the definition
of the ways in which workers organize. In Argentina the unions have been
and continue to be a powerful social force, and local legislation facilitates the
creation of unions with relative ease; meaning that on the one hand, before the
delivery platforms existed there was a pre-established union for the occupation
(ASIMM), and on the other hand, when a group of riders became dissatisfied
with that union, they were able to take the decision to form their own union
(APP). Although most delivery workers are young migrants with no prior
union experience, they set up their own union rather than alternative forms of
organization.

The second conclusion is that the characteristics of the trade union traditions
influenced the ways in which the unions organized the riders and acted on
their demands; these traditions enabled them to win partial victories but were
not sufficient in themselves to confront the power of the platform companies. In one case, APP developed strategies more akin to those of a rank and
file, participatory, direct action-oriented unionism, which permitted them to
accomplish some objectives, principally the construction of a workers' identity, placing the issue firmly on the public stage, and winning some immediate
demands (an increase of delivery rates), but which did not manage to overturn
the platforms' logic of refusing to recognize any employment relationship.
ASIMM, rooted in the bargaining tradition, attempted to negotiate the hiring
of workers with the companies, following established models of labour organization, with little success.

The third conclusion we can draw from this study is that the challenges
posed by platform companies have compelled these traditions to adopt greater
flexibility, and overhaul concepts, practices and strategies. In this regard, we
can observe that what here we describe as institutional plasticity is key to the
unions ability to respond to the new forms of capitalist production and new
worker subjectivities.

Similarly, a fourth conclusion, related to all those above, indicates that
while the unions were not immediately successful in the demands they brought
before the platform companies, their partial achievements were crucial to
advancing towards their goals in the longer term. In contrast with the discourse of entrepreneurialism, the self-identification of the workers as workers,
and raising the precarization of platform workers as a problem in the public

agenda, are key steps towards constructing the conditions that may enable them to gradually win their demands.

A fifth preliminary conclusion on the basis of this case, taking the political dynamics into consideration, is that the political-ideological orientation of the government is important, insofar as government support can contribute to achieving through political channels what cannot be resolved by direct action or bargaining with the companies. In this regard, while under a pro-business government (Mauricio Macri, 2015 to 2019) the companies enjoyed the opportunity to operate without regulation in Argentina, the change of government for one with a more worker-friendly orientation (Alberto Fernández from the end of 2019) seems to have presented the opportunity to establish a statute for platform work that would enshrine labour rights for delivery workers.

It is not possible to make generalizations from the Argentinian case; however, it does offer some dimensions of analysis which could have a favourable impact on workers' processes of organization and struggle, and which could fruitfully be incorporated into the field of union studies in platform capitalism, among them: the degree of power held by unions in society, the characteristics of trade union traditions, the degree of institutional plasticity demonstrated by the unions, the contributions of partial victories to the longer-term struggle, and the political-ideological orientations of governments.

NOTES

1. We have constructed our data on the basis of in-depth interviews: we conducted a first round of interviews with activists and leaders from the two unions studied between July and December 2018, when APP was at the height of its organization and struggle. Throughout 2019 we held a second round of interviews, with rank and file workers and again with union activists and leaders, in a period of retreat for APP. This diversity of experiences during the periods in which we were conducting our interviews enabled us to analyse the dynamics and complexities of the processes of union organization. Additionally, we have analysed union statutes and public discourse in the media and on social networks.
2. Neither of the two union confederations constitute a hegemonic block. The CGT in particular has been riven by internal disputes around a diversity of positions and strategies. In the 1990s a significant sector of the CGT strongly opposed market reforms but without formally abandoning their institutional affiliation.
3. Rappi was founded in Colombia in 2015 and arrived in Argentina in February 2018. Glovo was founded in Barcelona in 2005 and also arrived in Argentina at the beginning of 2018. PedidosYa was established in Uruguay in 2009, and from 2014 its main shareholder has been the German company Delivery Hero. PedidosYa has been running in Argentina since 2010 as an intermediary platform linking customers and businesses, and in 2017 incorporated its own delivery workers. In 2019 UberEats began operating, but given its short operational span so far, it is not an object of analysis in this chapter.

4. The 'Statute for On-Demand Platform Workers' is a project from the Argentinian Ministry for Labour. According to the draft we were able to review in March 2020, it is a statute specifically for riders. It establishes, among other things, regulations for maximum weekly working hours and rest time, a minimum guaranteed wage, a sickness and health and safety regime, and a regulatory framework for disciplinary action.

REFERENCES

Arias, C. (2010), 'Existencias precarizadas', *Gestión de las Personas y Tecnología*, **8**, 26–35.

Bunel, J. (1992), *Pactos y agresiones*, Buenos Aires: FCE.

Collier, R., Dubal, V. and Carter, C. (2017), 'Labor platforms and gig work: The failure to regulate', IRLE Working Paper No. 106–17. From http://irle.berkeley.edu/files/2017/labor-platforms-and-gig-work.pdf

Darlington, R. (2002), 'Shop stewards leadership, left wing activism and collective workplace union organization', *Capital and Class*, **76**, 95–126.

De Stefano, V. (2016), 'The rise of the "just-in-time" workforce: On demand work, crowdwork, and labor protection in the "gig economy"', Conditions of Work and Employment Series, ILO, 71. From https://wcd1.ilo.org/wcd1/groups/public/---ed_protect/---protrav/---travail/documents/publication/wcms_443267.pdf

Diana Menéndez, N. (2017), 'Representaciones inconclusas: dinámicas de constitución de identidades político sindicales en organizaciones gremiales', *Enfoques*, **27** (XV), 123–148.

Gilly, A. (1986), 'La anomalía argentina (Estado, corporaciones, trabajadores)', in P. González Casanova (ed.), *El Estado en America Latina. Teoría y práctica*, México: Siglo XXI, pp. 187–214.

Haidar, J., Diana Menéndez, N. and Arias, C. (2020), 'La organización vence al algoritmo (?) Plataformas de reparto y procesos de organización de los trabajadores de delivery en Argentina', *Revista Pilquen*, **23**, 15–28.

Hyman, R. (1975), *Industrial Relations. A Marxist Introduction*, Basingstoke: Palgrave Macmillan.

Jolly, C. (2016), 'Collective action and bargaining in the digital era', in M. Neufeind, J. O'Reilly & F. Ranft (eds), *Work in the Digital Age: Challenges of the Fourth Industrial Revolution*, London: Rowman and Littlefield International, pp. 209–223.

Kelly, J. (1998), *Rethinking Industrial Relations. Mobilization, Collectivism and Long Waves*, London: LSE/Routledge.

McKinney, J. (1966), *Constructive Typology and Social Theory*, New York: Appleton-Centrury-Crofts.

Möhlmann, M. and Zalmanson, L. (2017), 'Hands on the wheel: Navigating algorithmic management and Uber drivers autonomy', International Conference on Information Systems (ICIS 2017), Seoul. From https://www.researchgate.net/publication/319965259_Hands_on_the_wheel_Navigating_algorithmic_management_and_Uber_drivers%27_autonomy

Rosenblat, A. (2016), 'Algorithmic labor and information asymmetries: A case study of Uber's drivers', *International Journal of Communication*, **10**, 3758–3784.

Suriano, J. (2001), *Anarquistas. Cultura y Política Libertaria en Buenos Aires, 1890–1910*, Buenos Aires: Editorial Manantial.

Tassinari, A. and Maccarrone, V. (2019), 'Riders on the storm: Workplace solidarity among gig economy couriers in Italy and the UK', *Work, Employment and Society*, **34** (1), 35–54.

Tilly, C. (1978), *From Mobilization to Revolution*, Reading, MA: Addison-Wesley.

Vandaele, K. (2018), 'Will trade unions survive in the platform economy? Emerging patterns of platform workers collective voice and representation in Europe', *European Trade Union Institute, Working Paper 2018.5*. From https://www.etui.org/Publications2/Working-Papers/Will-trade-unions-survive-in-the-platform-economy-Emerging-patterns-of-platform-workers-collective-voice-and-representation-in-Europe

9. Collective resistance and organizational creativity amongst Europe's platform workers: a new power in the labour movement?

Kurt Vandaele

INTRODUCTION

This chapter explores and discusses labour agency in the platform economy in Europe.[1] The main research question is what this economy implies for the collective resistance and representation of platform workers, as well as for the relationship between them and established trade unions. The platform economy has induced pessimistic accounts of future labour agency, and it undoubtedly poses major challenges to unions. This chapter, however, develops a more positive appraisal. Emerging forms of collective resistance and representation are conceived here as a countervailing power *in the making* – at least in several European countries. A non-exhaustive mapping of this resistance and representation will be provided by utilizing 'grey literature'[2] and the burgeoning wealth of empirical studies on this subject. The argument is advanced that the distinctively disordered nature of the platform economy holds the promise of an epoch of organizational creativity and experimentation for labour (Murray et al. 2020), with possible cooperation between 'new' (informal) types of collective representation and existing unions. A threefold conceptual framework is used (depicted in Figure 9.1) to develop and elaborate on this argument, with concepts corresponding to different analytical levels.

A world-historical analysis of the labour movement places labour agency in the platform economy (in relation to capital mobility) within a historical perspective via the concept of spatio-temporal 'fixes' (Silver 2003). Fixes are various strategies of capital aiming to lessen labour costs and to maximize labour control. To understand the current restructuring of capitalism by digital labour platforms (henceforth 'platforms'), three fixes are studied here. The product fix relates to the shift of investments from old industries subject to strong competition to new ones. The technological/organizational fix is

Figure 9.1 *Heuristic concepts for studying labour agency in the platform economy*

understood as the introduction of new forms of management and methods of work arrangements. The spatial fix, rooted in labour geography, refers to the geographical relocation of capital to new areas in order to maximize profit and labour control. This concept of recurrent fixes helps to deconstruct the platforms' self-portrayal as mere technological start-ups. Fixes are only stable until the next regulation or crisis within capital accumulation, however, as a result of labour-capital dynamics within industries and countries. To analyse these dynamics, reference is made to the structural, associational and coalitional power of the platform workers (Vandaele 2018). The latter power resource is an element of societal power, as is discursive power, which has the potential to compensate for weaknesses in other power resources. Although some platforms might be likely sensitive to their public reputation, discursive power is not the major analytical focus in this chapter, as this would require another research design. Equally, although it is acknowledged that expressions of collective resistance and representation are also contingent on *prevailing* regulatory arrangements, institutional power is less studied here, mainly due to length considerations. Most platforms have also demonstrated an unwillingness or even refusal to accept existing or new regulation, while there has so far been little regulatory action by the state so far. Platform workers thus suffer from a lack of regulatory arrangements specifically tailored to their needs, implying that existing arrangements will have to suffice to fill the regulatory-institutional void – varying according to the context, particularly in the case of locally based platform work. Since the platform workers' associational and coalitional power reveals, respectively, organizational experimentation and diversity, it is worthwhile to demarcate two *ideal* representation approaches. While the workers' immediate needs and interests are central to the logic-of-membership approach, it is the relationship between the representative organization and its interlocutors that is key in the logic-of-influence approach (Offe and Wiesenthal 1980).

Three caveats should be made. First, the platform economy is here understood to be – or is narrowed down to – digital labour platforms, which are
exchanging labour and exercising high levels of labour control compared
to other platform types (Maffie 2020b). They are *typically* characterized by
a triangular relationship between the parties involved (Duggan et al. 2020).
Platforms are economic agents facilitating matching between providers of
labour and customers via online technologies based on algorithmic management which exerts disciplinary control over task allocation and performance.
Platforms reduce idle time at work by offering one-off 'jobs'[3] to workers who
are compensated on a task-by-task basis and who supply some of their own
means of production. A major bifurcation is the distinction between locally
based and online platform work. Second, it is acknowledged that workers' collective resistance is only one of the expressions of labour agency, and probably
not the most prevalent one for platform workers. Similar to the conventional
economy, other worker strategies for coping with working conditions are in all
probability more widespread than outright worker resistance in the platform
economy, though more hidden due to their often-individualized nature (see,
for instance, Heiland 2021). Third, little is currently known about the distinc-
tiveness of platform workers and employment dynamics within the platform
economy in European countries. Measuring its size and scope is difficult due
to the unclear taxonomy and measurement bias, inadequate data cleaning, and
self-selecting samples, which all impede accurate estimates. It is clear though
that there is a high turnover in platform work, making it a sizable workforce in
absolute terms, and that it provides an additional income for a growing number
of workers to top up their regular income. A marginal percentage of workers
regularly engage in platform work, earning at least 50 per cent of their total
income from it. Using this criterium of 50 per cent then, based on 16 countries,
the European simple average is estimated to have been at 1.4 per cent in 2018
(Urzì Brancati et al. 2020). Still, despite this low percentage, the product, tech-
nological/organizational and spatial fixes make clear that platforms warrant
specific study as they are relatively distinctive from other transformations
within capitalist development.

1   UNDERSTANDING THE SINGULARITY OF PLATFORMS VIA THREE FIXES

A shift in financial strategies has facilitated the emergence and rise of platforms
(Srnicek 2017). Their proliferation coincided with the crisis of the finance-led
accumulation regime in 2007–2008, with most platforms being established
in Europe after 2010 (Fabo et al. 2017).[4] The movement of capital to new
and promising profitable product lines and industries is labelled the 'product
fix'. Applying this fix to platforms is puzzling, however. First, the platforms'

return on investments have mostly only been high on paper so far. Yet their monopolistic tendencies, due to network effects fostered by large marketing budgets, hold the promise that they are less subject to intense competition in the long term (Langley and Leyshon 2017). Second, most platforms do not appear to create new products as they tap into existing services, although a technical formalization of previously informal labour is also common. Key to understanding the product fix is the use and potential valorization of the data-derived assets owned by the platforms, however (Badger and van Doorn 2020). 'Datafication' is built upon the extraction of data generated by the platform workers themselves. Therefore, apart from providing services (though not in a conventional way), their interaction with the platforms also makes them data workers.

The gathering, processing and analyzing of data is possible via another 'fix' that typifies platforms: their technological/organizational fix. This fix refers to new labour-saving technologies which enable labour control and enhance profitability by transforming the organization of production and labour processes. Management-by-algorithms meets this qualification: it facilitates and contributes to data accumulation while adjusting the algorithms via feedback loops. Algorithmic management can itself be traced back to various long-term changes in the management of work, culminating in digital Taylorism (Altenried 2020). Platforms act as a 'shadow employer' (Gandini 2019, p. 1049), as direct supervision is unwarranted: individual online ranking and reputation systems in particular, which often echo or even strengthen various types of discrimination, impel self-disciplining behaviour among workers, whereby they suffer from information asymmetries in favour of the platforms or clients. Reflecting findings on the labour process in the conventional economy, the sections below will demonstrate, however, that labour control via algorithmic management is never complete, which means that it can be subverted, opening up room for workers' resistance.

Motives for resistance are not only rooted in the technological fix of platform work but also in its organizational fix. This fix is especially associated with the instalment by platforms of a contractor relationship instead of an employment relationship. The contractor relationship should be understood in its spatio-temporal context; its application is largely influenced by existing country-specific classification schemes and institutional-regulatory contexts. Many of the organizational work practices in the platform economy are not new, and not necessarily limited to it alone (Finkin 2016; Stanford 2017). This also accounts for the contractor relationship and its regulatory ambiguity: it is reminiscent of other informal and triangular work arrangements during earlier capitalist development, such as 'piecework', meaning the production of goods at home. Operating with so-called 'independent contractors' can be understood as an 'emerging but incomplete' process of the subsumption of labour by capital (Joyce 2020). It installs a labour-capital relationship and hence a 'cash nexus' between the platforms and platform workers. More concretely, the contractor relationship implies that the regulations and securities that come with a genuine employment relationship do not apply to the platforms. There is general agreement that shortcomings in working conditions and social protection cannot be addressed by current anti-trust and competition regulation as they generally exclude or hinder the setting of minimum standards and collective bargaining for platform workers, the solo-self-employed and freelancers. Therefore, working conditions and social protection – normally provided by guaranteed minimum wages, regulations on working time, health and safety standards and anti-discrimination rules – are mostly meagre for platform workers. Employment benefits, training and career development opportunities are also largely evaded by the platforms. Aimed at pursuing profitability (Roy-Mukherjee and Harrison 2020), this shift of employment-related risks to workers holds particularly true if platform work is the main income. Although the anonymity of platform work can make it more inclusive, young people, migrants and women can still be exposed to health and safety risks or even discrimination. Only a few European countries, notably, France, Spain and Italy and to a certain extent Portugal, have enacted specific regulations aiming to improve platform workers' employment terms and conditions (Kilhoffer et al. 2020).

Finally, the spatial fix concerns the geographical mobility of production for facilitating profitability and controlling labour. To understand the platforms' spatial configurations, it is key to make a basic distinction regarding the geographical location of platform work (Johnson 2020). This can primarily either be performed online or locally.[5] Online platform work can be considered an individualized mode of service offshoring via 'one-person microproviders' instead of companies (Lehdonvirta et al. 2019). The platforms thereby act as active intermediaries between supply and demand, taking advantage of local differences in labour costs or skill availability. Relocation strategies are thus built in to the technological/organizational fix by default, triggering 'a new wave of international division of labour' (Anwar and Graham 2021). In practice, however, the work is clustered in certain zones, and is influenced by such factors as Internet access, labour costs, available skills, contextual knowledge, and cultural and linguistic proximity (Ettlinger 2017). Turning to locally based platforms, with their physical, time- and place-dependent tasks, these are impervious to successive relocations as they are 'geographically tethered' (Woodcock and Graham 2020, pp. 50–52). Such platforms are predominantly contingent on local consumers who can afford the platform-based personal services. Although the support facilities for couriers in locally based platforms (such as helpdesks) are prone to geographical mobility, this is not an option for their main services.[6] Locally based platforms are thus either temporally embedded and interrelated with specific regulatory frameworks – or not. If competitive pressures are too high or the technological/organizational fix comes under pressure via regulatory changes, or both, then such platforms tend to simply cease activities (or at least threaten to do so) in given localities. This distinction in the spatial fix between online and locally based platforms informs workers' structural power and, consequently, their disruptive capacity.

2   SOME VARIATION IN PLATFORM WORKERS' STRUCTURAL POWER

The structural power of platform workers relates to their workplace and marketplace bargaining power. Both are generally defined by external circumstances. Workplace bargaining power stems from a worker's specific position in distribution or production systems, whereas marketplace bargaining power is influenced by the desirability of a worker's skills to individual clients or companies, the degree of unemployment in general, or to what extent a worker can live from other non-market income sources (Silver 2003). In general, the platforms' recruitment policies, with their low-entry barriers to the tasks, guarantee a continuous influx of new workers. This structural over-supply and lack of tasks not only undermines marketplace bargaining power but also workplace bargaining power, as few platform workers are willing to threaten the withdrawal of their work in this case (Anwar and Graham 2021). Simultaneously, platform workers demonstrate different levels of attachment to the platforms, which also influences their incentives to engage in collective resistance and representation. Workers' structural power also varies according to the type of platform work. This is because the degree of labour control due to the technological/organizational fix is closely linked to the platform type (Pesole et al. 2018).[7] To elucidate this, it is helpful to simplify and classify platform work, which is heterogenous. Apart from the classification based on the spatial fix, different kinds of platform work can be further grouped, for instance, by skill level, task allocation or type of remuneration (Vallas and Schor 2020). Although overlaps cannot be excluded, looking through the lens of power resources approach, the most relevant defining factor for online platform work is who the actor initiating the transaction is (Howcroft and Bergvall-Kåreborn 2019), i.e. whether it is requester- or worker-initiated, whereas the contrast between private and public settings, i.e. where the tasks are performed, is more important for locally based platform work (Huws et al. 2017).

Table 9.1   Structural power of platform workers by platform types

Structural power	Online platform work		Locally based platform work	
	Requester-initiated	Worker-initiated	Private setting	Public setting
Workplace bargaining power	Weak	Weak/Intermediate	Weak	Strong
Marketplace bargaining power	Weak	Intermediate	Weak/Intermediate	Weak

Source: Own typology (inspired by Silver 2003).

Table 9.1 provides an appraisal of structural power in each type of platform work compared to the other types identified here, i.e. *not* in comparison with industries in the conventional economy. In requester-initiated platform work, workers agree (or not) with the price set by individual clients or private companies. They typically perform 'ghost work': specific, fragmented microtasks that are posted online, and which are often 'deskilled' in nature (Gray and Suri 2019). The disruptive capacity of such microworkers is almost non-existent: a work stoppage will have little impact on the flow of production. Their marketplace bargaining power is also weak: platforms based on requester-initiated work simply draw from a pool of cheap, flexible and geographically dispersed workers performing low-skilled tasks. Turning to worker-initiated platform work, this type shares many characteristics of profession-based freelance work, with the technological/organizational fix being more lenient compared to other platform types (Wood and Lehdonvirta 2021; Wood et al. 2018b). Online freelancers initiate the transaction by setting the price level, while the platform deducts a percentage upon transaction. A negotiated agreement is reached between the worker and the client through bidding for and winning the project-based task. Online freelancers may thus possess greater agency to shape their employment terms and conditions and in selecting platform tasks – especially in the Global South, as the spatial fix here allows for skill arbitrage, i.e. the workers are able to set a higher price via the platforms than what they would earn locally (Lehdonvirta et al. 2019; Sutherland et al. 2020). Since they often possess specialized skills, this theoretically provides them with some individual marketplace bargaining power, lowering the incentive for collective resistance and representation. Finally, their workplace bargaining power is a priori less clear-cut: it will largely depend on whether the specialist projects are part of vulnerable 'just-in-time' production systems or not.

Locally based platform work is particularly characterized by a prevalence of migrant domestic labour, which risks creating segmentation in labour markets along the lines of citizenship or ethnicity. Lower entry barriers in particular incentivize migrants to favour platforms over the conventional economy as the latter is regulated by immigration policies concerning employment and welfare (van Doorn et al. 2020). Platform work in private settings comprises manual labour like home repair work or (female-dominated) home-based services such as cleaning and child- or eldercare. Although platforms are instigating a formalization of often largely informal industries, the workplace bargaining power of platform workers providing personal services is weak due to difficulties in coordinating resistance across dispersed, small workplaces (Silver 2003, p. 120). Equally, marketplace bargaining power is generally weak given the large pool of workers with the necessary skills – although some skills might be scarce, meaning that marketplace bargaining could range from low to intermediate. Moving on to platform work in public settings, transportation is prominent here.[8] The workplace bargaining power of transportation workers in the conventional economy is relatively strong as they hold a strategic position in distribution networks, allowing for a considerable disruptive capacity (Silver 2003, pp. 97–103). The same applies, in all likelihood, to platform workers in transportation like delivery couriers or ride-hailing drivers. Although there is no empirical relationship between workplace bargaining power and the level of collective resistance, it can be expected that they are able to use their disruptive capacity given the 'spatial proximity and temporal synchronicity' (Woodcock and Graham 2020, p. 51) of their work. Unsurprisingly then, as a compromise, most collective bargaining agreements in the platform economy are in locally based platform work, especially in transportation (Kilhoffer et al. 2020, p. 119). Workplace bargaining power is, however, offset by marketplace bargaining power, which is generally muted, as demonstrated by their high turnover rate compared to other platform types (Urzì Brancati et al. 2020). Accounting for differences in platform workers' structural power is a starting point for analysing their disruptive capacity and the transcending of workplace or marketplace bargaining into associational power. The organizational morphology of this latter type of power, and whether this fits together with coalitional power, will be analysed in the next sections.

3   REQUESTER- AND WORKER-INITIATED ONLINE PLATFORM WORK

The spatial fix of online platform work implies that geographical mobility is entrenched from the very outset. Building collective resistance on local, regional or national levels is less effective since this organizationally and socially dispersed mode of work is strongly disembedded from local institutional-regulatory frameworks (Johnson 2020). Labour internationalism and regulatory provisions beyond these local levels are thus needed if online platforms are to be effectively challenged. Union strategies and other initiatives are thus primarily directed towards encouraging self-regulation by online platforms, counting on the importance of the platforms' public reputation to use it as leverage. The action-research project Fairwork Foundation, established in 2018 and based at the University of Oxford, thus produces a yearly report about fairness in the platform economy based upon evidence collected from platform workers across the globe (Graham et al. 2020). Similarly, IG Metall, the largest German union, launched the 'Fair Crowd Work' initiative in 2015.[9] A website, jointly run with the Austrian Chamber of Labour, the Austrian union confederation and the Swedish union, Unionen, informs platform workers about their rights and union membership, and introduces a rating system of the platforms' employment terms and conditions. Furthermore, three German-based platforms voluntarily signed a 'Crowdsourcing Code of Conduct' in 2015, and five other platform companies joined later. The signatory platforms, together with the German Crowdsourcing Association (Deutscher Crowdsourcing Verband) and IG Metall, have installed an ombudsman for a period of two years to enforce the Code and settle issues by consensus between workers and the platforms. These initiatives of IG Metall, based on a logic-of-influence approach, have strengthened its credibility among platform workers: in 2019, for example, the YouTubers Union, a self-organized group of professional content creators, set up a joint public campaign labelled 'FairTube' with IG Metall to make YouTube's algorithmic management and cash nexus fairer and more transparent (Niebler 2020).

The platforms themselves also provide a means for platform workers to share information and experiences amongst themselves via discussion forums and other types of online interaction. In practice, they control this digital architecture for community-building: community management is simply delegated to experienced platform workers who tend to orient themselves towards 'improving and optimising organizational performance' (Gegenhuber et al. 2021, p. 1495; Gerber 2021). This feeds into the view that online platform workers predominantly have an 'entrepreneurial orientation' (Vallas and Schor 2020, p. 5). Yet a significant proportion of platform workers in Europe (about 40 per cent) earning more than 50 per cent of their income from platform work report that they see themselves primarily as an employee – with minor variation between worker- or requester-initiated platform work (Urzì Brancati et al. 2019). This might be related to their dependency on the platform and hence their relative loss of autonomy compared to what they would experience in the conventional economy, especially regarding workers engaged in requester-initiated platform work (Wood et al. 2018b). Algorithmic management could also produce more uncertainty and precarity, although online workers might cope with this via 'creative strategies and new digital literacies to work with and around the platform' (Sutherland et al. 2020, p. 472).

Nevertheless, product and technological/organizational fixes are fuelling grievances and feelings of 'algorithmic injustice' among platform workers as well as generating a sense of shared identities and unified interests, all prerequisites for collectivism (Gerber and Krzywdzinkski 2019; Panteli et al. 2020; Wood and Lehdonvirta 2021; Wood et al. 2018a). For workers doing requester-initiated platform work, or in particular the solo self-employed, it is an empirical question as to whether they will opt for mutual aid or collective representation. 'Bread funds' in the Netherlands and (introduced at a later date) in the United Kingdom (UK) illustrate the importance of mutual aid. Resembling mutual insurance associations of the nineteenth century, these bottom-up small-scale funds, in which premiums are paid into risk-sharing pools, provide income protection in case of illness or injury, signifying that current social protection by the state is inadequate or that private initiatives are too expensive for the solo self-employed (Vriens and De Moor 2020). Beyond mutual aid and labour market intermediaries smoothing out the bumps in their non-standard career paths, options for collective representation could be either professional, business or employers' associations or unions. The solo self-employed in the conventional economy generally show no aversion towards collective representation, especially if it can help to mitigate inse-curities and the lack of social protection that comes with their labour market status (Murgia and Pulignano 2019). For instance, to look at the Netherlands again, precarious freelancers have a higher probability of unionizing than other types of solo self-employed workers (Jansen and Sluiter 2019), which seems to be driven by individual service needs, collective demands for better social protection and left-wing political orientations (Jansen 2020).

Organizing freelancers and the solo self-employed is certainly not new to most mainstream unions in Europe. Some union branches or unions have a long history of organizing them in particular industries where such contractor relationships are prevalent (Fulton 2018). There are nevertheless unions who have still not opened their doors to the solo self-employed, either because of existing legal barriers (which holds especially true for countries in Central and Eastern Europe), or due to internal rules or union attitudes. Apart from spe-cialist unions with a certain tradition in representing the solo self-employed, there are three other more recent union models that have been developed as unions have stepped up their efforts for this growing and heterogenous group. First, the dominant model in Italy is of separate unions organizing precarious non-standard workers, which are also, in theory, open to solo self-employed workers. This kind of model is also present in Slovenia, while grassroots unions in the UK and elsewhere are, in practice, also oriented towards these workers. Second, unions in Italy, the Netherlands and Spain have been spe-cially established for organizing the solo self-employed as a response to recent labour market developments in certain industries. Third, most mainstream unions have simply opened membership up to the solo self-employed, including platform workers; unions such as Ver.di in Germany and Unionen already did this prior to the rise of the platform economy, while others have begun to do likewise more recently. Examples of the latter include unions in France (who have welcomed, in particular, ride-hailing platform workers), IG Metall, the GMB in the UK, and union confederations in Norway and Spain.

Unions in Europe today generally lean towards a logic-of-influence approach, which prioritizes concluding collective agreements – and in several countries, unions are trying to include platform workers in these agreements. Agreements typically incorporate the solo self-employed, although they are restricted to specific professions or industries, or to those who are in bogus self-employment, or both (Fulton 2018). Some platforms are signing up to existing collective agreements in a few countries. New agreements at the company level have been concluded between the unions and platforms in Denmark (Ilsøe et al. 2020), while some platforms in Sweden have agreed to adhere to existing collective agreements for temporary agency workers in order to avoid reputational damage (Söderqvist and Bernhardtz 2019). Above all, however, unions are promoting tailored individual benefits and services to the solo self-employed and platform workers (Mori and Koene 2019), also because it is largely uncertain to what extent collective bargaining goes together which such an employment status. Examples include additional insurances, tax compliance, legal and other advice and professional support related to providing model contracts, reviewing contracts, and training. Some of these might become obsolete as 'selective incentives' for unionization if for-profit companies were to offer these benefits and services at a lower price, or states were to strengthen social protection via more coordination and harmonization with employee arrangements. Interestingly, the journalists' union in Finland, Suomen Journalistiliitto, set up the cooperative Mediakunta in 2017, which officially employs union members who work on journalism and media projects, invoicing clients on their behalf and handling their payroll (Fulton 2018). Furthermore, several unions and confederations have set up online platforms offering counselling and providing services for the solo self-employed. Ver.di has been operating such a platform for union members and the non-unionized solo self-employed – the latter being charged for the services – since the early 2000s (Haake 2017). Several similar initiatives have been launched in more recent years: in 2011 by a union organizing in the private services, affiliated to the Italian Labour Union (Unione Italiana del Lavoro) (Veronese et al. 2019); in 2016 by the French Democratic Confederation of Labour (Confédération française démocratique du travail), and reinforced three years later; in 2017 by the Workers' Commissions (Comisiones Obreras) and General Union of Workers (Unión General de Trabajadores) in Spain (Hermoso 2019); and in 2019 by the two main confederations in Belgium. All of them offer online tools for informing and advising the solo self-employed, including platform workers, about their rights in an attempt to help them overcome their geographical dispersion.

4   LOCALLY BASED PLATFORM WORK IN PRIVATE SETTINGS

Locally based platform work in private settings typically commodifies various forms of reproductive labour, which previously have been carried out at home or have been part of informal work in the conventional economy. The promise of platforms is that they can bring formalization and more transparency to this area. In practice, they reinforce existing risks and vulnerabilities for workers, as formalization is only partial, while the technological/organizational fix maintains or reinforces employment terms and conditions typical of the informal economy (Flanagan 2019; Ticona and Mateescu 2018). This same fix allows for clients easily to switch to platforms that provide services at lower costs or which are not affected by collective resistance. Such resistance seems unlikely, however, as professional loyalty towards individual clients and the direct, face-to-face contact between workers and clients make it harder to use their disruptive capacity (Silver 2003, pp. 119–122). Nevertheless, attracting client empathy to the workers' cause is also an important factor, as '"process transparency" matters: customers are more appreciative of workers when they can observe their labour' (Healy and Pekarek 2020, p. 164). Therefore, a key question is whether platforms will continue to favour one-off services or if locally based platform work in private settings will progress into worker-initiated platform work (Trojansky 2020). The latter would foster long-term interpersonal relationships between platform workers and clients and somewhat increase the structural power of workers. Furthermore, the prevalence of women and workers with a migrant background, sometimes undocumented, in care work and cleaning does not necessarily imply that union organizing efforts would be futile, quite the contrary (Tapia 2019).

Unions could also enhance trust between platform workers and clients in this type of platform work by setting higher standards. In the Netherlands, for example, a Dutch-owned platform which was active in the hospitality sector signed an agreement in 2018 of joint cooperation with the hospitality union, affiliated to the Federation of Dutch Trade Unions (FNV, Federatie Nederlandse Vakbeweging). This agreement, which aimed to strengthen the employment terms and conditions of the platform workers, was not signed without some internal tension within the FNV as it has been considered as legitimizing the technological/organizational fix. Also, Syndicom, the Swiss media and communications union, signed a code of conduct with a platform providing repair and tech services in 2019. A possible alternative way to uphold professional standards is self-organizing via a platform cooperative, as demonstrated by the Equal Care Co-op in the UK. Established as a pilot project in 2018 and inspired by the Dutch 'Neighbourhood care' (Buurtzorg), this co-op is active in social care work and self-governed by the care providers and receivers themselves; the collaborative platform aims to offer a standard employment contract in the future. So far, however, collective representation by (mainstream) unions in locally based platform work in private settings seems to be almost non-existent in Europe, and the same holds true for collective agreements. To the author's knowledge, the only real exception, reflecting a logic-of-influence approach, is the agreement concluded in 2018 between the Danish-owned platform Hilfr, which provides cleaning services in private households, and the United Federation of Danish Workers (3F, Fagligt Fælles Forbund), the largest union in Denmark.

Hilfr considers this agreement as part of its business strategy – i.e. to distinguish itself from its competitors, although a bigger market share has not been captured so far – and as a way of being socially responsible (Ilsøe 2020). The platform also joined the relevant employers' association. A government-led social dialogue body facilitated the negotiations, while the absence of any competing collective agreement in household cleaning made it easier for 3F to engage with the conclusion of an agreement at the company level. The agreement has been claimed to be the first one with a platform in the world, although similar collective agreements were concluded earlier on, such as one in Sweden in 2015 (Söderqvist and Bernhardtz 2019). Started as a one-year pilot project, the Danish agreement introduces a new category of workers, labelled 'Super Hilfr', besides the default 'Freelancehilfr'. Regarding the latter, the Danish Competition and Consumer Authority has concluded in 2020 that the minimum fee for 'Freelancehilfr' is at odds with competition law, however. Even so, workers with a 'Super Hilfr' status are entitled to a minimum hourly fee, a 'welfare supplement', holiday pay, sick leave pay and pension contributions paid by Hilfr. Just like freelance workers, 'Super Hilfr' workers can set their hourly fee themselves, although it has to be above a certain minimum. The agreement also touches upon the product fix by granting workers the right to request the removal of violating language or pictures from their online ranking and reputation profiles.

The status of 'Super Hilfr' is optional although almost automatically obtained: if a minimum of 100 hours of services are performed, then the collective agreement applies unless workers opt to retain their default status as 'Freelancehilfr'. Only about 17 per cent of the platform workers had obtained the special status of 'Super Hilfr' at the beginning of 2020, but they account for more than one-third of all cleaning tasks.[10] Workers can even apply to have this status before they have met the criterium, although the platform could reject this. In other words, if the collective agreement applies, obtaining this status is entirely up to the platform worker (although it should be noted that such a free choice of application is in fact not allowed by Danish labour law). There are also notable differences from similar collective agreements in the conventional economy: for instance, while disputes regarding the interpretation and infringement of an agreement are normally subject to labour court decisions, arbitration is the chosen procedure in the 'Hilfr agreement'. Also, the notice period is shorter compared to equivalent agreements at the industry level in the conventional economy. Furthermore, the minimum fee and social benefits are set at lower levels than the employment terms and conditions stipulated by agreements outside the platform economy. Nevertheless, negotiations for a new agreement for a three-year period are still ongoing at the time of writing, while an agreement at the industry level is being considered.

5   LOCALLY BASED PLATFORM WORK IN PUBLIC SETTINGS: THE CASE OF FOOD DELIVERY

A strike wave of platform-based food delivery couriers kicked off in London in the summer of 2016 (Cant 2019). Their strategic location in the distribution system meant that app-ordered food was prevented from being delivered from the ('ghost') restaurants to customers at the foreseen time. Ensuing local small-scale stoppages targeted other food delivery platforms in the UK, demonstrating the workplace bargaining power of the couriers. Strike action by food delivery couriers and low-paid hospitality workers connected precarious workers in the platform and conventional economies through the 2018 'Fast Food Shutdown' (Cant and Woodcock 2020), and resistance also spread transnationally to cities on the European continent. Motives for mobilization were very similar across cities and countries, being related to the cash nexus, meaning the shift from a genuine dependent employment relationship to a contractor status, together with a switch from hourly wages to a riskier payment-by-delivery system. Grievances and feelings of social injustice were perhaps not shared among all couriers: they experienced the work of food delivery differently depending on their individual circumstances, such as their life stage, need for income, and expectations of the work (Goods et al. 2019). Although struggles in platform-based food delivery have been variable across cities and rather ephemeral in most countries, resistance in the platform economy across the globe has nonetheless predominantly occurred in this industry, especially in Western Europe (Trappmann et al. 2020). Therefore, this section analyses the associational and coalitional power of food delivery couriers, the sector which the author is most familiar with; ride-hailing and local microtasking are not covered here.

*Table 9.2   The associational and coalitional power of platform-based
                     food delivery couriers in Western Europe*

| | | Activist groups and mainstream unions | |
		Conflictual relationship	Collaborative relationship
Grassroots unions	Absent	France, Italy, Spain	Austria, Belgium, Denmark, Finland, (France), Germany, Netherlands, Norway, Sweden, Switzerland
	Present	(France), Germany, (Italy), (Sweden), UK	(Finland)

Note: Countries in parentheses indicate that the feature is present but not dominant.
Source: Vandaele et al. (2019).

A critical mass of couriers is involved in online digital communities for discussing shared employment terms and conditions (Cant 2019; Tassinari and Maccarrone 2020).[11] Like in platform-based ride-hailing (Maffie 2020a), these hidden communities are virtually overcoming their spatial dispersion via real-time engagement and interaction facilitated by the Internet infrastructure. The spatial fix of food delivery work entails that couriers active in communities could also meet up offline in shared urban spaces. Easily recognizable by their platform-branded uniforms and equipment, they meet in waiting locations where there are clusters of restaurants, which stand in for a physical workspace. This facilitates social identification processes enabling the shaping of collective identities and offline organizing. While their digital communities and activist groups are initial indicators of associational power, the couriers could further increase their power via alliance-building with established organizations like unions. This coalitional power is variable, however, as it is influenced by the prevalence of grassroots unions and the couriers' subjective attitudes towards mainstream unions (or the inaccessibility of the latter due to these workers' legal status). Table 9.2 maps the *initial* or dominant patterns in the relationship between activist groups and grassroots or mainstream unions for most countries in Western Europe. The subsections below explain those relationships in more detail, and their connection with representation 'logics'.

A logic-of-membership approach: activist groups, cooperatives and grassroots unions
Activist groups of couriers have *initially* been the main drivers of resistance in France, Italy and Spain – countries which all have industrial relations systems characterized by a high degree of polarization between labour and capital. The relationship between these groups and mainstream unions can at least initially be considered a tense one. The couriers' attitudes towards unions were at first rather agnostic: young people (who represent the majority of couriers)

in the above-mentioned countries have demonstrated low levels of trust in mainstream unions since the financial crisis of 2007–2008 (Hyman 2015). It is no coincidence that, for instance, the couriers' resistance in Italy has been closer to 'some of the practices adopted by the Italian precarious workers' movements in the early 2000s' (Tassinari and Maccarrone 2017, p. 354) than to unions' 'repertoires of contention'. Although couriers have sought support from grassroots unions in Bologna and Milan, these attempts have largely failed due to disagreements about tactics and strategies, with Italian grassroots unions leaning more towards a logic-of-influence approach (Tassinari and Maccarrone 2018).

Apart from activist groups, which are active in the Paris region and Nantes, the grassroots union SUD (Solidaires Unitaires Démocratiques) and the General Confederation of Labour (Confédération Générale du Travail) are also organizing couriers, the latter especially in Bordeaux, Dijon and Lyon. Another element of this complex landscape in France is 'Coopcycle', which promotes, coordinates and federates local cooperative models across Europe as an alternative to food or other kinds of delivery platforms (Chagny 2019). By sharing knowledge about its model and providing support, Coopcycle assists companies whose delivery services are operated according to ecological and socially responsible principles, or couriers forming a platform-based cooperative in their locality. Its software is currently used by ten cooperatives in Belgium, France, Germany, Italy, Spain and the UK, although it is still very limited in terms of actual users: about 60 couriers in total were involved in spring 2019. To give one example of how it has been used, Deliveroo's retreat in Germany sparked ideas for a worker-led platform co-op among food delivery couriers in Berlin, which Coopcycle helped to turn into a reality in 2019.[12] Similar developments can be observed in Spain. Many smaller unions have been buttressing the activist group Riders for Rights (RidersXDerechos), although mainstream unions have also assisted in couriers' strikes as well as undertaken litigation actions (Fernàndez and Soliña Barreiro 2020). Riders for Rights explored the idea of a platform co-op funded by a crowdfunding campaign in 2018: *Mensakas* was set up in cooperation with Coopcycle a year later.

Small, independent grassroots unions have equally stepped up their organizing efforts towards food delivery platform workers in countries where such unions are prominent. A focus on organizing precarious workers, frequently with a migrant background, whether in the platform economy or not, is simply part of their union identity. Like the activist groups and platform co-ops, they lean towards a logic-of-membership approach, meaning that they foster an organizing approach centred around 'communities of struggle' for transformative change (Però 2020). Besides SUD, the Free Workers' Union (FAU, Freie Arbeiterinnen- und Arbeiter-Union) in Germany (although limited to Berlin),

Örestad LS in Sweden and, notably, the Independent Workers Union of Great Britain (IWGB) and, later on, the International Workers of the World, in the UK are all organizing food delivery couriers.[13] Resistance has not excluded litigation actions by some of these unions: changing the contractor set-up could reduce employment instability so that the couriers' marketplace bargaining power is strengthened and organizing efforts pay off. Supported by the transnational networks for union revitalization Alter Summit and ReAct, activist groups, with some of them backed by mainstream unions, and grassroots unions from 12 European countries, established the Transnational Couriers Federation in Brussels in 2018.[14] In contrast to traditional labour internationalism, the Federation has no elected leadership nor staff due to 'a combination of necessity and political desire' (Cant and Mogno 2020, p. 407). Mainly aiming to strengthen the transnational coordination of resistance in platform-based food delivery, the Federation may be considered a formalization of existing informal networks among couriers and their collective organizations.

A logic-of-influence approach: mainstream unions and labour market intermediaries

Lacking financial resources and infrastructures, activist groups have turned to mainstream unions in several countries. Although the latter also bring their organizational knowledge about mobilizing, they are mainly prioritizing regulatory solutions in the institutional realm. Unions have been typically choosing to start litigation actions to alter the contractor relationship, as an employee contract is a prerequisite for establishing works councils or collective bargaining. This logic-of-influence approach thus relies on the institutional logics of national systems of industrial relations, especially in countries with strong corporatist traditions. Simultaneously, from the unions' viewpoint, the activist groups can be considered pre-existing structures for organizing the couriers. Moreover, overlapping memberships are conceivable. Union activists can anonymously engage in the digital communities to identify the couriers' issues and needs, while unionized couriers can establish links between their groups and unions.

Foodora couriers in Vienna, for instance, have turned to Vida, the Austrian union organizing in transport and services, for help in electing a works council, which was set up in 2017. And for the first time in the country, bicycle couriers in a genuine employment relationship, either in the conventional or platform economy, have been covered by a collective agreement since 2020. Similarly, while FAU has been active in Berlin, couriers in the west of Germany have turned to the Food, Beverages and Catering Union (NGG, Gewerkschaft Nahrung-Genuss-Gaststätten) to help them set up a works council (Greef et al. 2020). Their Liefern am Limit campaign, focusing on improving employment terms and conditions, formally became an NGG project in 2018. The first works council in this industry was established in Foodora in Cologne in 2017, followed by a works council in Deliveroo in the same city a year later and other councils in various cities across Germany, although it is uncertain how active they actually are.[15] Couriers have also contacted the unions in Switzerland. Syndicom concluded a collective agreement in 2019, setting minimum wages and other employment standards for couriers, although food delivery platforms were not covered (Dunand and Mahon 2019). A proceeding initiated by Unia, the union organizing in the private service sector, has resulted in a court ruling obliging food-delivery platforms to reclassify its couriers as employees in the canton of Geneva in 2020, however.

Similarly, the autonomous Couriers Collective (Koerierscollectief/Collectif des Courier-e-s), established in Brussels in 2015, was able to depend on the unions' support in negotiating a collective agreement to improve the employment terms and conditions of couriers employed by the labour market intermediary and member-owned and -governed cooperative SMart (Société mutuelle des artistes) in 2017 (Charles et al. 2020). Notably, the couriers in Belgium, most of them students at the time that the collective was established, did not markedly differ in their attitudes towards unions from their counterparts in the conventional economy: the fact that most of them are not unionized reflected a lack of awareness and knowledge rather than outspoken feelings of antipathy towards unions (Vandaele et al. 2019). Negotiations on a collective agreement suddenly came to a halt when Deliveroo unilaterally decided to only work with ad hoc contracts and thus to end the 'SMart arrangement'. This arrangement put the couriers in a genuine employment relationship, providing them with an extra guarantee that legal minimum employment rights would be respected by Deliveroo. The unions considered the SMart arrangement as a second-best option in anticipation of the regulatory employment classification of the couriers. Unions are still awaiting a ruling about this, although a union litigation action has resulted in the overturning of a special tax regime encouraging platform work by the Constitutional Court in 2020 (Vandaele 2020). Likewise, a test case against Deliveroo looks promising for the FNV: a ruling stated that couriers should be considered employees instead of independent contractors in 2019 but the case is still ongoing; an organizing drive has therefore been helpful to identify evocative testimonies regarding the experience of couriers with management-by-algorithms (ibid.). The FNV is powering the now only virtually existing Riders Unions since mid-2018, which was previously an activist group established in 2017.

Turning to the Nordic countries, in Finland couriers launched a campaign called 'Justice4Couriers' in 2018, together with two grassroots unions, to improve their employment terms and conditions. The food couriers were later organized by Service Union United (Palvelualojen ammattiliitto) (Cant and Nicolson 2018). There has been little significant improvement so far, although the couriers are engaging with one of the platforms with which they have 'a constructive discussion relationship'.[16] Although opinions of the Finnish Labour Court are non-binding, the Court decided that couriers should be considered employees instead of freelancers in 2020. Meanwhile, negotiations for a collective agreement are ongoing between 3F and the Danish Chamber of Commerce, which is acting on behalf of Uber Eats, at the time of writing (Ilsøe 2020). The Transport Workers' Federation (NTF, Transportarbeiderforbund), affiliated to the Norwegian Confederation of Trade Unions, is organizing the couriers in Norway.[17] These couriers are in a genuine employment relationship, although on non-standard contracts (Ilsøe and Jesnes 2020). Negotiations for a collective agreement with Foodora first failed in 2019. After a five-week strike, however, an agreement was concluded, introducing, amongst other things, a minimum wage and reimbursement for equipment. Finally, platforms in Sweden are either the direct employer or use a so-called 'umbrella company', which means that couriers are employees and existing collective agreements can be applied to them (Söderqvist and Bernhardtz 2019).

Even in countries where the relationship between activist groups and mainstream unions is more tense, the latter are also catching up with the 'trend' of organizing food delivery and other couriers. Italian unions signed a local 'Charter of Fundamental Digital Workers' Rights in the Urban Context' in 2018, which introduces minimum employment terms and conditions for 'digital workers' in Bologna. Two local food delivery platforms signed up to it and a multinational pizza restaurant chain added their name later on (Veronese et al. 2019). Although international food platforms have so far refused to sign the Charter, it has inspired similar initiatives in other Italian regions, including legislation setting minimum terms and conditions for platform-based delivery couriers (Borelli 2019). There are also other examples of unions trying to compel food delivery platforms to respect the prevailing employment terms and conditions in Italy. A specific provision in a collective agreement in logistics, concluded in 2017, made couriers, irrespective of their employment status, part of the job classification system for the first time in Italy (Veronese et al. 2019); a new collective agreement guarantees that platform-based couriers are entitled to the same level of social protection as employees in 2020. Although the provision targets the platforms, not one of them has applied it, however, as the agreement is only binding for the signatory parties. Some progress has nevertheless been made when the food delivery platform Laconsegna established a work council and also signed a collective agreement introducing a dependent employment relationship for couriers in 2019. A number of Italian food delivery platforms also set up their own 'employers' association' annex lobby group, labelled 'Assodelivery', in 2018, and some of them signed a 'Food Delivery Values Charter' that same year, although they have only paid lip service to it. In a similar vein, thwarting bargaining strategies of the mainstream union confederations, Assodelivery concluded a collective agreement at the industrial level with the conservative, corporatist General Labour Union (Unione Generale Del Lavoro) in 2020: the agreement provides some social protection, but the technological/organizational fix is not addressed. Importantly, however, the court of Bologna ruled in 2020 that management-by-algorithm has been discriminating workers in case of absence including for taking industrial action. Furthermore, the scope of the collective agreement in catering and hospitality has been expanded in Spain: while food delivery platforms are in principle included, in practice the extension only concerns employees, meaning that platforms are not affected (Hermoso 2019). Lastly, while food delivery couriers are mainly organized by grassroots unions in the UK, the GMB concluded a collective agreement with the parcel courier company Hermes in 2019. The agreement enables couriers to opt for a new 'self-employed plus' status offering minimum wage guarantees, holiday pay and union representation, although it is noteworthy that they are in fact entitled to employment rights, as, according to an earlier tribunal case, they have been wrongly classified as self-employed (*Financial Times*, 26 February 2019).

CONCLUSION

This chapter has been underpinned by three key propositions about labour agency in the platform economy in Europe. First, platform work should be put in a historical perspective, in order to demystify its novelty. Platform work is simply one element of the increasingly fissured workplaces and precarious work arrangements that are becoming typical of the contemporary world. Such arrangements are rooted in the recommodification of labour in the Global North that took place from the 1970s onwards, and they imply a return to the default position of labour in capitalism, i.e. characterized by precarious work arrangements (Breman and van der Linden 2014). The crisis of the finance-led accumulation regime in 2007–2008 and subsequent austerity policies reinforced this recommodification in Europe, although standard employment is still dominant and persistent (Crouch 2019). At the same time, particular 'fixes' make platforms distinctive from other types of contingent and 'non-standard work'. The product fix is an indicator of how the promises of future revenue growth and market dominance lure investors to continue to financially support the platform business model. Insofar as the continuous circulation and accumulation of data becomes an arena for profit-making, then the product fix can also develop into financial expansion, or a 'financial fix'. In other words, the line between pure finance and speculation and venture-backed investments is a thin one in the case of platforms. At the time of writing, amidst the COVID-19 pandemic, it is still uncertain whether the economic downturn will catalyse the growth of (certain) platforms; food-delivery platforms seem to be in a good position here. Unemployment can feed a fresh reservoir of on-demand labour, and platforms might also benefit from shifting consumer preferences, new business strategies and the acceleration in remote work or facilitating state responses like the promotion of home-care provision.

The technological/organizational fix explains how platforms couple a relatively new type of labour management with old forms of work organization that frequently feature a contractor relationship. This fix is double-edged. On the one hand, platforms control the labour process by shifting a range of managerial responsibilities from humans to machines, thereby encouraging competition between platform workers via work allocation and performance rating systems. The algorithmic management thus also acts as a disincentive for collective resistance by platform workers as it encourages entrepreneurial interpretations of employment terms and conditions, thereby sustaining and reinforcing the existing work arrangements (Barratt et al. 2020). On the other hand, algorithmic management is simultaneously a source of frustration for workers as unilateral modifications of the algorithmic process affect employment terms and conditions and the 'cash nexus' (i.e. workers' pay). Although various governments across Europe have introduced special measures to cushion the loss of income for the solo self-employed since the pandemic, such measures have mainly been lacking for platform workers. Nevertheless, the coronavirus outbreak has transformed food delivery, personal care work and domestic work like cleaning, from low-status (invisible) work to so-called 'essential work'. Their non-entitlement to sick pay and other social benefits has undoubtedly put some of them in financial difficulties. The launch of health insurance schemes and support funds by some platforms, in a self-regulatory effort, is little more than a sticking-plaster solution, as the illness-related benefits they provide are generally inadequate (Fairwork 2020).

An analysis of platforms' spatial fixes makes the differences in geographical mobility clear between online and locally based platforms, with major consequences for labour agency. Relocation strategies as a response to collective resistance are nearly impossible for the (gendered) time- and place-bound work associated with locally based platforms. Compared to international operating platforms, locally based platforms might be more sensitive to pressure from political authorities to be transparent about their technological/organizational fix. The urban context could also unlock opportunities for forging coalitional power via alliance-building between platform workers, unions and other progressive communities or movements. Alliance-building between workers and consumers could also help to downgrade the importance of individual online ranking and reputation systems in locally based platform work. In contrast to online platform work, workers and consumers live in the same urban areas – this holds true especially for platform work in private settings, which could create more enduring human interactions. So far though, at least to the author's knowledge, not much more is known about self-organizing in this type of platform work. The development of online digital communities, for overcoming atomization and initiating social identification processes (along ethnic or citizenship lines or not), is similarly imaginable here like in platform-based transportation. Women will in all likelihood be the majority in such communities, reflecting the gender balance in cleaning and care which stands in contrast to the generally male-dominated transportation work in the platform economy. While platform workers in both private and public settings share the particular spatial fix of locally based platform work, however, it can be assumed that it is difficult for platform workers in private settings to gather physically during working time.

Second, based on a power resources theory approach, and in conjunction with the spatial fix, (visible) workers' resistance is typically expected to develop in locally based platform work in public settings, such as transportation in urban contexts, and less so in other types of platform work. Timed collective log-outs by couriers in the twenty-first century are mirroring the stopping of machines in the twentieth century. In fact, the seeds of cross-border cooperation and solidarity in the platform economy were first sown in transportation. A full understanding of emerging forms of collective resistance and representation requires also taking into account the platform workers' subjective situations in conjunction with their position in the labour market, the established organizational landscape of worker representation, the strategies of the platforms themselves and the institutional-regulatory context, especially regarding the employment relationship. It is apparent that unions in the Nordic countries, for instance, have managed to compel platforms to adhere to their prevailing institutional frameworks – although not without some difficulty, and the employment relationship is largely based on (precarious) non-standard contracts. Locally based platforms in other countries are moving heaven and earth to evade existing regulation on employment relations, but court decisions, also, in for instance Italy and Spain, seem increasingly not to their advantage as 'independent contractors' are reclassified as genuine employees.

Finally, the platform economy has ignited a (modest) spurt in collective organization-building. As in earlier examples, the new organizations show the imprint of their time in which they were created (Stinchcombe 1965). Today's organizations thus typically use the Internet infrastructure to engage with their members, revealing their foundation in the platform economy. Apart from this novelty, some imminent types of organization in the platform economy are quite reminiscent of older types of mutual aid and worker organization. With the exception of requester-initiated work in the online platform economy, it is apparent that cooperative models appear in all other types of platform work, although mostly in an embryonic stage. These models lack the disciplinary control and contractor relationship that are classical features of the technological/organizational fix. Union-led cooperatives have had a more supportive function, especially if the union action is only a half-hearted attempt to address the grey zones of the employment status of freelancers. Likewise, a more accommodative approach is also present in labour market intermediaries like SMart or co-op types of mutual aid such as Bread Funds. The worker-led co-op model has a greater transformative potential in locally based platforms where workers are owners (Scholz 2016). Since the current worker-led platform co-ops in food delivery seem to address the higher-end market, it remains to be seen whether they could be sustainable without the support of political authorities at the local level or beyond.

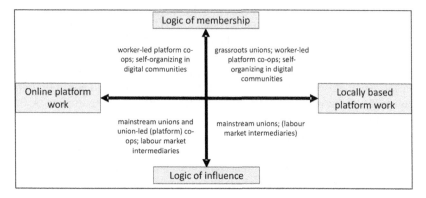

Figure 9.2   *Aligning old and 'new' forms of collective representation to representation logics*

These kinds of organizational experimentation hint at the possible coexistence of several models of unionism and new forms of collective representation – indeed, the latter requires widening the research lens beyond mainstream unions (Atzeni 2020). The degree of organizational fragmentation and cooperation between the old and 'new' will be subject to dynamics within industrial and national regulatory contexts (Hyman and Gumbrell-McCormick 2017). Figure 9.2 depicts the various models and forms and aligns them to the logic-of-membership and logic-of-influence approaches. So, the relationship between an organization and its members is considered central for self-organizing in digital communities and worker-led platform co-ops in both the locally based and online platform work and for grassroots unions in online platform work, although the latter are also involved in test cases and litigation actions. In fact, the number of European countries where grassroots unions are organizing platform workers is fairly limited (which might be in contrast to conventional wisdom). If no relevant grassroots unions are present in a country, then platform workers have either continued to organize themselves via their own groups of activists or they have approached mainstream unions. Mainstream unions, union-led co-ops and labour market intermediaries are all present in online platform work. They tend to focus on relationships with employers' associations and the state, which in the case of labour market intermediaries is a way to seek legitimacy for their model. Intermediaries seem absent in locally based platform work, with the exception of the short-lived SMart arrangement in Belgium. Only mainstream unions are present in this type of platform work if it concerns the logic-of-influence approach. Here, in locally based platform work, an emerging cooperation between activist groups and unions in platform-based food delivery can be detected in most but not all countries, whereby unions could be helpful in overcoming the 'liability of newness' (Stinchcombe 1965, p. 148) of these groups so that they continue to exist. While the effectiveness of the struggles to alter the platforms' technological/organizational fix is challenging, they have put pressure on states (and the European Union, see Countouris and De Stefano (2021)) to regulate the platform economy. Moreover, the cooperation between activist groups and unions, along with other types of organizations, could also point to a broader transition of unionism and its possible revitalization. Unions analysing their own 'big data', engaging with online digital communities and addressing issues of data transparency (and ownership) will therefore be key in the platform economy and beyond, as these developments will in all likelihood have a significant impact on the future of the labour movement in general.

NOTES

1. The chapter provides no systematic country-by-country analysis, and it is limited to selected European countries; countries in Central and Eastern Europe are mostly excluded. The European policymaking level is omitted from the analysis solely due to word limit constraints. However, that the European Commission is currently consulting how European competition law could be reconciled with collective bargaining rights for the self-employed, i.e. within and beyond the platform economy.
2. See https://www.eurofound.europa.eu/hu/data/platform-economy/initiatives
3. Such one-off jobs are being jargonized and popularized as 'gigs' – a slang term rejected here as it is originally associated with musical performance outside the platform economy. Such a positive connotation is not necessarily valid for platform work. The term 'gig economy' is particularly used in English-speaking countries, commonly just in reference to locally based platform work, whereas 'crowdwork' is dominant in German-speaking countries but only comprises online platform work.
4. Platforms based in the United States, which are among the largest ones, are exceptions as they have been active since an earlier time.
5. Although the proportion of online platform work might be overstated, due to the online survey methods, it looks like this type of work is more prevalent than locally

based platform work in Europe (Urzì Brancati et al. 2020). This stands in contrast to the academic and media attention being paid to the latter type of platform work, although the United Kingdom seems to be an exception as transportation services are dominant.

6. Alternatively, ride-hailing platforms could opt for a strategy of labour-saving automation via self-driving vehicles, or food delivery platforms could try to gain greater control over production via, for instance, 'dark kitchens' or 'ghost' restaurants, which are businesses in inexpensive areas set up for delivery only.
7. Labour control might also differ within the same platform type.
8. It could involve offline microwork that has far less visibility, such as taking photos of objects.
9. In addition, the Frankfurt Declaration on Platform-Based Work of 2016 was signed by unions in Europe and the USA.
10. No data are available on the number of unionized workers, although it is speculated to be very low.
11. The platforms themselves initially also set up digital communities for passing on and clarifying information for the couriers.
12. See https://kolyma2.coopcycle.org. 'FoodFairies' is another food delivery platform aiming to be a post-Deliveroo co-op in Berlin; see https://foodfairies.de
13. The International Transport Workers' Federation, in a move towards 'glocalism', set up a project funding two full-time London-based organizers in 2019.
14. Similarly, in ride-hailing, a first convening of the International Alliance of App-Based Transport Workers took place in London in early 2020, with participants from 23 countries across the globe.
15. The works council in Cologne had already become obsolete before Deliveroo stopped its business in Germany in 2019 as the platform reduced the number of permanent staff so that legal requirements were no longer met for a works council.
16. See https://www.justice4couriers.fi/2020/02/24/our-second-meeting-with-wolt/
17. NTF merged with the United Federation of Trade Unions (Fellesforbundet) in 2020.

REFERENCES

Altenried, M. (2020), 'The platform as factory: Crowdwork and the hidden labour behind artificial intelligence', *Capital & Class*, **44** (2), 145–158.

Anwar, M.A. and M. Graham (2021), 'Between a rock and a hard place: Freedom, flexibility, precarity and vulnerability in the gig economy in Africa', *Competition & Change*, **25** (2), 237–258.

Atzeni, M. (2020), 'Worker organisation in precarious times: Abandoning trade union fetishism, rediscovering class', *Global Labour Journal*, **11** (3), 311–314.

Badger, A. and N. van Doorn (2020), 'Platform capitalism's hidden abode: Producing data assets in the gig economy', *Antipode*, **52** (5), 1475–1495.

Barratt, T., C. Goods and A. Veen (2020), '"I'm my own boss ...": Active intermediation and 'entrepreneurial' worker agency in the Australian gig-economy', *Environment and Planning A: Economy and Space*, **52** (8), 1643–1661.

Borelli, S. (2019), 'Italy', in I. Daugareilh, C. Degryse and P. Pochet (eds) *The platform economy and social law: Key issues in comparative perspective*, Working Paper 2019.10, Brussels: ETUI, pp. 63–73.

Breman, J. and M. van der Linden (2014), 'Informalizing the economy: The return of the social question at a global level', *Development and Change*, **45** (5), 920–940.

Cant, C. (2019), *Riding for Deliveroo. Resistance in the new economy*, Cambridge: Polity Press.

Cant, C. and C. Mogno (2020), 'Platform workers of the world, unite! The emergence of the Transnational Federation of Couriers', *South Atlantic Quarterly*, **119** (2), 401–411.

Cant, C. and M. Nicolson (2018), 'Justice for couriers: An interview with a Finnish Foodora worker', accessed 27 July 2020 at https://notesfrombelow.org/article/justice-for-couriers-finnish-foodora-worker

Cant, C. and J. Woodcock (2020), 'Fast food shutdown: From disorganisation to action in the service sector', *Capital & Class*, **44** (4), 513–521.

Chagny, O. (2019), 'France. Case study report, Don't GIG Up! Project', accessed 27 July 2020 at www.dontgigup.eu/wp-content/uploads/2019/11/Casestudy_FR.pdf

Charles, J., I. Ferreras and A. Lamine (2020), 'A freelancers' cooperative as a case of democratic institutional experimentation for better work: A case study of SMart-Belgium', *Transfer: European Review of Labour and Research*, **26** (2), 157–174.

Countouris, N. and V. De Stefano (2021), 'The labour law framework: Self-employed and their right to bargain collectively', *Bulletin of Comparative Labour Relations*, accessed 18 January at https://papers.ssrn.com/sol3/papers.cfm?abstract_id= 3763214

Crouch, C. (2019), *Will the gig economy prevail?*, Cambridge: Polity.

Duggan, J., U. Sherman, R. Carbery and A. McDonnell (2020), 'Algorithmic management and app-work in the gig economy: A research agenda for employment relations and HRM', *Human Resource Management Journal*, **30** (1), 114–132.

Dunand, J.-P. and P. Mahon (2019), 'Switzerland', in I. Daugareilh, C. Degryse and P. Pochet (eds) *The platform economy and social law: Key issues in comparative perspective*, Working Paper 2019.10, Brussels: ETUI, pp. 107–113.

Ettlinger, N. (2017), 'Paradoxes, problems and potentialities of online work platforms', *Work Organisation, Labour & Globalisation*, **11** (2), 21–38.

Fabo, B., M. Beblavý, Z. Kilhoffer and K. Lenaerts (2017), *An overview of European platforms: Scope and business models. JRC science for policy reports*, Luxembourg: Publications Office of the European Union.

Fairwork (2020), *The gig economy and Covid-19: Fairwork report on platform policies*, Oxford: The Fairwork Project.

Fernàndez, A. and M. Soliña Barreiro (2020), 'The algorithm is not my boss anymore: Technological appropriation and (new) media strategies in Riders x Derechos and Mensakas', *Contracampo*, **39** (1), 65–83.

Finkin, M. (2016), 'Beclouded work, beclouded workers in historical perspective', *Comparative Labor Law and Policy Journal*, **37**, 603–618.

Flanagan, F. (2019), 'Theorising the gig economy and home-based service work', *Journal of Industrial Relations*, **61** (1), 57–78.

Fulton, L. (2018) *Trade Unions protecting self-employed workers. Why self-employed workers need better rights? What unions are doing? Which priorities for the future?*, Brussels: European Trade Union Confederation.

Gandini, A. (2019), 'Labour process theory and the gig economy', *Human Relations*, **72** (6), 1039–1056.

Gegenhuber, T., M. Ellmer and E. Schüßler (2021), 'Microphones, not megaphones: Functional crowdworker voice regimes on digital work platforms', *Human Relations*, **74** (9), 1473–1503.

Gerber, C. (2021), 'Community building on crowdwork platforms: Autonomy and control of online workers?', *Competition & Change*, **25** (2), 90–211.

Gerber, C. and M. Krzywdzinski (2019), 'Brave new digital work? New forms of performance control in crowdwork', in S. Vallas and A. Kovalainen (eds) *Work and labor in the digital age. Research in the sociology of work*, Vol. 33, Bingley: Emerald, pp. 121–143.

Goods, V., A. Veen and T. Barratt (2019), '"Is your gig and good?' Analysing job quality in the Australian platform-based food-delivery sector', *Journal of Industrial Relations*, **61**, (4), 502–527.

Graham, M., J. Woodcock, R. Heeks, P. Mungai, J.-P. Van Belle, D. du Toit, S. Fredman, A. Osiki, A. van der Spuy and S.M. Silberman (2020), 'The Fairwork Foundation: Strategies for improving platform work in a global context', *Geoforum*, **112**, 100–103.

Gray, M.L. and S. Suri (2019), *Ghost work. How to stop Silicon Valley from building a new global underclass*, Boston, MA: Houghton Mifflin Harcourt.

Greef, S., W. Schroeder and H.J. Sperling (2020), 'Plattformökonomie und Crowdworking als Herausforderungen für das deutsche Modell der Arbeitsbeziehungen', *Industrielle Beziehungen*, **2**, 205–226.

Haake, G. (2017), 'Trade unions, digitalisation and the self-employed – inclusion or exclusion?', *Transfer: European Review of Labour and Research*, **23** (1) 63–66.

Healy, J. and A. Pekarek (2020), 'Work and wages in the gig economy: Can there be a high road?', in A. Wilkinson and M. Barry (eds) *The future of work and employment*, Cheltenham, UK and Northampton, MA, USA: Edward Elgar pp. 156–173.

Heiland, H. (2021), 'Controlling space, controlling labour? Contested space in food delivery gig work', *New Technologies, Work and Employment*, **36** (1), 1–16.

Hermoso, M. (2019), 'Spain. Case study report. Don't GIG Up! Project', accessed 27 July 2020 at http://www.dontgigup.eu/wp-content/uploads/2020/01/Casestudy_ES .pdf

Howcroft, D. and B. Bergvall-Kåreborn (2019), 'A typology of crowdwork platforms', *Work, Employment and Society*, **33** (1), 21–38.

Huws, U., N.H. Spencer, D.S. Syrdal and K. Holts (2017), *Work in the European gig economy: Research results from the UK, Sweden, Germany, Austria, the Netherlands, Switzerland and Italy*, Brussels: Foundation for European Progressive Studies.

Hyman, R. (2015), 'Austeritarianism in Europe: What options for resistance?', in D. Natali and B. Vanhercke (eds) *Social policy in the European Union: State of play 2015*, Brussels: ETUI, pp. 97–126.

Hyman, R. and R. Gumbrell-McCormick (2017), 'Resisting labour market insecurity: Old and new actors, rivals or allies?', *Journal of Industrial Relations*, **59** (4), 538–561.

Ilsøe, A. (2020), *The Hilfr agreement. Negotiating the platform economy in Denmark*, FAOS Research Paper 176, Copenhagen: Employment Relations Research Centre.

Ilsøe, A. and K. Jesnes (2020), 'Collective agreements for platforms and workers – two cases from the Nordic countries', in K. Jesnes and S.M. Nordli Oppegaard (eds) *Platform work in the Nordic models: Issues, cases and responses*, Copenhagen: Nordic Council of Ministers, pp. 57–67.

Ilsøe, A., K. Jesnes and M. Hotvedt (2020) 'Social partner responses in the Nordic platform economy', in K. Jesnes and S.M. Nordli Oppegaard (eds) *Platform work in the Nordic models: Issues, cases and responses*, Copenhagen: Nordic Council of Ministers, pp. 68–78.

Jansen, G. (2020), 'Solo self-employed and membership of interest organizations in the Netherlands: Economic, social and political determinants', *Economic and Industrial Democracy*, **41** (3), 512–539.

Jansen, G. and R. Sluiter (2019), 'The matter of representation: Precarious self-employment and interests organizations', in W. Conen and J. Shippers (eds) *Self-employment as precarious work. A European perspective*, Cheltenham, UK and Northampton, MA, USA: Edward Elgar, pp. 216–237.

Johnson, H. (2020), 'Labour geographies of the platform economy: Understanding collective organizing strategies in the context of digitally mediated work', *International Labour Review*, **159** (1), 25–45.

Joyce, S. (2020), 'Rediscovering the cash nexus, again: Subsumption and the labour–capital relation in platform work', *Capital & Class*, **44** (4), 541–552.

Kilhoffer, Z., W.P. De Groen, K. Lenaerts, I. Smits, H. Hauben, W. Waeyaert, E. Giacumacatos J.-P. Lhernould and S. Robin-Olivier (2020), *Study to gather evidence on the working conditions of platform workers*, Luxembourg: Publications Office of the European Union.

Langley, P. and A. Leyshon (2017), 'Platform capitalism: The intermediation and capitalisation of digital economic circulation', *Finance and Society*, **3** (1), 11–31.

Lehdonvirta, V., O. Kässi, I. Hjorth, H. Bernard and M. Graham M. (2019), 'The global platform economy: A new offshoring institution enabling emerging-economy microproviders', *Journal of Management*, **45** (2), 567–599.

Maffie, M.D. (2020a), 'The role of digital communities in organizing gig workers', *Industrial Relations*, **59** (1), 123–149.

Maffie, M.D. (2020b), 'Are we "sharing" or "gig-ing"? A classification system for online platforms', *Industrial Relations Journal*, **51** (6), 536–555.

Mori, A. and B. Koene (2019), 'Continuity and discontinuity in collective representation', in R. Semenza and F. Pichault (eds) *The challenges of self-employment in Europe. Status, social protection and collective representation*, Cheltenham, UK and Northampton, MA, USA: Edward Elgar, pp. 178–205.

Murgia, A. and V. Pulignano (2019), 'Neither precarious nor entrepreneur: The subjective experience of hybrid self-employed workers', *Economic and Industrial Democracy*, https://doi.org/10.1177/0143831X19873966

Murray, G., C. Lévesque, G. Morgan and N. Roby (2020), 'Disruption and re-regulation in work and employment: From organisational to institutional experimentation', *Transfer: European Review of Labour and Research*, **26** (2), 135–156.

Niebler, V. (2020), '"YouTubers unite": Collective action of content Creators on YouTube', *Transfer: European Review of Labour and Research*, **26** (2), 223–227.

Offe, C. and H. Wiesenthal (1980) 'Two logics of collective action: Theoretical notes on social class and organizational form', *Political Power and Social Theory*, **1** (1), 67–115.

Panteli, N., A. Rapti and D. Scholarios (2020), '"If he just knew who we were": Microworkers' emerging bonds of attachment in a fragmented employment relationship', *Work Employment and Society*, **34** (3), 476–494.

Però, D. (2020), 'Indie unions, organizing and labour renewal: Learning from precarious migrant workers', *Work, Employment and Society*, **34** (5), 900–918.

Pesole, A., M.C. Urzì Brancati, E. Fernández-Macías, F. Biagi and I. González Vázquez (2018), *Platform workers in Europe. Evidence from the COLLEEM survey*, Luxembourg: Publications Office of the European Union.

Roy-Mukherjee, S. and M. Harrison (2020), 'The shifting boundaries of capitalism and the conflict of surplus value appropriation within the gig economy', in R. Page-Tickell and E. Yerby (eds) *Conflict and shifting boundaries in the gig economy*, Bingley: Emerald Publishing, pp. 45–62.

Scholz, T. (2016), *Platform cooperativism. Challenging the corporate sharing economy*, New York: Rosa Luxemburg Stiftung.

Silver, B. (2003), *Forces of labor: Workers' movements and globalization since 1870*, Cambridge: Cambridge University Press.

Söderqvist, C.F. and V. Bernhardtz (2019), *Labor Platforms with unions. Discussing the law and economics of a Swedish collective bargaining framework used to regulate gig work*, Working Paper 2019:57, Stockholm: Swedish Entrepreneurship Forum.

Srnicek, N. (2017), *Platform capitalism*, Cambridge: Polity Press.

Stanford, J. (2017), 'The resurgence of gig work: Historical and theoretical perspectives', *The Economic and Labour Relations Review*, **28** (3), 382–401.

Stinchcombe, A. (1965) 'Social structure and organizations', in J.G. March (ed.) *Handbook of organizations*, Chicago: Rand-McNally, pp. 142–193.

Sutherland, W., M. Hossien Jarrahi, M. Dunn and S.B. Nelson (2020), 'Work precarity and gig literacies in online freelancing', *Work, Employment and Society*, **34** (3), 457–475.

Tapia, M. (2019), '"Not fissures but moments of crises that can be overcome": Building a relational organizing culture in community organizations and trade unions', *Industrial Relations*, **58** (2), 229–250.

Tassinari, A. and V. Maccarrone (2017), 'The mobilisation of gig economy couriers in Italy: Some lessons for the trade union movement', *Transfer: European Review of Labour and Research*, **23** (3), 353–357.

Tassinari, A. and V. Maccarrone (2018), 'Varieties of unionism meet the platform economy: A comparison of gig workers' organizing practices and trade union responses in Italy and the UK', paper presented at Industrial Relations in Europe Conference (IREC), KU Leuven, 11 September.

Tassinari, A. and V. Maccarrone (2020), 'Riders on the storm: Workplace solidarity among gig economy couriers in Italy and the UK', *Work, Employment and Society*, **34** (1), 35–54.

Ticona, J. and A. Mateescu (2018), 'Trusted strangers: Carework platforms' cultural entrepreneurship in the on-demand economy', *New Media & Society*, **20** (11), 4384–4404.

Trappmann, V., I. Bessa, S. Joyce, D. Neumann, M. Stuart and C. Umney (2020), *Global labour unrest on platforms. The case of food delivery workers*, Berlin: FES.

Trojansky, A. (2020), *Towards the 'Uber-isation' of care? Platform work in the sector of long-term home care and its implications for workers' rights*, Brussels: European Economic and Social Committee.

Urzì Brancati, C.U., A. Pesole and E. Fernández-Macías (2019), *Digital Labour Platforms in Europe: Numbers, profiles, and employment status of platform workers. JRC Technical reports*, Luxembourg: Publications Office of the European Union.

Urzì Brancati, C.U., A. Pesole and E. Fernández-Macías (2020), *New evidence on platform workers in Europe. Results from the second COLLEEM survey*, Luxembourg: Publications Office of the European Union.

Vallas, S. and J. Schor (2020), 'What do platforms do? Understanding the gig economy', *Annual Review of Sociology*, **46** (1), 1–22.

Vandaele, K. (2018), *Will trade unions survive in the platform economy? Emerging patterns of platform workers' collective voice and representation in Europe*, Working Paper 2018.05, Brussels: ETUI.

Vandaele, K. (2020) *From street protest to "improvisational unionism". Platform-based food delivery couriers in Belgium and the Netherlands*, Berlin: FES.

Vandaele, K., A. Piasna and J. Drahokoupil (2019), *'Algorithm breakers' are not a different 'species': Attitudes towards trade unions of Deliveroo riders in Belgium*, Working Paper 2019.06, Brussels: ETUI.

van Doorn, N., F. Ferrari and M. Graham (2020) *Migration and migrant labour in the gig economy: An intervention*, accessed 27 July 2020 at https://ssrn.com/abstract=3622589

Veronese, I., A. Pirastu, P. Richini and F. Ludicone (2019), 'Italy. Case study report. Don't GIG Up! Project', accessed 27 July 2020 at http://www.dontgigup.eu/wp-content/uploads/2020/02/Casestudy_IT.pdf

Vriens, E. and T. De Moor (2020), 'Mutuals on the move: Exclusion processes in the welfare state and the rediscovery of mutualism', *Social Inclusion*, **8** (1), 225–237.

Wood, A. and V. Lehdonvirta (2021), 'Antagonism beyond employment: how the 'subordinated agency' of labour platforms generates conflict in the remote gig economy', *SSRN* accessed 27 July 2020 at https://osf.io/preprints/socarxiv/y943w/

Wood, A., V. Lehdonvirta and M. Graham (2018a), 'Workers of the Internet unite? Online freelancer organisation among remote gig economy workers in six Asian and African countries', *New Technology, Work and Employment*, **33** (2), 95–112.

Wood, A.J., M. Graham, V. Lehdonvirta and I. Hjorth (2018b), 'Good gig, bad gig: Autonomy and algorithmic control in the global gig economy', *Work, Employment and Society*, **33** (1), 56–75.

Woodcock, J. and M. Graham (2020) *The gig economy: A critical introduction*, Cambridge: Polity Press.

10. Digital platform work in Latin America: challenges and perspectives for its regulation[1]

Graciela Bensusán and Héctor Santos

INTRODUCTION

During the first two decades of the twenty-first century, a diverse range of companies offering services through digital platforms and intelligent techno-logical devices connected to the internet emerged globally. These companies encouraged those willing to provide services to sign up as self-employed workers. In some cases, this business model obscured the labour relationship between companies and workers and exemplifies what is known as the 'the disappearance of the employer' (Degryse 2019). That is, companies who fail to register workers with social security systems and to recognize their labour rights, thus contributing to labour informality in the countries in which they operate (Berg and De Stefano 2016). The issue of digital platform employment is thus an important one in the study of labour markets and constitutes an enor-mous challenge for both the state and social actors in Latin America.

Some specialists argue that platforms are an opportunity for labour for-malization as their growth in developing countries, in addition to generating employment, will inevitably lead to their regulation (Buenadicha et al. 2017). In contrast, others suggest that the prevalence of weak states in these countries allows offline platforms[2] to operate at the margins of employment and other regulations. Digital platforms therefore have no incentive to encourage job formalization or to recognize workers' rights (Robinson 2015).

In light of this debate, in this chapter we argue that the quality of jobs gen-erated by offline digital platforms will depend both on the characteristics of the platforms themselves, as well as on the opportunities and restrictions faced by states and social actors (unions, principally) to regulate the platforms and counterbalance the unilaterality of their actions. Both factors stem from the structural conditions of labour markets, as well as from power relations and political decisions, and are likely to have important consequences for workers' well-being and social inequality in the region. Thus, although some type of state intervention intended to curb the most detrimental social effects of the digital economy can be expected, precisely as occurred in previous industrial revolutions, responses are likely to vary and will depend largely on the instruments used as well as their scope and orientation. In fact, various countries across the region have already begun this process, and efforts to regulate work done through platforms are particularly advanced in certain developed countries, as we will show.

As a result of the evidence gathered in this chapter, we argue that platform work is often considered to be low quality but workers in Latin America seem quite satisfied with it; it offers better opportunities in terms of pay and autonomy than the local labour markets, particularly for better educated workers. At the same time, platform work threatens to further informalize the already highly informal labour markets in Latin America and to further increase already high levels of inequality. This further informalization will result in a growing percentage of the working population living in conditions of insecurity since informal workers are not covered by social security arrangements such as unemployment benefits, pensions or sickness benefits, which are often linked to formal employment in Latin America.

Platform work takes the form of informal work due to the workers being generally treated as self-employed, even though in many cases they should really be classified as employees. There is a lack of regulation and enforcement here. Weak states and weak social actors (unions) along with the refusal of the platforms to recognize their employment responsibility are at the root of this problem.

There is no single solution to these problems, which also arise in the rest of the world. However, some experiences in Latin America and further afield show that the state and social actors have a range of options with which to better regulate the platform economy and reduce informality.

To develop these arguments, this chapter is organized as follows. Section 1 provides a brief overview of the main characteristics of Latin American labour markets: informality and job insecurity. Section 2 presents the main findings of two quantitative investigations into platform work. One includes Mexico, Chile, Brazil and Colombia. The other focuses on Argentina. We also present some perceptions of various actors in Mexico on the advisability of regulating work on platforms. Section 3 examines the central issues of this debate, as well as the main approaches to the role of the state and collective actors with regards to regulating platforms. We argue that decisions will depend upon the orientation of the different governments as well as the local characteristics and socio-political arrangements of the world of work, which will create more or less favourable structures of political opportunities for workers' protection.

The fourth section reviews current forms of state intervention into the regulation of digital platforms, taking into account different governmental branches (legislative, judicial and administrative) and orientations (those that recognize the subordinate status of these workers as well as those that view platform workers as self-employed). We examine the situation both regionally and internationally. Here, the case of Mexico serves to illustrate how a change in governmental political orientation can create favourable conditions for the protection of the most vulnerable. Finally, our conclusions are presented.

1　　THE LABOUR MARKET IN LATIN AMERICA: INFORMALITY AND INEQUALITY

A study conducted by CEPAL (2010, p. 160) asserts that the social and economic inequality characterizing the region is mainly due to the poor performance of labour markets and the disparities that arise as a consequence. One example is that in Latin America for every hour worked, women receive on average 17 per cent less income than men (OIT 2019a). Another significant inequality is that 18 per cent of 15–24-year-olds are unemployed, which is the more than twice the overall rate of unemployment in the region, which was 8.4 per cent in the same year (ILO 2020). Young people also registered a 62.4 per cent rate of labour informality in 2019, which is 10 per cent higher than the general rate in Latin America (ILO 2020).

Labour informality, understood as jobs outside of contributory social security systems, persists and is a serious issue in Latin America, despite the fact that some governments were able to improve levels of formality between 2003 and 2013. During this period, the regional average percentage of workers enrolled in social security systems increased from 38.3 per cent to 45.2 per cent (BID 2015). Despite this, in 2018, five out of ten employed persons worked in informal employment (OIT 2018), and eight out of ten self-employed workers were informally employed (OIT 2015). According to the ECLAC-ILO (CEPAL-OIT 2019), in 2018, self-employed work accounted for 48 per cent of employment at a regional level. It has been noted that in Latin America, paid informal work is largely involuntary, although this is also true for a significant proportion of self-employed workers (Perry et al. 2007). Given the prognosis of low economic growth for the region in the upcoming decade, and the probable limited creation of new positions of paid work, self-employed work, partly associated with work on digital platforms, is likely to increase (CEPAL-OIT 2019). Hence, there is a need to prevent workers who sign on to digital platforms from falling into involuntary informality.

In Latin America, labour market inequalities are linked to access to or exclusion from social security systems, according to the type of employment. In general terms, there are two varieties of social protection schemes in Latin

America. One is contributions-based social security, linked to standard formal employment and with a low rate of coverage. Among its benefits are pensions and health insurance. In order to finance this scheme, workers and employers make income-based contributions. The other variant is non-contributory social security, which provides coverage to those who do not have formal employment. It provides more limited benefits than contributory schemes, but it differs from these in the scope of the benefits, and the source of funding is public spending (OIT 2018, p. 15). Currently, the persistent and elevated rate of informality in the region has led to a recognition that social risks should be responded to with a combination of contributory and non-contributory social security schemes (OIT 2018).

The third issue, job insecurity, defined as unstable and insecure working conditions (affecting access to work benefits), is expressed in rates of employee turnover. In Latin America, one in four employed persons between the ages of 24 and 54 have worked in their current job for a year or less, compared to one in eight in OECD countries. Furthermore, the average length of service in Latin America is 40 per cent less than in OECD countries (BID 2015). Among the possible causes for such instability are labour informality (CONEVAL 2018), low productivity, minimal training for workers and low wages, resulting in a cycle of 'poor quality jobs' (BID 2015, p. 20).

As a result of this, digital platforms in the region are inserted into a segmented labour market, but it is not clear to what extent they could influence the tendencies described. In this sense, the platforms play an as yet uncertain role in relation to the social and economic inequality that characterizes the region and that is produced in the labour market, as CEPAL points out (2010).

2   LATIN AMERICAN EXPERIENCES WITH PLATFORM WORK

With the aim of examining the degree to which emerging work on platforms follows the trends described above, we now present findings from two quantitative studies. The first study focuses on Uber drivers in Mexico, Chile, Brazil and Colombia (Azuara et al. 2019), while the second looks at workers registered on a variety of platforms in Argentina (Madariaga et al. 2019). While anticipating further studies incorporating a wider range of countries, these studies provide at least an initial, general profile of platform workers. Complementarily, we present some perceptions of various actors in Mexico on the advisability of regulating work on platforms, the scope of this, as well as the advantages and disadvantages of doing so (Bensusán 2020).

2.1 Uber in Mexico, Chile, Brazil and Colombia[3]

The study produced by Azuara, González and Keller (2019) analyses the case of Uber in Mexico, Chile, Brazil and Colombia, analysing the results of a survey conducted with 5,251 Uber drivers in those four countries.

The average age of Uber drivers in those countries is 38, 93 per cent of whom are men. In these countries, 55 per cent of workers have a university degree. In general, they are workers in the prime of their working life with a good level of education.

On a regional level, almost half the Uber drivers had been informally employed before joining the company (45 per cent) (Azuara et al. 2019). This data supports Robinson's (2015) argument that regional state regulatory weakness facilitates the platforms operating at the margins of labour legislation or other laws, and thereby reproduces the tendency for informality in the region's labour markets. In addition, it partly explains the difficulty faced by these workers to organize and gain recognition as workers with rights.

Azuara and colleagues (2019, p. 14) survey shows that income levels from digital platforms are a significant incentive, equivalent to three times the national minimum wage in Mexico, Chile, Brazil and Colombia. It is also worth highlighting that, in these countries the 'average duration in the use of the platform is 19 hours per week, and the majority of Uber drivers uses it less than 30 hours per week' (Azuara et al. 2019, p. 11). Either way, this is less than the 48 hours per week legal limit in Mexico and does not even constitute the minimum of 35 hours of a full working week according to the criteria of the National Institute of Statistics and Geography (INEGI).[4] In addition, it should be noted that 66 per cent of digital platform workers identify the option of flexible hours as an important motive for signing onto, and continuing to work on, these platforms. It is surprising that only 40 per cent of these workers stated that they would leave these jobs if they were offered other paid work, suggesting that the majority are satisfied with their working conditions. It should also be noted that 28 per cent are employed on more than one platform (Azuara et al. 2019).

Finally, considering the lack of asset ownership as a key indication of the nature of the relationship between workers and platforms, the fact that half of the region's Uber drivers do not own their vehicle suggests that they should be considered as subordinate workers. However, this does not necessarily mean that the platform is the employer, as workers could be considered to be in a subordinate relationship with the owner of the vehicle they rent. In summary, most of the above data challenges the digital platforms' claim that workers are self-employed, despite the fact that a significant proportion of workers may be satisfied with this condition.

The above coincides with the findings of Eisenmeier's case study (2018) of Uber drivers in Mexico. In this case, the drivers' satisfaction is much more evident among those who have been excluded from the formal labour market, mainly due to age, and who own their vehicles. However, the author points out that this satisfaction is in decline in the face of growing competition between drivers and among platforms (Eisenmeier 2018).

Although concerns regarding the regulation of platform workers' rights could at first be seen as purely academic and lacking social support, as long as satisfaction with Uber's working conditions continues to decline, that situation could change.

2.2   Work on Digital Platforms in Argentina

The report for the International Labour Organization and Interamerican Bank of Development prepared by Madariaga et al. (2019), analyses the results of a survey conducted with 603 workers from ten different types of platforms. It found that the age of platform workers in Argentina is between 18 and 49, 73.7 per cent of whom are men. In this country, 37 per cent of workers have university degrees (Madariaga et al. 2019). Just like in the case of Uber drivers, in general, they are workers at the beginning of their working life with a good level of education.

In Argentina's platform economy only 55 per cent of workers contribute to social security. Almost 90 per cent of them do so as independent taxpayers, a tax regime created in Argentina for self-employed workers long before the rapid expansion of digital platforms.

In relation to work insecurity, workers from a heterogeneous group of platforms reported having been working on platforms for an average of 15 months, longer than four out of ten workers in the region who have less than a year's continuity in their current job (BID 2015). With regards to hours worked per week, 35.9 per cent of the survey's respondents reported that they work less than 20 hours, and 31.6 per cent report more than 45 hours. On average, workers on the ten platforms included in the study worked a little over 32 hours weekly (Madariaga et al. 2019, p. 100).

In terms of motives for seeking employment on these platforms, the main one reported by 30.2 per cent of respondents was the possibility of additional earnings. Furthermore, it should be noted that 29.1 per cent of digital platform workers identify the option of flexible hours as an important motive for signing onto, and continuing to work on, these platforms (Madariagae et al. 2019, p. 93).

Work through digital platforms constitutes the main source of income for 61 per cent of these workers. This contradicts the assumption that these jobs are secondary occupations, preventing workers from claiming their labour rights.

Furthermore, in this country 22 per cent of workers surveyed are employed on more than one platform.

This suggests that most workers, by earning at least 75 per cent of their income from a single platform, meet the criterion of economic dependence used to establish workers' rights. The majority also meet the criterion of exclusivity. It has also been argued however that these characteristics distinguish a third category of work, falling between subordinated work and self-employment, as discussed below.

2.3   The Opinions of Actors Involved in Platform Work in Mexico[5]

The results of interviews conducted in Mexico with various social and governmental actors, as well as with Uber drivers and Rappi food deliverers show a general agreement for the need to regulate these jobs. Respondents also agreed that legislation was needed to establish the criteria that would determine the circumstances under which a (subordinate) employment relationship existed between platforms and workers. They also shared the concern of digital platform work becoming a new path to informality.

Respondents were given three options regarding the recognition of platform workers' rights: to decouple social security from employment status, to create new categories of workers between subordinated and self-employed work (i.e. dependent contractor in Britain, Sánchez-Urán 2018, p. 72), or to consider such workers to be subordinate in all cases, with all the rights that this would entail. Interestingly, some digital platform workers emphatically stated that they would not sacrifice their autonomy for labour rights, reflecting the dominant argument against regulation.

Finally, it was recognized that relations between the platforms and the actors interested in labour regulation (federal governments and the government of Mexico City) have been sporadic and have failed to produce results (Bensusán 2020). According to respondents, and as is common knowledge, this is largely due to the fact that platforms generally oppose regulation. Government authorities and the legislative branch are thus attempting various ways of overcoming this resistance, as shown below.

To recapitulate, evidence suggests that Latin American labour market tendencies extend to digital platform work, although more precise studies are needed to corroborate this. This would entail improving available statistical sources and considering the inclusion of emerging occupations in the digital economy in national surveys of occupation and employment. On the other hand, the high levels of satisfaction, flexible hours and income level of workers on digital platforms need to be considered when designing labour regulations. As will be seen, this is a highly contentious issue. Nevertheless, these opinions also show that much still needs to be done in order for both platforms and workers to appreciate that flexibility for workers does not necessarily need to imply a lack of labour rights, as correctly expressed by the OECD (2019). Without a doubt, there are many reasons workers may be satisfied with their situation, especially when comparing it with that of the many poorer-quality jobs available within a context of low economic growth. Nevertheless, this should not relegate the discussion regarding regulatory alternatives to a secondary question or one without justification, as argued by the platforms.

3   REGULATING THE PLATFORM ECONOMY: WHY AND HOW

It is worth mentioning that the lack of employment formalization in Latin American countries is critical, because, as mentioned above, there is no universal social security system independent of employment status. The debate around this issue reveals various positions regarding the regulation of digital work; specifically, whether it should be regulated, and if so, how. Two key questions emerge: the heterogeneity of platforms (are they true service providers or simply technological intermediaries), and the nature of the relationship between platforms and their service providers (are workers self-employed or subordinate). However, while there is consensus regarding the need to prevent digital platform work from expanding the 'cycle of poor-quality jobs' (BID 2015) and aggravating existing labour market tendencies, a variety of theoretical perspectives exist regarding how to approach this, and what the rationale and scope of state intervention should be. Equally, a range of positions question the capacity and interest of unions to defend platform workers, as well as the willingness of these workers to organize.

The nature of digital platforms and the social connections between them and their service providers are at the centre of the debate around the need to regulate, and more importantly, around what instruments the state should use in order to do this (Rodríguez-Piñero 2018).

Another debate in relation to digital platforms revolves around to what extent the economy and social relations could be platformized. There are two perspectives with regards to this issue. On the one hand, it is argued that the digital platforms with their particular business models and algorithmic management drastically reduce the transactional costs of economic and social exchanges. As a consequence, a new managerial rationality emerges from the intensive use of algorithms, replacing human managers. Thus, traditional companies will tend to adopt a business and managerial model comparable to that used by digital platforms (Kilpi 2015, cited in Degryse 2019). From the other perspective, critical of the former, it is asserted that the digital platforms have developed a narrative which legitimates their status as technological intermediaries between an autonomous worker and a customer who requires a particular service. In other words, the platforms' narrative conceals their condition of being companies that provide services, while their actions reveal that, in fact, they are. This would imply that there is a shift in business narratives rather than a change in practices as a result of digital technology (Tomasseti 2016, cited in Degryse 2019).

Other areas of debate centre around whether these platforms generate new forms of job insecurity or simply reproduce existing insecurity (CEPAL-OIT 2019). It is worth asking whether existing labour institutions that protect subordinate work are still useful or if new mechanisms of inclusion are needed (OIT 2019b).

A particular feature of the platforms is that they take advantage of intermediate technologies for the organization and management of work in traditional sectors such as transportation, domestic work, courier services, food delivery services and even professional activities. Those who argue that platform work reflects a continuity in the nature of work, rather than a rupture, maintain that digital workers have more in common with traditional agricultural labourers or domestic workers in the region (CEPAL-OIT 2019). While it may be true that platforms facilitate the reproduction of traditional informality and insecurity with a new face, technology can also be used as a tool to monitor and neutralize negative aspects, such as the evasion of tax and employer responsibilities. Workers could also make use of these platforms to establish flexible forms of organization and networks, which could, to some degree, counterbalance the isolation they may experience in their work. The obstacle of isolation acquires particular importance for workers on platforms such as Uber, Cabify or Didi. This is due to the fact that these workers do not share any space facilitating face-to-face gatherings which would enable them to establish social bonds around their work, something that delivery workers for Rappi have established in their interactions outside restaurants. Personal interaction is a key factor for the emergence of collective action, as it has an impact on the construction of a shared identity (Haidar et al. 2020).

3.1 The Heterogeneous Nature of the Platforms and the Scope of their Operations

Given its heterogeneity, there is no single answer regarding what to do in the face of the expanding platform economy. For example, platforms offer services which may be performed virtually or face to face; some offer specific services, while others have a wide range of services, and the scope of their operations are both national and international (Todolí 2017). Furthermore, there are also differences in the level of qualifications needed in order to offer services (Drahokoupil and Fabo 2016). Nevertheless, the most salient characteristic in deciding on regulation is whether locally implemented platforms operate exclusively as technological intermediaries, or if they organize service providers, as will be discussed below.

The purpose of all digital platforms, despite their diversity, is to be a technological intermediary in online space, between the supply and demand for a particular service. This is done through the use of algorithms and an interface (app) on which service users can register and connect with suppliers (Todolí 2017). However, it has been found that not all limit their functions to technological intermediation, but also assume other functions, which would equate them with service provider companies.

According to Goerlich and García (2018), a platform is considered to be a service-providing company when it unilaterally designs the characteristics of a service and organizes and establishes the conditions under which the service is provided. Another feature of these platforms is that they assume control and supervision of the provision of services through some form of evaluation. Furthermore, platforms are considered to be service providers when they fix the cost of the service, as would be done by the key asset owner (CEPAL-OIT 2019). On the other hand, if the price is determined by the service provider, it is agreed upon with the client, and if the provider designs and determines the service, the platform is considered to be an intermediary.

The classification of platforms as service providers or as technological intermediaries is only the starting point in establishing whether the relationship between platforms and workers is of a subordinated nature. Although service provider platforms tend to forge subordinated relationships with their workers, this does not necessarily result in them legally recognizing their responsibilities as employers. On the other hand, the characterization of platforms as solely technological intermediaries also does not rule out all employment responsibilities in relation to their service providers (Goerlich and García 2018).

3.2   Employer Evasion and the Commodification of Labour

Regardless of the classification of platforms, there is consensus that in reality they are business models that avoid labour protection for paid work. Degryse (2019, p. 28) considers this 'the organized irresponsibility of companies to disappear the figure of an employer, deny labour relations and make collective agreements inapplicable'. From this point of view, the consequence of the expansion of the platform economy is the abandonment of social-labour relations developed in conventional companies, legitimized, in theory, by the opportunities for flexibility offered by the platforms. According to this approach, one of the main problems of platform work is the commodification of labour relations though adhesion contracts (hiring agreements) that may define false self-employment, i.e. that may conceal subordinate employment relationships. This is because they are contracts the clauses of which are unilaterally defined by the digital platforms, in which any indication that could provide justification for considering these workers as subordinate to the platforms is excluded, even when in practice they maintain control over and supervise the work (for the case of Mexico see Bensusán 2020).

In sum, according to Degryse (2019), what is of concern regarding work on digital platforms and the fourth industrial revolution is not the end of work, but rather the possibility that employers will begin to evade their responsibilities by hiding behind technology and the commodification of labour.

In this respect, both Latin America and the rest of the world face two key challenges. The first is to differentiate between platforms that limit their activities to technological intermediation and those that broaden their operations to include the provision of services. This first step in identifying subordinate working relationships is important as it avoids locating the heterogeneity of platforms within homogenous regulatory schemes. The second challenge is to identify the employers in order to avoid the negative social and employment consequences of them hiding behind technology and the heterogeneity of these businesses (Degryse 2019; Rodríguez-Piñero 2016). In sum, it is necessary to establish the responsibility that digital platforms have towards their workers. This will largely depend on whether traditional attributes of subordinate labour apply, and whether these criteria should be made more flexible as the nature of work transforms with new technology and business models. This will be addressed in the next section.

3.3   The Role of the State

As stated in the introduction, there are various perspectives on the role of the state in a digital economy characterized by the heterogeneity of platforms and uncertainty regarding their legal nature and the way in which they should be regulated. A first, and among the most optimistic theoretical approaches, was proposed by Arun Sundararajan (2017), who indicates that rather than intervene in the regulation of what he refers to as 'platform capitalism', the state should restrict itself to collaborating with and delegating regulatory responsibility to the platforms themselves, their workers, civil society organizations, consumers and other stakeholders. His proposal consists of generating digital trust networks that self-regulate through a certification granted to the platforms by the government and civil society organizations and the clear definition of the faculties of all involved parties. However, the author himself recognizes that emerging self-regulation by digital trust networks can be complemented by the state. Given the tendency to substitute subordinate work for self-employment, he suggests that new social contracts and models of regulation are required in which protections and rights can be transferred when workers move from one platform to another. Such a contract would have a universal reach and thus would be linked to citizenship and not employment. As we shall see, this proposal has generated significant support.

Based on a political economy approach, Rogers (2016) argues that the dichotomy between dependent and independent work needs to be overcome, founded on the principles of a democratic political order. In his view, the whole labour force should be guaranteed rights and civil liberties, individual dignity and distributive justice regardless of employment status. In this case, while the criteria commonly used to identify legal or economic dependence would indicate whether a worker is in a subordinate relationship with their employer, they should not necessarily determine the employment status. He proposes returning to the basic sense of rights and labour regulations – to reduce asymmetries – which would enable 'fomenting a more egalitarian and democratic political economy' (ibid., p. 483).

Rodríguez-Piñero (2016) offers another approach by arguing that the digital platform economy is in a pre-regulatory stage in which uncertainty prevails regarding the categorization of work on platforms (in part due to contradictory judicial rulings) and the scarcity of legislative activity to regulate it. This perspective poses the question of how to reformulate regulations across various legal systems – labour, fiscal, administrative and competence – in order to deal with the issues raised by digital platforms. This task would entail confronting at least four challenges: dealing with situations of illegality; resolving legal uncertainty in the classification of workers; adopting means of protection for genuinely self-employed workers; and moving from bilateral labour models to multilateral models.

3.4 Proposals for Public Intervention

Even among proposals that agree on the need for state intervention into the platform economy, different approaches exist. The first is to create a universal employment relationship (Countouris 2019). This proposal is particularly important in countries where access to social security is currently conditioned upon a subordinate employment relationship, as is the case in Latin American countries. A universal employment relationship would extend currently legislated labour rights to all workers, independent of their legal status. In other words, this would entail the dominance of fact over form as the general criterion to access labour rights. Thus, many of the employment relationships currently located in labour market grey areas, due to informality, poor classification, or because they do not strictly fulfil the characteristics of a subordinate employment relationship, would still be covered by social protection.

Another proposal from the ILO (OIT 2019b) centres around people. Informed by this principle, state intervention should aim to promote people's capabilities and strengthen labour institutions and programmes that incentivize decent work. The singularity and merit of this proposal lies in the fact that it argues for the need for global labour governance for platforms. In addition, it also highlights the need to establish legal responsibility for companies using algorithms to organize work. It coincides with previous proposals by focusing social protection on people, independently of how their occupation is contractually characterized.

Similarly, the OECD (2019) argues that while new forms of work can provide companies and workers with high degrees of flexibility, this should not result in job insecurity and the weakening of labour and social protections for workers. This position is reflected in the seven areas of social protection proposed by the OECD. In contrast to the previous two proposals, the OECD does not argue for the universality of social protection, although it does emphasize the need to strengthen it, including the creation of intermediate categories of work.

3.5   Collective Actors: Perspectives and Experiences

One commonly agreed upon aspect is the importance of collective bargaining with digital platforms in order to secure the protection of workers' rights. This brings us to the issue of collective action on digital platforms. Hyman (2015) argues that given the tendency towards job insecurity, including work on digital platforms, limits need to be placed by either the political elite or by unions who have played a historical role in counteracting inequality. In response, contrasting views exist, both optimistic, related to studies of union revitalization (Murray 2016), as well as pessimistic, viewing unions as actors with exclusively economic interests whose sole focus is the interests of their members (Standing 2011). As such, if unions are to assume their role as principal actors in the struggle against poverty and inequality and to protect the most vulnerable, they will need to change their traditional forms of organization for less hierarchical ones, return power to their rank and file and link affiliation to individuals, who would thereby be able to maintain their membership regardless of occupation (Hyman 2015; Hayter and Stoevska 2011). Without a doubt, technology could be an indispensable tool for overcoming obstacles and countering isolation, even though these conditions did not impede the organization of others in similar situations, such as agricultural or domestic workers. However, the relationships of organizations with their rank and file members, political parties, the state and civil society are embedded in socio-political and institutional configurations. These factors can obstruct, facilitate or, under exceptional circumstances, remain neutral in the face of union transformation.

It is thus imperative to consider the broad institutional environment and labour laws in each country as they shape what unions are, what they do, the organizational problems they face, as well as workers' expectations and decisions regarding affiliation and participation (Godard 2008).

Given the different socio-political and institutional configurations, union cultures and trajectories, as well as the varied relationships with the state in the region, the opportunities for and limitations on collective action vary substantially. These range from state corporativism less inclined to opening up to other movements or new categories of workers (Argentina and Mexico), to corporativism of a more social nature, which maintains broad alliances with social movements and seeks the affiliation of workers affected by the insecurity of working and living conditions, such as in Uruguay and Brazil (Bensusán 2019). Thus, while in some countries it can be expected that the state (executive, legislative and/or judicial branches) will spearhead efforts to halt job insecurity, in others the leading role could be played by collective organizations.

Either way, for workers in the digital economy, a first step is ensuring access to the full enjoyment of collective rights. However, this is not a sufficient condition for platform workers to organize and negotiate collectively with platforms. On the contrary, various factors explain the slow progress in organizing digital platform workers, not only in the region.

First, collective action for digital workers needs to be based more on solidarity than on a shared identity given the heterogeneous or temporary nature of their activities, even though the experience of Argentinian workers shows that the construction of an identity is possible and politically productive (Haidar et al. 2020). Evidence shows that many workers are not aggrieved by their lack of recognized labour rights and may even express satisfaction with the conditions of this type of work. Second, platforms are reluctant to recognize themselves as employers. Third, the work is isolated, generating individualistic behaviours that may hinder – though not prevent – opportunities for collective action, as they inhibit an understanding that organizing may be a path towards countering the insecurity associated with the lack of rights (Díaz Santana 2020).

Finally, as has already been mentioned, the idea that the flexibility that workers enjoy is not compatible with access to rights, hampers organizing efforts. Nevertheless, some evidence indicates that interest in collective action and the formation of unions also varies according to the type of platform. For example, deliverers of food and other merchandise show a greater disposition to organize than workers in private passenger transport platforms (Bensusán 2020). Without a doubt, information regarding impediments to collective action, and particularly on variations by country, type of platform and activities, is still relatively scarce and further research is required.

One experience of organization and collective action[6] is provided by APP (the Association of Platform Workers), founded in 2018 in Argentina by organized workers on the Rappi platform. Haidar et al. (2020) analyse the case from the perspective of workers' resources of power. They examine an action which they describe as being similar to a strike, organized through WhatsApp communities, and conclude that an essential factor in its success was the face-to-face gatherings of workers outside the businesses while they waited for work. These gatherings play a crucial role in overcoming the workers' lack of power in the labour market. It is important to note that these workers constructed a collective identity on the basis of discovering shared interests, and transforming them into demands such as the legal recognition of their subordinate employment relation with their employer (Rappi) and access to labour rights.

This process involved transforming the delivery workers' perception of themselves as self-employed and constructing a workers' identity. The organized workers also drew on resources such as discursive power, challenging the company's image and hoping that public opinion would pressure the platform into conceding to the workers' demands. Another resource of power they harnessed, although not without difficulties, was the formation of coalitions with pre-existing union organizations (Haidar et al. 2020). This experience shows that the platforms' algorithmic management generates a dual movement: it is the source of labour grievances, but at the same time it opens up the possibility of converting these grievances into politically productive actions through a key actor in the world of digital work – the unions.

4   LATIN AMERICA IN THE INTERNATIONAL CONTEXT: VARIATIONS IN PROTECTION

The theoretical approaches mentioned above identify various paths and orientations of state intervention in the digital economy. The different alternatives for intervention also reflect the political orientation of governments regarding the protective or liberal role they choose to play in labour relations. However, in Latin America, low taxation and poor tax collection capacity severely limit the ability of governments to implement what is generally considered to be one of the best methods of avoiding exclusion from social protection – the adoption of universal social security systems, which would include the whole population regardless of employment relations. This possibility remains pending, and lacks any substantial progress, even by governments with a left-leaning political ideology (Reygadas and Filgueiras 2011).

4.1   The Role of Labour Judges: Method of Indicators[7] and Legal Interpretation

Given minimal legislative progress and the obstacles to moving towards universal social security, judicial interpretation – a traditional but expensive method for distinguishing between subordinate work and self-employment – has been the main way of determining access to rights for platform-based workers (Sánchez-Urán 2018). However, this method depends on an initial demand from workers and generates significant uncertainty, as the legal interpretation of classification criteria may vary within a single country for similar cases, as will be shown in the cases of Spain, the United States and Argentina (Bensusán 2020). Thus, many propose a legislative path, though this would also be subject to the same issue of legally interpreted criteria.

On an international level, judges use traditional criteria (Table 10.1) to classify the nature of work on digital platforms. One of the variants in their deliberations is the rigidity or flexibility with which they interpret these criteria, as rulings tend to use different combinations of the indicators in Table 10.1. We refer here generically to the indicators of dependence and independence as it is beyond the scope of this chapter to detail all these combinations. While the particularities of each ruling may be lost, we nevertheless show the interpretative variation of the indicators.

Table 10.1   Indicators of subordination or independence on digital platforms

Dependence and subordination	Autonomy/Independence
Power of direction, control and discipline	a) Time and place of work freely chosen by the worker
a) Disconnection from the platform (dismissal)	b) Power to reject services
b) Systems of evaluation	c) Contact with the market
c) Work guidelines	d) Assume business risk
d) Contracts of services/commercial contracts unilaterally developed by the platform	e) Agree work guidelines
	f) No exclusiveness
Necessary and sufficient conditions	g) Secondary activity
e) Recruitment processes and selection of workers	
f) Cannot deny services	
g) Price setting by platform	
h) Platform owns assets	
i) Remuneration and personal nature of work	
j) Exclusiveness	
k) Place and time of work	
l) Training	
m) Use of logos	

Source: Adapted from Bensusán (2020, p. 19).

Contrasting interpretations are a source of uncertainty. According to judicial rulings emitted in Valencia[8] in 2018 (Deliveroo) and in Madrid[9] in 2019 (Glovo), an employment relationship was recognized between the platforms and its delivery workers. The first case was based on the principle of the primacy of facts (in light of the indicators of dependence and subordination) regarding the way in which the involved parties described their relationship. In contrast, the ruling in Madrid offered a new interpretation of the indicator of 'workplace', understanding it as 'all that can be the object of geolocalization' and that of 'working time' as 'all that in which the activity can be realised using ICT'. However, contrary to the above, another court in Madrid[10] in 2019 ruled that the relationship between Glovo and one of its deliverers was of a commercial nature, and the worker was thus considered to be independent of their employer. In this case, the judge argued, taking a stringent approach, that indicators of dependence did not apply.

Another illustrative case comes from the United States. In 2018, a judge in Pennsylvania (BCNC 2018) applied the 'Donovan Factors' test, which, with some variation, endorses the indicators of dependence/subordination presented in Table 10.1. The judge found that as Uber did not control nor direct drivers, no employment relationship existed between the platform and the driver. In contrast, in 2018, a judge in New York (Van den Bergh 2019), taking into consideration some of the indicators of dependence and subordination, ruled that Uber exercised control over its workers and, consequently, their relationship was of an employment nature. One of the arguments in the ruling was that indicators needed to be loosely interpreted, given that labour relations evolve over time and thus need to be considered in context.

In the Latin American context, at least two rulings, one in Uruguay[11] (2019) and the other in Brazil[12] (2017) recognized the dependent and subordinate character of the relationship between Uber and plaintiff drivers, subscribing to the primacy of fact over form based on the criterion from the control that Uber exercises over its drivers. Regarding more general arguments, the judge in Brazil maintained that platforms represent a new type of employer, and that the employment relationship presents new characteristics that need to be taken into account in order to protect workers. For its part, the Uruguayan ruling emphasized that work should be seen as a 'social, dynamic, changing and evolving fact [… with] new ways of organizing work, taking advantage of new technologies', to which legal procedures needed to adapt.

Contradictory interpretations are also evident in Argentina regarding the nature of work on digital platforms. The Federal Administration of Public Income (AFIP) regards Uber as the type of business anticipated in the Employment Contract Law, and thus argues that it should fulfil its tax and social security obligations. However, criminal law rulings (economic, conventional and misdemeanours) found that Uber was limited to intermediating the supply and demand of transport and thus its workers are self-employed (La Nación 2019).

In sum, specialists (Rodríguez-Piñero 2016, 2018; Pérez de los Cobos 2018; Sánchez-Urán 2018) tend to agree that legal uncertainty in the platform economy is the result of a diversity of interpretations of the indicators of independence and subordination, even regarding the same platform. In the face of such uncertainty, the role of legislators is fundamental.

4.2   The Incipient Role of Employment Legislation

Upon reviewing international labour legislation, at least three countries were found with laws regulating platform work: France (Daugareilh 2019), the regions of Lazio and Piamonte in Italy (Borelli 2019), and the state of California in the USA (Solís 2019; BCNC 2018). In the French case, platform workers are considered to be self-employed, although they do have access to social security, as is the case in the other two countries. In Italy, legislation classifies work on all platforms as subordinate and dependent, while in the US case, labour laws are limited to drivers on transport platforms.

Two countries recognize intermediate work categories in their employment legislation, although these were not specifically designed for work on digital platforms. In England, the equivalent category is 'dependent contractor' or 'worker' (Mason 2019), while the Italian concept is of 'para-subordinate' workers (Borelli 2019). With their respective variations regarding the indicators that substantiate this third category, all provide limited rights to workers. The literature discusses the degree to which these categories are viable for platform work.

The Mexico case illustrates how, within a context of union weakness or disinterest following decades of neo-liberal policies, a change in government political orientation following the 2018 elections resulted in a greater top-down demand to protect vulnerable groups in the labour market.[13] Mexican legislative initiatives concerning both labour regulations (not passed) as well as tax regulations (passed) are signs of a new phase of legislative activism that may favour platform workers.

Although still to be approved, Mexico has two legislative initiatives (Alemán 2019; Padilla 2019) and Colombia has one (Lara 2018) that aim to regulate work on digital platforms. The main difference between them relates to the recognition of a subordinate work relationship between platforms and workers in the Mexican case and the categorization of this work as self-employment in Colombia. These initiatives thus differ regarding the obligations of the platforms and the rights of workers.

Despite these differences, a central concern of both countries' initiatives is access to social security. A key difference is that in Colombia, contribution payments for social security are equally divided between platforms and workers, while in Mexico, by recognizing workers on platforms as subordinate and thus granting them full rights as established in the labour law, contributions are paid by employers, workers and the state. One of the shortcomings of the Mexican initiatives is that they do not specify the indicators needed to recognize platform workers as subordinate, which are necessary in order to confront the uncertainty of the legal classification of these occupations. In contrast, the Colombian initiative includes specific criteria for the proposed intermediate employment category for platform work.

4.3   Other Regulations

Interest in regulating platforms goes beyond concerns related to labour rights and has increasingly adopted a restrictive, if not prohibitive, nature. Various Latin American countries have already reformed their tax schemes or have reform initiatives underway regarding the Value Added Tax (VAT) for digital economy activities with rates that vary between 9 per cent and 22 per cent, depending on the country (Chile, Costa Rica, Uruguay, Colombia, Argentina and Mexico) (CEPAL 2019). With their own individual characteristics, each country has included mechanisms to ensure the effective levying of VAT in their reforms. For example, Argentina identifies the cell-phone code from which a service is requested as the mechanism for detecting and levying VAT. In Mexico workers are obliged to request that the platforms provide them with proof of tax contributions from their income.

In Peru and Uruguay, the tax schemes related to income tax have been modified to include digital services. In 2003, Peru legally established that platforms' income should be levied for income tax at a rate of 30 per cent (CEPAL 2019, p. 76). In 2017, Uruguay established a law that levied the total income obtained by digital platforms at a rate of 12 per cent (CEPAL 2019). In contrast to these two countries, where the income of the platforms is taxed, in Mexico the current scheme for levying income tax in the platform economy applies to workers' income.

An alternative way to regulate digital platforms has been at a sectoral level as, for example, with the private transport platforms in Mexico City. This strategy assumes that these platforms overlap with the traditional industry of regulated taxis, reshaping the sector. For example, taxi drivers must comply with certain administrative regulations, and assume economic costs in order to provide transport services, which is not the case with digital platforms. This legal inequality has led to an inter-sectoral dispute between taxis and transport platforms around the inequality of conditions of competition between sectors. Another inter-sectoral disparity relates to the tax obligations of taxis and Uber. The latter is obligated to retain taxes from its drivers and declare to the tax authorities, while taxi concession holders are not. On the other hand, the generalized labour informality of taxi drivers (Pogliaghi 2012) overlaps with that of Uber drivers (Hernández and Galindo 2016).

Regulating on a sectoral level has the advantage of countering the heterogeneity of digital platforms and is an alternative consistent with Rodríguez-Piñero's (2016) argument that the platform economy requires the reorganization of various legal fields (Santos 2020).

CONCLUSIONS

In the face of the expansion of digital platforms, the challenge is how to formalize the jobs generated by these without affecting the benefits that they offer workers, particularly given the limited or null economic and formal employment growth in the region. These benefits include minimal entry barriers and a degree of work flexibility.

In this chapter we have argued that the quality of work generated by digital platforms will depend both on their characteristics as well as on the opportunities and restrictions faced by states and social actors (primarily unions) to regulate the platforms and to counteract the unilaterality of their actions. The debate around protection is far from settled and while Latin America may have been slow to respond, various countries are now responding to the challenge, through either legislation or legal interpretations, in order to relax the criteria for categorizing work as subordinate employment and enable workers to claim their rights. Overcoming the uncertainty that currently characterizes employment relations with the platforms is imperative in order to avoid the spread of informality, job insecurity and inequalities in the labour market.

As has been shown in this chapter, in the face of the profound transformations experienced in these markets, and the increasing urgency to promote a transition to models of social incorporation that do not depend on the nature of employment status, two types of problems exist. On one hand, there is the issue of financing, and on the other, the risk of weakening the protection of subordinate work – by decreasing rights – for the sake of extending this to all workers, encouraging employers to evade their employment responsibilities.

Although platform workers themselves may be somewhat satisfied with their working conditions and convinced of the advantages of this type of work over others, this should not legitimize the position of platforms, which resist assuming their responsibilities and successfully disseminate the argument that flexibility necessarily correlates with the absence of rights. It is up to the state, the unions and society in general to reject this, as well as to find the best way of protecting workers without ignoring the importance of platforms as sources of employment nor nullifying the advantages derived from their lower entry barriers.

NOTES

1.   An extended version of the content of this chapter can be found in Bensusán (2020). Also included are some of the findings from research conducted by Santos (2020) as part of his master's thesis (Instituto de Investigaciones Dr. José María Luis Mora) funded by a scholarship from the National Council for Science and Technology.
2.   All digital platforms offer their services through the internet. The difference lies in how the services are performed: 'online' being without the physical presence of the person providing the service, and 'offline' with (Todolí 2017).
3.   Uber announced that from 1 February 2020 it would withdraw from Colombia as a consequence of the judicial ruling which ordered the company to suspend its operations in the country, which indicated that Uber had failed to comply with the existing competency regulations (Cuevas 2020). However, in July 2020 Uber obtained a ruling in its favour from the Supreme Court in Bogotá, enabling its return (Torres Reina 2020).
4.   See the INEGI glossary at https://www.inegi.org.mx/app/glosario/default.html?p= ENOE15 (accessed on 7 June 2020).
5.   Twenty-two interviews were conducted with various actors, including Uber drivers, and 20 questionnaires were completed by Rappi workers between August and October 2019. See Bensusán (2020).
6.   Other experiences developed in Mexico with the Independent Union of App Delivery Workers SIRA APPS (legally a coalition according to articles 354 add 355 of the Federal Labour Law), and in Chile with the Chilean Union of Uber Drivers.
7.   This consists of judges assessing the facts of a particular employment situation by interpreting a set of legal indicators that determine their legal nature.
8.   Ruling No. 6/244, *Juzgado no. 6 de Valencia no. 244*, 1 June 2018.
9.   Ruling No. 53/19 [Glovo], *Juzgado de lo Social No. 33 de Madrid*, Spain.
10.   Ruling No. 715/2019 [Glovo], *Tribunal Superior de Justicia de Madrid Sección 04 de los Social,* Spain.
11.   Ruling No. 77 Montevideo. C/UBER TECHNOLOGIES URUGUAY S.A. Y OTRO. PROCESOLABORAL ORDINARIO (LEY 18.572). Sheet 2–3894/2019.
12.   Ruling passed in case 0011359–34.2016.5.03.0112 [Uber], *33 Juzgado del Trabajo de Belo Horizonte, Brazil.*
13.   In addition to significant increases to the minimum wage in December 2018 and 2019, reforms were passed aimed at protecting workers in matters related to freedom of association, labour law and domestic work. There are also initiatives to restrict outsourcing and protect telework (Bensusán 2020).

REFERENCES

Alemán, M. C. (2019), 'Iniciativa que reforma diversas disposiciones de la Constitución Política de los Estados Unidos Mexicanos; y de las leyes del Impuesto Sobre la Renta, y Federal del Trabajo a cargo de la Diputada María Alemán Muñoz Castillo' (grupo parlamentario del PRI), México: Cámara de Diputados LXIV Legislatura.
Azuara, O., S. González and L. Keller (2019), '¿Quiénes son los conductores que utiliza las plataformas de transporte en América Latina?, Perfil de los conductores de Uber

en Brasil, Chile, Colombia y México', Washington DC: División de Mercados Laborales del Banco Interamericano de Desarrollo.

BCNC (Biblioteca del Congreso Nacional del Chile) (2018), 'Uber y conductores. Legislación comparada sobre la relación laboral, Asesoría Técnica Parlamentaria', accessed 10 October 2019 at https://www.bcn.cl/obtienearchivo?id=repositorio/10221/25909/2/BCN_Uber_laboral_actualizado_PA_CW_GW__2_.docx

Bensusán, G. (2019), 'Trade unions and politics in Latin America', in Harry E. Vanden and Gary Prevost (eds), *Encyclopedia of Latin American politics*, Oxford: Oxford University Press.

Bensusán, G. (2020), 'Ocupaciones emergentes en la economía digital y su regulación en México', Serie Macroeconomía del Desarrollo, Santiago: Comisión Económica para América Latina y El Caribe (CEPAL).

Berg, J. and V. De Stefano (2016), '¿Se quiere mejorar el crowdwork? Entonces hay que regularlo', *Global Labour Column*, **240**, 3.

BID (Banco Interamericano de Desarrollo) (2015), 'Empleos para crecer', Washington DC: Banco Interamericano de Desarrollo.

Borelli, S. (2019), 'Italy', in Isabelle Daugareilh, Christophe Degryse and Philippe Pocher (eds), *The platform economy and social law: Key issues in comparative perspective*, Brussels: European Trade Union Institute (ETUI).

Buenadicha, C., A. Cañigueral and I. De León (2017), 'Retos y posibilidades de la economía colaborativa en América Latina y el Caribe', División de competitividad, tecnología e innovación, Washington, DC: Banco Interamericano de Desarrollo.

CEPAL (Comisión Económica para América Latina y el Caribe) (2010), 'La hora de la igualdad: brechas por cerras, caminos por abrir', Brasilia del 30 de mayo a 1 de junio de 2010, Santiago, Chile.

CEPAL (Comisión Económica para América Latina y el Caribe) (2019), 'Panorama Fiscal de América Latina y el Caribe 2019: políticas tributarias para la movilización de recursos en el marco de la Agenda 2030 para el Desarrollo Sostenible', Santiago, Chile.

CEPAL-OIT (Comisión Económica para América Latina y el Caribe) Organización Internacional de Trabajo) (2019), 'El futuro del trabajo en América Latina y el Caribe: antiguas y nuevas formas de empleo y los desafíos para la regulación laboral', *Coyuntura Laboral en América Latina y el Caribe*, **20**, mayo de 2019, Santiago, Chile.

CONEVAL (Consejo Nacional de Evaluación de la Política de Desarrollo Social) (2018), *Estudio diagnóstico del derecho al trabajo 2018*, México: CONEVAL.

Countouris, N. (2019), *Defining and regulating work relations for the future of work*, Geneva: International Labour Organization.

Cuevas, S. (2020), 'Uber anuncia su salida de Colombia, luego de orden para suspender operaciones', accessed 10 January 2020 at https://www.elfinanciero.com.mx/tech/uber-se-va-de-colombia-a-partir-del-1-de-febrero

Daugareilh, I. (2019), 'France', in Isabelle Daugareilh, Christophe Degryse and Philippe Pocher (eds), *The platform economy and social law: Key issues in comparative perspective*, Brussels: European Trade Union Institute (ETUI).

Degryse, C. (2019), 'Introduction', in Isabelle Daugareilh, Christophe Degryse and Philippe Pochet (eds), *The platform economy and social law: Key issues in comparative perspective*, Brussels: European Trade Union Institute (ETUI).

Díaz Santana, M. (2020), *Trabajo en plataformas digitales: Estado y acción colectiva*, Tesis de Doctorado [borrador], México: Flacso-México.

Drahokoupil, J. and B. Fabo (2016), 'The platform economy and the disruption of the employment relationship', *Policy Brief No. 5 European Economic, Employment and Social Policy*, Brussels: European Trade Union Institute (ETUI).

Eisenmeier, S. (2018), 'The contradictory effect of on-demand ridesharing on labour: The cause of Uber in Mexico City', paper presented at Seminario de la Ciudad de Mexico: Pasado y Presente, Instituto Mora, June 2018.

Godard, J. (2008), 'Union formation', in Paul Blyton, Nicolas Bacon, Jack Fiorito and Edmund Heery (eds), *The Sage handbook of industrial relations*, Thousand Oaks, CA: SAGE Publishing.

Goerlich, J. M. and M. A. García (2018), 'Indicios de autonomía y laboralidad en los servicios de los trabajadores de plataforma', in Francisco Pérez de los Cobos (Dir.), *El trabajo en plataformas digitales. Análisis sobre su situación jurídica y regulación futura*, España: Wolters Kluwer.

Haidar, J., N. Diana-Menéndez and C. Arias (2020), 'De la app a la APP. La gestión algorítmica y los procesos de organización y lucha de los trabajadores de reparto', in Héctor García y Lucas Caparrós (comps.), *El trabajo en la economía de plataformas*, Buenos Aires: EDIAR.

Hayter, S. and V. Stoevska (2011), *Social dialogue indicators, international statistical inquiry 2008–09*, Geneva: International Labour Organization.

Hernández, Y. and R. Galindo (2016), 'Modelo de gestión del servicio de transporte UBER ¿Quién pierde y quién gana?', *Revista Estudios Públicos*, **19** (47), 147–175.

Hyman, R. (2015), 'Tres hipótesis sobre el futuro de las relaciones laborales en Europa', *Revista Internacional del Trabajo*, **134** (1), 5–15.

ILO (International Labour Office) (2020), *Global employment trends for youth 2020: Technology and the future of jobs*, Geneva: ILO.

La Nación (2019), *La AFIP determinó que Uber debe $358 millones en tributos y cargas sociales*, accessed 20 October 2019 at https://www.lanacion.com.ar/economia/deuda-millonaria-la-afip-determino-uber-debe-nid2242513

Lara, R. (2018), *Proyecto de ley número 082 de 2018 Cámara, por medio de la cual se regula el Trabajo Digital en Colombia y se dictan otras disposiciones*, accessed 5 september 2019 at https://congresovisible.uniandes.edu.co/proyectos-de-ley/por-medio-de-la-cual/9526/#tab=2

Madariaga, J., C. Buenadicha, E. Molina and C. Ernst (2019), *Economía de plataformas y empleo. ¿Cómo es trabajar en una APP en Argentina?*, Buenos Aires: CIPPEC, BID, OIT.

Mason, L. (2019), 'United Kingdom', in Isabelle Daugareilh, Christophe Degryse and Philippe Pocher (eds), *The platform economy and social law: Key issues in comparative perspective*, Brussels: European Trade Union Institute (ETUI).

Murray, G. (2016), 'Union renewal: What can we learn from three decades of research?', *Transfer: European Review of Labour and Research*, **23** (1), 9–29.

OECD (Organisation for Economic Co-operation and Development) (2019), 'Policy responses to new forms of work', paper prepared for the second meeting of the G20 Employment Working Group under the Japanese G20 Presidency in Tokyo, 22–24 April 2019.

OIT (Oficina Internacional del Trabajo) (2015), *Trabajar para un futuro más prometedor. Comisión Mundial sobre el Futuro del Trabajo*, Ginebra: OIT.

OIT (Organización Internacional del Trabajo) (2018), *Panorama Temático Laboral. Presente y Futuro de la Protección Social en América Latina y El Caribe*, Lima: Oficina Regional para América Latina y El Caribe.

OIT (Organización Internacional del Trabajo) (2019a), *Panorama Laboral 2019, América Latina y el Caribe,* Lima: OIT, Oficina Regional para América Latina y el Caribe.

OIT (Organización Internacional del Trabajo) (2019b), *Trabajar para un futuro más prometedor,* Ginebra: Comisión Mundial sobre el Futuro del Trabajo.

Padilla, J. (2019), *Iniciativa por la que se reforma la ley federal del trabajo para regular a los trabajadores de las empresas de servicios por medio de aplicaciones digitales* (Grupo Parlamentario del Partido del Trabajo), México: Senado de la República.

Pérez de los Cobos, F. (dir.) (2018), *El trabajo en plataformas digitales. Análisis sobre su situación jurídica y regulación futura,* España: Wolters Kluwer.

Perry, G., W. Maloney, O. Arias, P. Fajnzylber, A. Mason, J. Saavedra-Chanduvi and M. Bosch (2007), *Informalidad: escape y exclusión, estudios del Banco Mundial sobre América Latina y el Caribe,* Washington, DC: Banco Mundial.

Pogliaghi, L. (2012), 'La problemática del trabajo, la identidad y la organización colectiva en los taxistas de la ciudad de México', in Enrique De La Garza Toledo (coord.), *Trabajo no clásico, organización y acción colectiva,* México: UAM-I/ Plaza y Valdés Editores, pp. 209–250.

Reygadas, L. and F. Filgueiras (2011), 'Desigualdad y crisis de incorporación: la caja de herramientas de políticas sociales de la izquierda', in Gonzalo Abad Ortiz (coord.), *América Latina y el Caribe: Escenarios posibles y políticas sociales,* Montevideo: Flacso/Editor Theutonio Dos santos, pp. 133–160.

Robinson, W. (2015), 'Can digital sharing economy platforms pull Latin America's informal sector into the mainstream? No', accessed 15 November 2019 at http:// www.americasquarterly.org/content/can-digitalsharing-economyplatforms-pull -latin-america%E2%80%99s-informal-sector-mainstream-no

Rodríguez-Piñero, M. (2016), 'El trabajo 3.0 y la regulación laboral: por un enfoque creativo en su tratamiento legal', *Creatividad y Sociedad,* **26**, 24–68.

Rodríguez-Piñero, M. (2018), 'La figura del trabajador de plataforma: las relaciones entre las plataformas digitales y los trabajadores que prestan sus servicios', in Francisco Pérez de los Cobos (dir.), *El trabajo en plataformas digitales. Análisis sobre su situación jurídica y regulación futura,* España: Wolters Kluwer.

Rogers, B. (2016), 'Employment rights in the platform economy: Getting back to basics', *Harvard Law & Policy Review,* **10**, 480–520.

Sánchez-Urán, Y. (2018), 'El trabajo en plataformas ante los tribunales: un análisis comparado', in Francisco Pérez de los Cobos (dir.), *El trabajo en plataformas digitales. Análisis sobre su situación jurídica y regulación futura,* España: Wolters Kluwer.

Santos, H. (2020), *El Estado y los conflictos laborales y de competencia en el sector del transporte de particulares: la irrupción de Uber en México,* Tesis de Maestría [borrador], México: Instituto de Investigaciones Dr. José María Luis Mora.

Solís, V. (2019), 'Fuerte golpe a Uber y Lyft: California aprueba iniciativa para reclasificar a contratistas como empleados', accessed 15 December 2019 at https:// www.univision.com/local/san-francisco-kdtv/fuerte-golpe-a-uber-y-lyft-california -aprueba-iniciativa-para-reclasificar-a-contratistas-como-empleados

Standing, G. (2011), *The precariat: The new dangerous class,* London: Bloomsbury Academic.

Sundararajan, A. (2017), *The collaborative economy: Socioeconomic, regulatory and policy issues,* Policy Department: Economic and Scientific Policy, Brussels: European Parliament.

Todolí, A. (2017), *El trabajo en la era de la Economía Colaborativa*, España: Editorial Tirant lo Blanch.

Torres Reina, Guillermo (2020), 'El regreso de Uber a Colombia, la próxima pelea', in *Semana*, 19 de julio, https://www.semana.com/tecnologia/articulo/regreso-de-uber-a-colombia-la-proxima-pelea/683938

Van den Bergh, K. (2019), 'United States', in Isabelle Daugareilh, Christophe Degryse and Philippe Pocher (eds), *The platform economy and social law: Key issues in comparative perspective*, Brussels: European Trade Union Institute (ETUI).

Index